America Now
Short Readings from Recent Periodicals
Second Edition

Edited by

ROBERT ATWAN

Exercises prepared with the assistance of

Nancy Canavera
Charleston Southern University
Liz deBeer
Middlesex County College
Jennifer Ivers
Boston University

Bedford Books   ≈   Boston

For Bedford Books
President and Publisher: Charles H. Christensen
General Manager and Associate Publisher: Joan E. Feinberg
Managing Editor: Elizabeth M. Schaaf
Developmental Editor: Beth Castrodale
Editorial Assistant: Joanne Diaz
Production Editor: Maureen Murray
Production Assistant: Deborah Baker
Copyeditor: Barbara Sutton
Text Design: Jean Hammond
Cover Design: Hannus Design Associates
Cover Photograph: Martin Paul, Ltd.

Library of Congress Catalog Card Number: 96–86758

Manufactured in the United States of America
1   0   9   8   7
f   e   d   c   b

For information, write: Bedford Books, 75 Arlington Street, Boston, MA
02116 (617–426–7440)

ISBN: 0–312–13410–X

Acknowledgments

"AIDS Faces" (advertisement). United Colors of Benetton. Concept: O. Toscani.
Fall/Winter 1994.
American Indian College Fund (advertisement). "I'll Never Fight for Women's Rights."
Print ad developed by Wieden and Kennedy for the American Indian College
Fund's public-service advertising campaign.
Dominique Apollon, "A Quest for Justice." Reprinted by permission of the author and
the *Cavalier Daily.*
Jonathan Bailey, "A Different Drummer," *Stanford,* September 1995. Reprinted by
permission of *Stanford* and by permission of the author.
Maggie Bandur, "Women Play the Roles Men Want to See," (c) *The Daily Northwest-
ern.* Reprinted by permission of the author and *The Daily Northwestern.*

*Acknowledgments and copyrights are continued at the back of the book on
pages 297–99, which constitute an extension of the copyright page. It is a violation of the law to reproduce these selections by any means whatsoever
without the written permission of the copyright holder.*

Preface for Instructors

People write for many reasons, but one of the most compelling is to express their views on matters of current public interest. Browse any newsstand or library magazine rack and you'll find an overabundance of articles, features, and opinion columns written in response to current issues or events. Even reflective essays on subjects that aren't necessarily timely are often pegged (sometimes ingeniously) to a current issue or trend.

The second edition of *America Now,* like its predecessor, is designed to involve introductory writing students in the give-and-take of current public discussion. Its forty-seven selections are drawn from forty recent periodicals and address such controversial topics as violence in the media, affirmative action, gender differences, censorship, English-only laws, TV talk shows, interracial relationships, and date rape. Two chapters also feature controversial advertisements. All of the selections appeared in print within the past few years and all of the topics remain in the news. Originally published in some of our most popular and respected newspapers and magazines, the selections illustrate the variety of personal, informative, and persuasive writing read daily by millions of readers.

New to this edition are seventeen published student essays — most drawn from college newspapers across the country. These recent essays reveal student writers confronting, in a public forum, the same topics and issues that challenge some of our leading social critics and commentators. These selections are intended to show how student writers can enter into and influence public discussion. In this way, *America Now* invites students to view the act of writing as a form of personal and public empowerment. Too frequently, students see the writing they do in a composition course as having little connection with real-world problems and issues. Many selections in this book prove that writing can make a difference.

Almost all of the student pieces in the second edition were located on the Internet, making *America Now* the first composition reader to draw heavily on this new and important resource for readers, writers, and anyone interested in discussing current political and cultural affairs. As Web pages, chat rooms, and other discussion sites proliferate, students will find a wide-open environment for sharing information, opinions, and concerns. All kinds of public forums are rapidly growing more convenient and accessible (most periodicals, for example, now welcome e-mail responses). Today, student writers can enter the public sphere as never before.

Student essays not only make up a large percentage of this new edition but they also shape the volume's contents. A wide spectrum of college newspapers were consulted (and sometimes polled) to discover the most commonly discussed issues and topics. Some issues — like affirmative action, censorship, and bilingualism — had provoked so much student response that they could have led to entire single-topic collections. Many college papers did not restrict themselves to news items and editorial opinion but found room for personal essays as well. Some favorite student topics on the personal side were roommates, campus life, identity, and gender stereotypes.

America Now intends to get students reading, thinking, talking, and writing. The overriding instructional principle — which informs everything from the choice of selections and topics to the design of apparatus — is that participation in informed discussion helps to stimulate and improve student writing. The book encourages both instructors and students to view reading, discussion, and writing as interrelated activities. It assumes that: (1) attentive reading will lead to informed discussion; (2) participation in open and informed discussion will lead to a broadening of viewpoints; (3) an awareness of different viewpoints will lead to thoughtful compositions. To further promote discussion, *this edition now features a prereading assignment for each selection.* The questions in "Before You Read" will help students explore a few of the avenues that lead to fruitful discussion and interesting papers. A full description of the advantages gained by linking reading, writing, and classroom discussion can be found in my introduction to the instructor's manual.

To facilitate group discussion and in-class work, *America Now* features both bite-sized chapters and relatively brief selections (some no longer than two pages). These tightly focused chapters permit instructors to cover a broad range of themes and issues in one semester. Each chapter can be conveniently handled in one or two class periods. The chapters move from very accessible, personal topics (for example, physical appearance and sharing space) to more complex, public issues, thus accommodating teachers who prefer to start with personal writing and gradually progress to exposition, analysis, and argument. *The book concludes with two new chapters on argument:* an all-student discussion of affirmative action, followed by a focused debate on date rape in which one writer responds specifically to the opinions of the other. For instructors who prefer to organize selections by writing modes and methods, *this edition includes an alternate rhetorical table of contents.*

The apparatus of *America Now* supports both discussion-based instruction and more individualized approaches to reading and writing. Taking into account the increasing diversity of students (especially the growing number of non-native speakers) in today's writing programs, the apparatus includes extensive help with college-level vocabulary. *Another new feature of this edition is a "Words to Learn" list preceding each selection.* This vocabulary list with brief definitions will allow students to isolate some of the words they may have difficulty with as they read; encountering the word later in context will help lock it into memory. It's unrealistic, however, to think that students will acquire a fluent knowledge of new words by memorizing a list; therefore, the apparatus following each selection includes "Discussing Vocabulary / Using a Dictionary," a set of questions that introduces students to prefixes, suffixes, connotations, denotations, tone, and some etymology.

Along with the discussion of vocabulary, the questions that follow individual selections emphasize reading comprehension ("Discussing Meaning") and writing strategies ("Discussing Writing"). In addition, the selection apparatus includes "In-Class Writing Activities" and "Challenging the Selection," a cluster of questions that ask students to take a critical stance toward the essay. Realizing that beginning students can sometimes be too trusting of what they see in print, especially in textbooks, the "Challenging the Selection" questions invite them to take a more skeptical attitude toward their reading and to form the habit of questioning a selection from both an analytical and an experiential point of view.

In addition to the selection apparatus, *America Now* contains unit apparatus designed to encourage discussion and writing. The unit apparatus approaches the reading material from topical and thematic angles with an emphasis on group discussion. A brief introduction to each unit helps students understand the main discussion points and the way selections are linked together. The end of each unit features three sets of interlocking study questions and tasks: (1) a suggested topic for discussion; (2) clusters of questions and ideas to help students prepare for class discussion; and (3) several writing assignments which ask students to move from discussion to writing — that is, to develop papers out of the ideas and opinions expressed in class discussion. Finally, instructors with very diverse writing classes may find "Topics for Cross-Cultural Discussion" a convenient way to encourage an exchange of perspectives and experiences that could also lead to ideas for writing.

Aside from the instructional aids noted above, this edition of *America Now* features two ancillaries: an instructor's manual, *From Discussion to Writing: Instructional Resources for* AMERICA NOW, and a workbook, *Developmental and ESL Exercises to Accompany* AMERICA NOW.

Liz deBeer of Middlesex County College prepared the instructor's manual, bringing to the task not only a familiarity with the text but years of classroom experience at all levels of composition instruction. The manual contains journal activities, numerous collaborative activities, classroom projects (including introductory research assignments), and additional writing assignments. Anyone using *America Now* should be sure to consult the manual before designing a syllabus, framing a discussion topic, or even assigning an individual selection. Professor deBeer also contributes to the instructor's manual a helpful essay on designing student panels ("Forming Forums") and advice on using the book's apparatus in both developmental and mainstream composition classes.

Developmental and ESL Exercises to Accompany AMERICA NOW, prepared by Jennifer Ivers of Boston University, will expand the instructional utility of *America Now*. This workbook — which follows *America Now* chapter by chapter and draws on its selections for exercises — helps students improve their grammar, vocabulary, and sentence-level skills. The workbook also includes activities to generate thoughtful, coherent paragraphs and essays. Concluding with additional vocabulary exercises and an appendix that defines idiomatic expressions and other terms that may be challenging to ESL students, Professor Ivers's workbook is an enormously useful addition to the *America Now* composition package.

Acknowledgments

While putting together the second edition of *America Now* I was fortunate to receive the assistance of many talented individuals. In addition to their work on the instructor's manual and workbook, Liz deBeer and Jennifer Ivers offered many useful suggestions for the book's instructional apparatus. I am also grateful to Nancy Canavera of Charleston Southern University for applying her extensive classroom experience to the book. Along with her son, college student Mark Canavera, she read and responded to all of the selections and helped draft relevant discussion questions. Matthew Howard, managing editor of the *Boston Review* (and a recent college graduate), helped me keep selections and questions oriented to student interests and concerns. For months, Matthew closely monitored campus issues and student writing on the Internet; he found many more essays than we were finally able to include in this collection.

To revise a text is to entertain numerous questions: What kind of selections work best in class? What types of questions are most helpful? How can reading, writing, and discussion be most effectively intertwined? This edition profited immensely from the following instructors who generously took the time to respond to the first edition: Nancy Canavera, Charleston Southern University; Linda Currivan, University of Hawaii-Leeward Community College; Sheri Divers, Georgia Southern University; Mary M. Dossim, SUNY-Plattsburgh; John Gibney, Landmark College; Peggy Kocoras, Assumption College; Dawn L. Leonard, Charleston Southern University; Mark Lindemer, College of Southern Idaho; Nancy McCabe, University of Nebraska; Edward Mack, Sullivan County Community College; Alison McNeal, Slippery Rock University; Frank Noji, Kapiolani Community College; Mary J. Page, San Jose City College; William Roney, Rutgers University-New Brunswick; Natasha Saltrup, Rutgers University-Newark; Robin Schore, Mercer County College; and Warren B. Seekamp, University of Louisville.

Other people helped in various ways. I'm indebted to Barbara Gross of Rutgers University (Newark) for her excellent work in preparing the instructor's manual for the first edition. Two good friends, Charles O'Neill and Jack Roberts, both of St. Thomas Aquinas College, went over my early plans for the book and offered many useful suggestions. I appreciate the advice and suggestions of: Mary Ann Ardeline, Northampton Community College; Nancy Bailey, Metropolitan State College; David Borofsky, Northampton Community College; Mary Ann Hofer, University of Findlay; Kate Mangelsdorf, University of Texas–El Paso; Evelyn J. Posey, University of Texas–El Paso; Barbara Rayman, Arapahoe Community College; Ann Rohovec, Dona Ana College; Nancy Troutman, Northampton

Community College; and Janet Vucinich, Santa Fe Community College. Many of the comments they offered during the book's planning stages remain relevant.

As always, it was a pleasure to work with the superb staff at Bedford Books. *America Now* began with Bedford's associate publisher, Joan E. Feinberg, who conceived of the idea — and I thank her for it. Jane Betz, my editor on the first edition, shaped the book in lasting ways and helped with the planning of the revision. Of all the people acknowledged, I owe the most gratitude to this edition's developmental editor, Beth Castrodale. Her insightful suggestions, remarkable good sense, and uncanny ability to keep track of so many minute details made this collection a pleasure to work on from start to finish. I appreciate, too, the efforts of several other people at Bedford: Joanne Diaz, John Pent, and Maura Shea, who tackled a variety of editorial tasks. Liza Ferrell cleared permissions under a tight deadline. Maureen Murray guided the book through production with patience and care, staying on top of many details; Deborah Baker provided production assistance; and Elizabeth Schaaf managed the production process with her usual attentiveness. I was fortunate to receive the careful copyediting of Barbara Sutton. In the advertising and promotion department, manager Donna Dennison, as well as Susan Pace and Miranda Pinckert, deserve warm thanks for their work.

Finally, I would like to thank Bedford's publisher, Charles H. Christensen, for his deep and abiding interest in college composition. It is a great pleasure and privilege to work with him.

R. A.

Contents

1 How Do You See Yourself?   1

What is your self-image? Is it positive or negative? Are you inclined to make yourself miserable over physical characteristics that other people may not even notice? One of the world's most famous cartoonists finds that he is stuck with a childhood self-image that no longer reflects the way he looks. . . . A Pulitzer-Prize winning African American reporter discusses a painful topic many blacks would rather not confront. . . . In a personal essay that helped gain him admission to Stanford, a college applicant describes the process of transforming a physical liability into a life-enhancing talent.

2 Sharing Space: Can We Learn to Live with Others?   17

Is it possible to find the ideal living companion or roommate? What are the pressures and problems of sharing space with other people? An American Catholic living in India tells how she successfully shares a life with her Hindu husband. . . . A

4 What Are We Afraid Of?   60

The list of things Americans fear seems to grow daily — violent crime, environmental hazards, natural disaster, fatal illness, poverty, and unemployment represent only a few. Are these fears justified or are they irrational? A young New York City journalist describes how the AIDS epidemic has led to widespread distrust and hysteria.... A Benetton advertisement reflects mass anxiety about AIDS.... An African American attorney provides a horrifying account of a senseless and brutal crime.... With antigovernment sentiments on the rise, a Wake Forest University student wonders whether Americans have any real reasons to fear the federal government.

5 Can We Resist Stereotypes?   83

Why are we so quick to label people? Where do our stereotypes come from? What harm can they do? A young Korean American questions the validity of Asian male stereotypes. . . . A prominent Columbia University sociologist examines how the poor are used as scapegoats for social problems.... A Northwestern University speech major asks why some women still conform to female stereotypes.

6 Can Interracial Relationships Succeed?   100

Given America's growing ethnic diversity, it's no surprise that
interracial marriages and relationships are also on the rise. But
are they now viewed more positively, and should they be encouraged? An Asian American law professor wonders why
one's romantic life should be limited to members of the same
race. . . . A white college student discusses the social pressures
that she and her black boyfriend face. . . . An African American
college magazine invites a cross-section of students to speak out
on interracial dating.

7 Do Gender Differences Really Exist?   120

Do men and women behave as though they are from different
planets? Are their differences biologically innate or caused by
social forces? A prominent writer and linguistics professor examines the different attitudes men and women have toward
computers. . . . A well-known newspaper columnist asks if the
media are dividing along gender lines. . . . A University of Michigan English major considers why males tend to dominate classroom discussion even in courses where they are outnumbered.

8 Can We Just Say "No" to Addictions?   138

When we think of addictive behavior we usually focus on drugs.
Yet our everyday world reveals all sorts of addictions. A news
commentator speaks out against the way state lotteries try to
lure America's poorest people. . . . A public-policy reporter
makes a sober assessment of college drinking. . . . Are college
students spending an excessive amount of time in cyberspace?
asks a *Washington Post* reporter. . . . A Northwestern University theater and economics major explains why young people
will never quit smoking.

9 Do Words Matter?   162

"Sticks and stones can break my bones, but names will never
hurt me" — is the old childhood rhyme true? Or can words seriously injure? Can they have far-reaching effects on our behavior
and self-image? Two communications professionals show how
the habitual use of one very common word can leave us powerless. . . . A contributor to a prominent gay magazine proposes a
new word for "homosexual". . . . What may seem like a trivial
detail can actually be politically significant, argues a University
of South Florida student who takes issue with his cafeteria's
menu.

10   Can We Say What We Want?   178

Is our right to free speech limited or unlimited? What kinds of restraints can be placed on speech, and who decides what can or cannot be expressed? A noted commentator for *Time* magazine finds it hard to believe that someone could be fired for wearing a T-shirt the boss doesn't like.... An award-winning syndicated columnist believes that colleges have gone too far in suppressing speech.... Has the quest for political correctness left us afraid of talking to each other? asks a columnist for Colgate University's student paper.

11   Should English Be the Official Language?   196

Unlike some nations, the United States has never had an official language. Many influential politicians think the time has finally come to establish English-only legislation. But is an official language a good idea? Based on his personal experiences, a *Wall Street Journal* reporter explains why bilingual education fails Spanish-speaking students.... A young Korean American novelist recalls his mother's difficulties in coping with an English-speaking society. . . . The former president of the University of

Rochester's Spanish and Latin student association argues that an official language would be "un-American."

12   TV Talk Shows — What's Their Appeal?   213

Why are television talk shows so popular? What do Oprah, Ricki, Sally Jessy, and Geraldo tell us about ourselves? A national news commentator compares television talk programs to the sleazy carnival freak-shows of an earlier time. . . . A communications professor maintains that by airing views which might otherwise be suppressed, talk shows serve a useful political purpose. . . . A Boston University communications major asks why people who claim to dislike talk shows find it so hard to stop watching them.

13   Do the Media Promote Violence?   234

Few people would dispute the fact that violence is now a main feature of American music, television, and cinema. But whether violence on the screen actually causes violence on the street is a hotly disputed topic, one that has become a serious political issue. How should the government respond to the increase in media violence? asks one of our print media's most influential figures. . . . Violence toward women is nothing new in American

15 Opposing Views: What Should Be Done about Date Rape?   276

What is date rape and what should be done about it? When it occurs, who should be held more responsible—the man or the woman? One of America's most controversial authors argues that today's victim-oriented feminism has not prepared young women to behave responsibly and realistically when confronted with male sexual aggression. . . . Responding directly to this selection, a magazine editor contends that such thinking only perpetuates gender stereotypes and antagonism.

Rhetorical Table of Contents

For the convenience of instructors who prefer to assign some or all of the readings in *America Now* according to types of writing, the following table of contents groups the selections into the rhetorical modes or categories most frequently used in composition classes. Selections that effectively demonstrate various modes may appear under more than one category.

Comparison and Contrast

Division and Classification

Definition

Process Analysis

Introduction:
The Empowered Writer

How to Read this Book

America Now collects recent articles carefully selected to stimulate reading, discussion, and writing. The articles come from two
main sources — popular periodicals and college newspapers available
on the Internet. Written by journalists and columnists, public figures
and activists, as well as professors and students from all over the
country, the selections illustrate the types of material read by millions
of Americans every day. The book covers fifteen of today's most
widely discussed issues and topics. In reading, discussing, and writing
about the selections, you will be actively taking part in some of the
major controversies of our time.

Participation is the key to this collection. I encourage you to view
reading and writing as a form of participation. I hope you will read
the selections attentively, think about them, be willing to discuss
them in class, and use what you've learned from your reading and
discussion as the basis for your papers. If you do these things, you
will develop three skills necessary for successful college work: the
ability to read critically, to discuss topics intelligently, and to write
persuasively.

America Now invites you to see reading, discussion, and writing
as closely related activities. As you read a selection, imagine that you
have entered into a discussion with the author. Take notes as you
read. Question the selection. Challenge its point of view or its evidence. Compare your experience with the author's. Consider how
different economic classes or other groups are likely to respond.

Remember, just because something appears in a newspaper or
book doesn't make it true or accurate. Form the habit of challenging
what you read. Don't be persuaded by an opinion simply because it
appears in print or because you believe you should accept it. Trust
your own observations and experiences. Though logicians never say

so, personal experiences and keen observations often provide the basis of our most convincing arguments.

When your class discusses a selection, be especially attentive to what others think of it. It's always surprising how two people can read the same article and reach two entirely different interpretations. Observe the range of opinion. Try to understand why and how people arrive at different conclusions. Do some seem to be missing the point? Do some distort the author's ideas? Have someone's comments forced you into rethinking the selection? Keep a record of the discussion in your notebook. Then, when you begin to draft your paper, consider your essay as an extension of both your imaginary conversation with the author and the actual class discussion. If you've taken detailed notes of your own and the class's responses to the selection, you should have more than enough information to get started.

Participating in Class Discussion: Six Basic Rules

Discussion is a learned activity. It requires a variety of essential academic skills: speaking, listening, thinking, and preparing. The following six basic rules are vital to healthy and productive discussion.

1. *Take an active speaking role.* Good discussion demands that everyone participates, not (as so often happens) just a vocal few. Many students remain detached from discussion because they are afraid to speak in a group. This fear is quite common — so common that psychological surveys show that speaking in front of a group is generally one of our worst fears. A leading communication consultant suggests that people choke up because they are more worried about how others will respond than about what they themselves have to say. It helps to remember that most people will be more interested in *what* you say than in how you say it. Once you get over the initial fear of speaking in public, your speech skills will improve with practice.

2. *Listen attentively.* No one can participate in group discussion who doesn't listen attentively. This may sound obvious, but just think of how many senseless arguments you've had because either you or the person with whom you were talking completely misunderstood what was said. A good listener not only hears what someone is saying but understands why he or she is saying it. One of the most important things about listening is that it leads to one element that lively discus-

sion depends on: good questions. When the interesting questions begin to emerge, you know good discussion has truly begun.

3. *Examine all sides of an issue.* Good discussion requires that we be patient with complexity. Difficult problems rarely have obvious and simple solutions, nor can they be easily summarized in popular slogans. Complex issues demand to be turned over in our minds so that we can see them from a variety of angles. Group discussion will broaden our perspective and deepen our insight into difficult issues and ideas.

4. *Suspend judgment.* Class discussion is best conducted in an open-minded and tolerant spirit. To fully explore ideas and issues, you will need to be receptive to the opinions of others even when they contradict your own. Remember, discussion is not the same as debate. Its primary purpose is communication, not competition. In discussion you are not necessarily trying to win everyone over to your point of view. The goal of group discussion should be to open up a topic so that everyone in the group will be exposed to a spectrum of attitudes. Suspending judgment does not mean you shouldn't hold a strong belief or opinion about an issue; it means that you should be willing to take into account rival beliefs or opinions. An opinion formed without an awareness of other points of view — one that has not been tested against contrary ideas — is not a *strong* opinion but merely a stubborn one.

5. *Avoid abusive or insulting language.* Free and open discussion can only occur if we respect the beliefs and opinions of others. If we speak in ways that fail to show respect for differing viewpoints — if we resort to name-calling or use demeaning and malicious expressions, for example — we not only embarrass ourselves but we close off the possibility for an intelligent and productive exchange of ideas. Contrary to what you might gather from some popular radio and television talk shows, shouting insults and engaging in hate-speech are signs of verbal and intellectual bankruptcy. They are usually the last resort of someone who has nothing to say.

6. *Come prepared.* Discussion is not merely random conversation. It demands a certain degree of preparation and focus. To participate in class discussion, you must consider assigned topics beforehand and read whatever is required. You should develop the habit of reading with pen in hand, underlining key points and jotting down questions, impressions, and ideas in your notebook. The notes you bring to class will be an invaluable aid in group discussion.

Group Discussion as a Source of Ideas

Group discussion can stimulate and enhance your writing in several important ways. First, it supplies you with ideas. Let's say that you are participating in a discussion about how we express our identities (see Chapter 3). One of your classmates mentions some of the problems a mixed ethnic background can cause. But suppose you also come from a mixed background, and, when you think about it, you believe that your mixed heritage has given you more advantages than disadvantages. Hearing her viewpoint may inspire you to express your differing perspective on the issue. Your perspective could lead to an interesting personal essay.

Suppose you now start writing that essay. You don't need to start from scratch and stare at a blank piece of paper or computer screen for hours. Discussion has already given you a few good leads. First, you have your classmate's opinions and attitudes to quote or summarize. You can begin your paper by explaining that some people view a divided ethnic identity as a psychological burden. You might expand on your classmate's opinion by bringing in additional information from other student comments or from your reading to show how people often focus on only the negative side of mixed identities. You can then explain your own perspective on this topic. Of course, you will need to give several examples showing *why* a mixed background has been an advantage for you. The end result can be a first-rate essay, one that takes other opinions into account and demonstrates a clearly established point of view. It is personal, and yet it takes a position that goes beyond one individual's experiences.

Whatever the topic, your writing will benefit from reading and discussion, which will give your essays a clear purpose or goal. In that way, your papers will resemble the selections found in this book: They will be a *response* to the opinions, attitudes, experiences, issues, ideas, and proposals that inform current public discourse. This is why most writers write; this is what most newspaper and magazines publish; this is what most people read. *America Now* consists entirely of such writing. I hope you will read the selections with enjoyment, discuss the issues with an open mind, and write about the topics with purpose and enthusiasm.

The Practice of Writing

Suppose you wanted to learn to play the guitar. What would you do first? Would you run to the library and read a lot of books on music? Would you then read some instructional books on guitar playing? Might you try to memorize all the chord positions? Then would you get sheet music for songs you liked and memorize them? After all that, if someone handed you an electric guitar, would you immediately be able to play like Jimi Hendrix or Eric Clapton?

I don't think you would begin that way. You would probably start out by strumming the guitar, getting the feel of it, trying to pick out something familiar. You would probably want to take lessons from someone who knows how to play. And you would practice, practice, practice. Every now and then your instruction book would come in handy. It would give you basic information on frets, notes, and chord positions, for example. You might need to refer to that information constantly in the beginning. But knowing the chords is not the same as knowing how to manipulate your fingers correctly to produce the right sounds. You need to be able to *play* the chords, not just know them.

Learning to read and write well is not that much different. Though instructional books can give you a great deal of advice and information, the only way anyone really learns to read and write is through constant practice. The only problem, of course, is that nobody likes to practice. If we did, we would all be good at just about everything. Most of us, however, want to acquire a skill quickly and easily. We don't want to take lesson after lesson after lesson. We want to pick up the instrument and sound like a professional in ten minutes.

Wouldn't it be a wonderful world if that could happen? Wouldn't it be great to be born with a gigantic vocabulary so we instantly knew the meaning of every word we saw or heard? We would never have to go through the slow process of consulting a dictionary whenever we stumbled across an unfamiliar word. But, unfortunately, life is not so easy. To succeed at anything worthwhile requires patience and dedication. Watch a young figure skater trying to perfect her skills and you will see patience and dedication at work; or watch an accident victim learning how to maneuver a wheelchair so he can begin again an independent existence; or observe a new American struggling to learn English. None of these skills is quickly and easily acquired. Like building a vocabulary, they all take time and effort. They all require practice. And they require something even more important: the willingness to make mistakes. Can someone learn to skate without taking a spill? Or learn a new language without mispronouncing a word?

Writing as a Public Activity

Many people have the wrong idea about writing. They view writing as a very private act. They picture the writer sitting all alone and staring into space waiting for ideas to come. They think that ideas come from "deep" within and only reach expression after they have been fully articulated inside the writer's head.

These images are part of a myth about creative writing and, like most myths, are sometimes true. A few poets, novelists, and essayists do write in total isolation and search deep inside themselves for thoughts and stories. But most writers have far more contact with public life. This is especially true of people who write regularly for magazines, newspapers, and professional journals. These writers work within a lively social atmosphere in which issues and ideas are often intensely discussed and debated. Nearly all the selections in this book illustrate this type of writing.

As you work on your own papers, remember that writing is very much a public activity. It is rarely performed alone in an "ivory tower." Writers don't always have the time, the desire, the opportunity, or the luxury to be all alone. They may be writing in a newsroom with clacking keyboards and noise all around them; they may be writing at a kitchen table, trying to feed several children at the same time; they may be writing on subways or buses. The great English novelist D. H. Lawrence grew up in a small coal miner's cottage with no place for privacy. It turned out to be an enabling experience. Throughout his life he could write wherever he happened to be; it didn't matter how many people or how much commotion surrounded him.

There are more important ways in which writing is a public activity. Much writing is often a response to public events. Most of the articles you encounter every day in newspapers and magazines respond directly to timely or important issues and ideas, topics that people are currently talking about. Writers report on these topics, supply information about them, discuss and debate the differing viewpoints. The chapters in this book all represent topics now regularly discussed on college campuses and in the national media. In fact, all of the topics were chosen because they emerged so frequently in college newspapers.

When a columnist decides to write on a topic like affirmative action, she willingly enters an ongoing public discussion about the issue. She didn't just make up the topic. She knows that it *is* a serious issue, and she is aware that a wide variety of opinions have been expressed about it. She has not read everything on the subject but usually knows enough about the different arguments to state her own position or attitude persuasively. In fact, what helps make her writing persuasive is that she takes into account the opinions of others. Her own essay, then, becomes a part of the continuing debate and discussion, one that you in turn may want to join.

Such issues are not only matters for formal and impersonal debate. They also invite us to share our *personal* experiences. Many of the selections in this book show how writers participate in the discussion of issues by drawing on their experiences. For example, the essay by the Korean American novelist Chang-rae Lee, "Mute in an English-Only World" (Chapter 11), is written entirely from Lee's own point of view, though the topic — English as an official language — is one widely discussed and debated by politicians and educators. Nearly every chapter of *America Now* contains an example of personal writing to illustrate how you can use your experiences to discuss and debate an issue.

Writing is public in yet another way. Practically all published writing is reviewed, edited, and re-edited by different people before it goes to press. The author of a magazine article has most likely discussed the topic at length with colleagues and publishing professionals and may have asked friends or experts in the field to look it over. By the time you see the article in a magazine, it has gone through numerous readings and probably quite a few revisions. Though the article is credited to a particular author, it was no doubt read and worked on by others who helped with suggestions and improvements. As a beginning writer, it's important to remember that most of what you read in newspapers, magazines, and books has gone through a writing process that involves the collective efforts of several people besides the author. Students usually don't have that advantage and should not feel discouraged when their own writing doesn't measure up to the professionally edited materials they are reading for a course.

What Is "Correct English"?

One part of the writing process may seem more difficult than others — correct English. Yes, nearly all of what you read will be written in relatively correct English. Or it's probably more accurate to say "corrected" English, since most published writing is revised or "corrected" several times before it appears in print. Even skilled professional writers make mistakes that require correction.

Most native speakers don't actually *talk* in "correct" English. There are numerous regional patterns and dialects. As the Chinese American novelist Amy Tan says, there are "many Englishes." What we usually consider correct English is a set of guidelines developed over time to help standardize written expression. This standardization — like any agreed-upon standards such as weights and measures — is a matter of use and convenience. Suppose you went to a vegetable stand and asked for a pound of peppers and the storekeeper gave you a half pound but charged you for a full one. When you complained, he said, "But that's what *I* call a pound." What if you next bought a new compact disc you've been waiting for, and when you tried to play it you discovered it wouldn't fit your CD player. Life would be very frustrating if everyone had a different set of standards: Imagine what would happen if some places used a red light to signal "go" and a green one for "stop." Languages are not that different. In all cultures, languages — especially written languages — have gradually developed certain general rules and principles to make communication as clear and efficient as possible.

You probably already have a guidebook or handbook that systematically sets out certain rules of English grammar, punctuation, and spelling. Like our guitar instruction book, these handbooks serve a very practical purpose. Most writers — even experienced authors — need to consult them periodically. Beginning writers may need to rely on them far more regularly. But just as we don't learn how to play chords by merely memorizing finger positions, we don't learn how to write by memorizing the rules of grammar or punctuation.

Writing is an activity, a process. Learning how to do it — like learning to ride a bike or prepare a tasty stew — requires *doing* it. Correct English is not something that comes first. We don't need to know the rules perfectly before we can begin to write. As in any activity, corrections are part of the learning process. You fall off the bike and get on again, trying to "correct" your balance this time. You sample the stew and "correct" the seasoning. You draft a paper about the neighborhood you live in and as you (or a classmate or teacher) read it over, you notice that certain words and expressions could stand some improvement. And step by step, sentence by sentence, you begin to write better.

Writing as Empowerment

Writing is one of the most powerful means of producing social and political change. Through their four widely disseminated gospels, the first-century evangelists helped propagate Christianity throughout the world; the writings of Adam Smith and Karl Marx determined the economic systems of many nations for well over a century; Thomas Jefferson's Declaration of Independence became a model for countless colonial liberationists; the books and essays of numerous feminists have altered twentieth-century consciousness. In the long run, many believe, "the pen is mightier than the sword."

Empowerment does not mean instant success. It does not mean that your opinion or point of view will suddenly prevail. It does mean, however, that you have made your voice heard, that you have given your opinions wider circulation, that you have made yourself and your position a little more visible. And sometimes you get results: A newspaper prints your letter; a university committee adopts your suggestion; people visit your Web site. Throughout this collection you will encounter writing specifically intended to inform and influence a wide community.

Such influence is not restricted to professional authors and political experts. This collection features a large number of student writers who are actively involved with the same current topics and issues that engage the attention of professionals — affirmative action, bilingualism, media violence, free speech, gender differences, labeling and stereotyping, and so on. The student selections, all of them previously published, are meant to be an integral part of each chapter, to be read in conjunction with the professional essays, and to be criticized and analyzed on an equal footing. The student writing holds up.

The student essays were written for a wide variety of reasons — some personal, some public. The writers had little idea how their work would be received. Jonathan Bailey wrote his short personal essay "A Different Drummer" as part of the application process for Stanford University. It not only helped him get accepted, but it ended up being featured in Stanford's alumni magazine as one of five admission essays selected out of fifteen thousand. Erin Mansur-Smith got to read her essay on affirmative action, "It's Not Whether You Win or Lose — It's Whether or Not You're Allowed to Play the Game," on National Public Radio. Both writers reached far larger audiences than they ever imagined. In fact, none of the student writers appearing in this collection ever expected their work to be selected for a college text and be read by students throughout the country.

America Now urges you to voice your ideas and opinions — in your notebooks, in your papers, in your classrooms, and, most importantly, on your campus and in your communities. Reading, discussion, and writing will force you to clarify your observations, attitudes, and values, and as you do so you will discover more about yourself and the world you live in. These are exciting times. Don't sit on the sidelines of controversy. Don't retreat into invisibility and silence. Jump in and confront the ideas and issues currently shaping America.

1

How Do You See Yourself?

The Scottish poet Robert Burns once wrote: "Oh, would some power the Giver give us / To see ourselves as others see us!" The idea is that it would be a welcome gift from God if we could expand our self-perception and see ourselves through the eyes of others. Yet, what if we *do* see ourselves exactly as others perceive us and the view is not very flattering? Do we then always see ourselves in a negative light, or do we try to look at ourselves in new ways? The following selections show three people in the process of coming to terms with their appearance.

In "My Inner Shrimp," the famous creator of "Doonesbury," Garry Trudeau, describes a psychological condition many of us are familiar with: No matter how much we've changed, we continue to see ourselves as we once were. Our appearance can also be connected to serious racial issues. In "Light Skin versus Dark," Charisse Jones brings up a painful topic within the African American community: Having a dark complexion, she is especially sensitive to "colorism," which she defines as "being rejected by your own people because your skin is colored cocoa and not cream, ebony and not olive." Stanford student Jonathan Bailey introduces us to yet another aspect of appearance: Born with no fingers on his left hand, he describes in "A Different Drummer" how learning to play the drums helped dramatically improve his self-image.

GARRY TRUDEAU

My Inner Shrimp

[THE NEW YORK TIMES MAGAZINE / March 31, 1996]

Before You Read

Until he was seventeen, the author was one of the shortest boys in his class. Though he grew to be over six feet tall, he still thinks of himself as a short person. At one point in his essay he writes, "Not growing forces you to grow up fast." As you read, consider what Trudeau means by this remark. Can you apply his lesson to other kinds of childhood experiences?

Words to Learn

diminutive (para. 1): very small; tiny (adj.)

irrespective (para. 1): without regard to (adj.)

harrowing (para. 1): distressing or traumatic (adj.)

warren (para. 2): a crowded-together complex of living spaces (n.)

contingent (para. 10): a group sharing the same goals or traits (n.)

ignominiously (para. 10): with shame or disgrace (adv.)

ancillary (para. 11): less important; subordinate (adj.)

subtext (para. 12): underlying meaning (n.)

GARRY TRUDEAU *(b. 1948), creator of the popular comic strip "Doonesbury," has also contributed articles to such publications as* Harper's, Rolling Stone, *and* The New Republic. *A graduate of Yale University, where he received bachelor's and master's degrees, Trudeau won a Pulitzer Prize in 1975 and in 1994 received the award for best comic strip from the National Cartoonists Society.*

9/4/01

For the rest of my days, I shall be a recovering short person. Even from my lofty perch of something over six feet (as if I don't know within a micron), I have the soul of a shrimp. I feel the pain of the diminutive, irrespective of whether they feel it themselves, because my visit to the planet of the teenage midgets was harrowing, humiliating, and extended. I even perceive my last-minute escape to have been flukish, somehow unearned — as if the Commissioner of Growth Spurts had been an old classmate of my father.

My most recent reminder of all this came the afternoon I went hunting for a new office. I had noticed a building under construction in my neighborhood — a brick warren of duplexes, with wide, westerly-facing windows, promising ideal light for a working studio. When I was ushered into the model unit, my pulse quickened: The soaring, twenty-two-foot living room walls were gloriously aglow with the remains of the day. I bonded immediately.

I am still recalled as the Midget I myself have never really left behind.

Almost as an afterthought, I ascended the staircase to inspect the loft, ducking as I entered the bedroom. To my great surprise, I stayed ducked: The room was a little more than six feet in height. While my head technically cleared the ceiling, the effect was excruciatingly oppressive. This certainly wasn't a space I wanted to spend any time in, much less take out a mortgage on.

Puzzled, I wandered down to the sales office and asked if there were any other units to look at. No, replied a resolutely unpleasant receptionist, it was the last one. Besides, they were all exactly alike.

"Are you aware of how low the bedroom ceilings are?" I asked.   5

She shot me an evil look. "Of course we are," she snapped. "There were some problems with the building codes. The architect knows all about the ceilings.

"He's not an idiot, you know," she added, perfectly anticipating my next question.

She abruptly turned away, but it was too late. She'd just confirmed that a major New York developer, working with a fully licensed architect, had knowingly created an entire twelve-story apartment building virtually uninhabitable by anyone of even average height. It was an exclusive high-rise for shorties.

Once I knew that, of course, I couldn't stay away. For days thereafter, as I walked to work, some perverse, unreasoning force would draw me back to the building. But it wasn't just the absurdity, the stone silliness of its design that had me in its grip; it was something

far more compelling. Like some haunted veteran come again to an
ancient battlefield, I was revisiting my perilous past.

When I was fourteen, I was the third-smallest in a high school   10
class of one hundred boys, routinely mistaken for a sixth grader. My
first week of school, I was drafted into a contingent of students ignominiously dubbed the "Midgets," so grouped by taller boys presumably so they could taunt us with more perfect efficiency. Inexplicably,
some of my fellow Midgets refused to be diminished by the experience, but I retreated into self-pity. I sent away for a book on how to
grow tall, and committed to memory its tips on overcoming one's genetic destiny — or at least making the most of a regrettable situation.
The book cited historical figures who had gone the latter route —
Alexander the Great, Caesar, Napoleon (the mind involuntarily
added Hitler). Strategies for stretching the limbs were suggested —
hanging from door frames, sleeping on your back, doing assorted
floor exercises — all of which I incorporated into my daily routine
(get up, brush teeth, hang from door frame). I also learned the importance of meeting girls early in the day, when, the book assured me,
my rested spine rendered me perceptibly taller.

For six years, my condition persisted; I grew, but at nowhere
near the rate of my peers. I perceived other problems as ancillary, and
loaded up the stature issue with freight shipped in daily from every
corner of my life. Lack of athletic success, all absence of a social life,
the inevitable run-ins with bullies — all could be attributed to the
missing inches. The night I found myself sobbing in my father's arms
was the low point; we both knew it was one problem he couldn't fix.

Of course what we couldn't have known was that he and my
mother already had. They had given me a delayed developmental
timetable. In my seventeenth year, I miraculously shot up six inches,
just in time for graduation and a fresh start. I was, in the space of a
few months, reborn — and I made the most of it. Which is to say that
thereafter, all of life's disappointments, reversals, and calamities still
arrived on schedule — but blissfully free of subtext.

Once you stop being the butt, of course, any problem recedes, if
only to give way to a new one. And yet the impact of being literally
looked down on, of being *made* to feel small, is forever. It teaches
you how to stretch, how to survive the scorn of others for things that
are beyond your control. Not growing forces you to grow up fast.

Sometimes I think I'd like to return to a high-school reunion to
surprise my classmates. Not that they didn't know me when I finally
started catching up. They did, but I doubt they'd remember. Adoles-

cent hierarchies have a way of enduring; I'm sure I am still recalled as the Midget I myself have never really left behind.

Of course, if I'm going to show up, it'll have to be soon. I'm starting to shrink. 15

Discussing Vocabulary / Using a Dictionary

1. A key word in the essay is "short." How many synonyms for the word can you find in the essay? Make a list. Are all of the words interchangeable? Divide your list into synonyms that seem neutral and those that seem insulting.

2. How would you distinguish between a "harrowing" experience and a "humiliating" (para. 1) one?

3. You probably won't find "flukish" in a dictionary. What does it mean? What word is it based on? Can you substitute a different word with a similar meaning? Have you experienced something "flukish" in your own life?

4. Several difficult vocabulary terms come together when Trudeau writes that he was part of a "contingent of students ignominiously dubbed the 'Midgets'" (para. 10). Can you rephrase Trudeau's statement in simpler terms?

5. Trudeau writes that "adolescent *hierarchies* have a way of enduring" (para. 14). What is a hierarchy? Can you think of a few hierarchies in your own life?

6. The word "ancillary" is a useful one that appears in many different contexts. Textbook publishers, for example, often produce "ancillary" materials such as workbooks, diagnostic tests, and teacher's manuals to supplement the main text. Try using the word in another context. The word also has an unusual origin. What is it?

Discussing Meaning

1. What does Trudeau mean when he says "my visit to the planet of the teen-age midgets was harrowing, humiliating, and extended" (para. 1)? Why do you think he uses this expression?

2. Of what importance is the scene in the apartment building? How is it connected to Trudeau's main point? Why is the receptionist

"unpleasant"? Why does Trudeau find the building "compelling"?

3. What does Trudeau mean in paragraph 13 when he states: "Not growing forces you to grow up fast"? Can you express this concept in another way? Why is this expression especially appropriate? How does the author play on two senses of a word?

Discussing Writing

1. Why do you think Trudeau chose for his title the word "shrimp," a slang term for a short person, instead of a term like "small" or "short"? What other terms does Trudeau use for short people? Do you think these words are insulting or demeaning? Why or why not?

2. In paragraph 9 Trudeau uses the following image to describe what fascinated him about the apartment building: "Like some haunted veteran come again to an ancient battlefield, I was revisiting my perilous past." What does the image suggest about Trudeau's boyhood experience?

3. In what way is the "battlefield" image important to Trudeau's word choices? Try locating other terms and references in the next few paragraphs that evolve out of the battlefield image.

4. Is Trudeau's tone serious or sarcastic? Do you think he writes in a different tone when he writes about his adolescent and adult experiences? List words that reflect his tone.

Challenging the Selection

1. Trudeau's title suggests a phrase popular in today's "Recovery Movement," where people sometimes speak of their "inner child" as a presence that always remains inside them. Trudeau plays on this movement again when he lets us know in his opening sentence that he will forever "be a recovering short person." Do you think Trudeau is serious in viewing his teenage height in the same terms one would use in discussing child abuse or addictions?

2. Trudeau says that in school he was part of a group of short students "ignominiously dubbed the 'Midgets'" (para. 10). Why is the word "ignominious"? Who is degrading or debasing the

"Midgets"? Why would one group label another group "igno-miniously"?

In-Class Writing Activities

1. Select the one sentence in the essay that you think best captures Trudeau's main point. Then in a few sentences explain why you chose that particular sentence. Compare your choice with those of your classmates.

2. One of Trudeau's points is that he will never get past a negative self-image. Write him a one-paragraph letter offering him your best advice.

CHARISSE JONES

Light Skin versus Dark

[GLAMOUR / October 1995]

Before You Read

In junior high school, the author discovered that she was a victim of "colorism," a color bias among her fellow African Americans for those of lighter complexion. Because this rejection came from her own people, Charisse Jones believes it is more hurtful than white racism. Before you read, consider your own attitude with respect to this issue: Do you think that a "light complexion" is a physical advantage?

Journalist CHARISSE JONES (b. 1965), a 1987 graduate of the University of Southern California, writes for the New York Times *and has also contributed to* Vibe *and* Essence *magazines. Formerly a reporter for the* Los Angeles Herald *and the* Los Angeles Times, *she shared a Pulitzer Prize for coverage of the 1992 Los Angeles riots. Jones says her mission as a journalist is to "give a form to the voices of people who are normally not heard."*

Words to Learn

lexicon (para. 4): terminology used by a particular group (n.)

hue (para. 4): shade of color (n.)

nuance (para. 12): slight or subtle

degree of difference (n.)

eradicate (para. 13): to completely eliminate

I'll never forget the day I was supposed to meet him. We had only spoken on the phone. But we got along so well, we couldn't wait to meet face-to-face. I took the bus from my high school to his for our blind date. While I nervously waited for him outside the school, one of his buddies came along, looked me over, and remarked that I was going to be a problem, because his friend didn't like dating anybody darker than himself.

When my mystery man — who was not especially good-looking — finally saw me, he took one look, uttered a hurried hello, then disappeared with his smirking friends. I had apparently been pronounced ugly on arrival and dismissed.

That happened nearly fifteen years ago. I'm thirty now, and the hurt and humiliation have long since faded. But the memory still lingers, reinforced in later years by other situations in which my skin color was judged by other African Americans — for example, at a cocktail party or a nightclub where light-skinned black women got all the attention.

A racist encounter hurts badly. But it does not equal the pain of "colorism" — being rejected by your own people because your skin is colored cocoa and not cream, ebony and not olive. On our scale of beauty, it is often the high yellows — in the lexicon of black America, those with light skin — whose looks reap the most attention. Traditionally, if someone was described that way, there was no need to say that person was good-looking. It was a given that light was lovely. It was those of us with plain brown eyes and darker skin hues who had to prove ourselves.

I was twelve, and in my first year of junior high school in San Francisco, when I discovered dark brown was not supposed to be beautiful. At that age, boys suddenly became important, and so did your looks. But by that time — the late 1970s — black kids no longer believed in that sixties mantra, "Black is beautiful." Light skin, green eyes, and long, wavy hair were once again synonymous with beauty.

5

Colorism — and its subtext of self-hatred — began during slavery on plantations where white masters often favored the lighter-skinned blacks, many of whom were their own children. But though it began with whites, black people have kept colorism alive. In the past, many black sororities, fraternities, and other social organizations have been notorious for accepting only light-skinned members. Yes, some blacks have criticized their lighter-skinned peers. But most often in our history, a light complexion has been a passport to special treatment by both whites *and* blacks.

Some social circles are still defined by hue. Some African Americans, dark and light, prefer light-skinned mates so they can have a "pretty baby." And skin-lightening creams still sell, though they are now advertised as good for making blemishes fade rather than for lightening whole complexions.

A light complexion has been a passport to special treatment by both whites and blacks.

In my family, color was never discussed, even though our spectrum was broad — my brother was very light; my sister and I, much darker. But in junior high, I learned in a matter of weeks what had apparently been drummed into the heads of my black peers for most of their lives.

Realizing how crazy it all was, I became defiant, challenging friends when they made silly remarks. Still, there was no escaping the distinctions of color.

In my life, I have received a litany of twisted compliments from fellow blacks. "You're the prettiest dark-skinned girl I have ever seen" is one; "you're pretty for a dark girl" is another.

A light-complexioned girlfriend once remarked to me that dark-skinned people often don't take the time to groom themselves. As a journalist, I once interviewed a prominent black lawmaker who was light-skinned. He drew me into the shade of a tree while we talked because, he said, "I'm sure you don't want to get any darker."

Though some black people — like film-maker Spike Lee in his movie *School Daze* — have tried to provoke debate about colorism, it remains a painful topic many blacks would rather not confront. Yet there has been progress. In this age of Afrocentrism, many blacks revel in the nuances of the African American rainbow. Natural hairstyles and dreadlocks are in, and Theresa Randle, star of the hit film *Bad Boys,* is only one of several darker-skinned actresses noted for their beauty.

That gives me hope. People have told me that color biases among blacks run too deep ever to be eradicated. But I tell them that is the kind of attitude that allows colorism to persist. Meanwhile, I do what I can. When I notice that a friend dates only light-skinned women, I comment on it. If I hear that a movie follows the tired old scenario in which a light-skinned beauty is the love interest while a darker-skinned woman is the comic foil, the butt of "ugly" jokes, I don't go see it. Others can do the same.

There is only so much blacks can do about racism, because we need the cooperation of others to make it go away. But healing ourselves is within our control.

At least we can try. As a people we face enough pain without in-   15
flicting our own wounds. I believe any people that could survive slavery, that could disprove the lies that pronounced them less than human, can also teach its children that black is beautiful in all of its shades.

Loving ourselves should be an easy thing to do.

Discussing Vocabulary / Using a Dictionary

1. In paragraph 4, the author refers to "the *lexicon* of black America." What is a lexicon? Find a few other words in her essay that belong to this "lexicon."

2. What does "hue" mean and why is the word a useful one for the author?

3. In what sense does the writer use the word "foil" (para. 13)? What other words might she have used to convey a similar meaning?

4. The author wants to "eradicate" (para. 13) color bias among blacks. What else should be eradicated from American society?

Discussing Meaning

1. What does the author mean by "colorism" (para. 4), and how does it differ from racism? What are the word's origins?

2. What does the author mean by "twisted compliments" (para. 10)? Why are her examples of such compliments "twisted"?

3. Toward the conclusion of her essay, the author says that she's hopeful that "colorism" is declining. What gives her hope? How convincing do you find her examples?

Discussing Writing

1. Do you think the author imagines she is writing for mainly white or mainly black readers? Point to elements of the essay that indicate a white audience. What elements indicate that she is addressing fellow African Americans?

2. The author begins with a personal story about a high school experience. Can you think of other ways she might have started her essay? What other paragraph in the essay might have offered an effective opening?

3. Jones's article was published in *Glamour,* a magazine for young women that contains articles on fashion, beauty, and lifestyles. What other audiences could learn from this article? What other publications would be good vehicles for its important message?

Challenging the Selection

1. Do you think gender plays any part in "colorism"? In other words, would the author feel that a light complexion is a greater advantage to African American women than it is to men?

2. Why does the author believe that "colorism" is more painful than racism? Do you agree with her on this point? What were your thoughts on this topic before you read the essay? Has reading the essay changed your views?

In-Class Writing Activities

1. Charisse Jones gives several examples of what she calls "twisted compliments." Write a single paragraph in which you introduce an example of how such a "compliment" works.

2. Toward the end of her essay, the author says that she does what she can to change attitudes about "colorism." In small groups of three to five students, review her efforts in this direction. Make a list of additional ways "colorism" can be resisted.

3. The author distinguishes between the problems that require cooperation of others to solve and those we can heal from within ourselves. Separate some of the real problems in your life or in the world into two groups — those that require cooperation and those that you (and perhaps your social or cultural group) can heal from within. Do certain problems fit into both groups?

JONATHAN BAILEY

A Different Drummer

[STANFORD / September 1995]

Before You Read

Born with no fingers on his left hand, the author grew up feeling ashamed and fearful of rejection. But then he discovered the drums and learned to see himself in a new, positive way. As you read, consider the details that Bailey chooses to include in his brief self-portrait and those he doesn't.

Words to Learn

envelop (para. 3): to wrap or enclose (v.)
pulsating (para. 3): throbbing; beating (adj.)

I was born a little bit different from everyone else. I have no fingers, only a thumb, on my left hand. Throughout much of my life I was ashamed of my physical distinction. I believed that people would judge my character based on what my hand looked like, and I feared rejection. One thing in particular helped to change my perspective: the drums.

When I was thirteen, as my stepmother and I stood in the kitchen talking, I began to tap on the table. My stepmother, who was once a musician, immediately noticed a good sense of rhythm in my counter-tapping endeavor and suggested we consider starting me on the drums. I was surprised that she would even suggest such a thing.

JONATHAN BAILEY *(b. 1977) plans to double-major in complete science and studio art and design at Stanford University, for which he wrote the following essay as part of his admissions application. The essay was reprinted in "The Write Stuff," a special section of* Stanford, *the university's alumni magazine.*

Drums required two hands — and I had only one. However, the very next day, the two of us were off to the music store to purchase a pair of drumsticks and a "practice pad." Six months later we purchased my drum set.

I'll never forget the first time I sat on the throne of my new drum set. My entire body shook with excitement. I had always wanted to play the drums, but I never believed I could. I thought my "disability" would stop me. Now, before me lay not just one drum, but an entire drum set, beckoning me to play. I cautiously picked up my drumsticks and, ever so gently, began tapping on first one, and then all of the drums and cymbals. Then I let loose. I sounded awful, but I didn't care. It was one of the most romantic experiences of my life. Never had I been so enveloped in a blanket of pulsating frequencies and tones. I was in love. My parents, however, were not, and we quickly agreed that I could continue playing the drums only if I took lessons. It was settled. I started my lessons and began to practice.

I was born a little bit different from everyone else.

Drums were not only a source of pleasure and joy for me, they became the means by which I realized that I could use my left hand productively. By being able to play the drums, I discovered that my left hand could be used to produce something beautiful, something useful, and I realized its unique importance. Instead of hating my hand, I began to respect it — to respect me.

Through my drums, my hand and I have become one. Now, when I meet new people, I no longer fear that the first part of me a person sees will be my hand. That person may see my heart, as I share with him a poem I have just finished. Another person will see my mind, as I discuss with her Newton's Law of Universal Gravitation. Another will see me, sitting behind the fruit of my passion, the drums, driving a punk quartet or the school jazz band. And if that person does see my hand — what of it? It is with this hand that I make music. It is with this hand that I write a poem, or do a calculus problem, or stroke a kitten. What more could I possibly want? I am complete.

5

Discussing Vocabulary / Using a Dictionary

1.   Bailey says that he was ashamed of his "physical distinction" (para. 1). What does "distinction" mean in this sense?

2. What does Bailey mean by "pulsating" (para. 3)? What is the root of that word? How is the word related to "pulse"?

Discussing Meaning

1. Why did learning to play the drums help Bailey transform his self-image? What did he learn from his new accomplishment?
2. "I am complete," writes Bailey to conclude his essay. What do you think he means by that remark?

Discussing Writing

1. In paragraph 3, why does Bailey refer to sitting on the "throne" of his new drum set? What does the image suggest?
2. Note Bailey's final paragraph. Why does he introduce these other interests? What effect do they have on your perception of him?
3. How does Bailey's last paragraph show his sensitivity to gender stereotypes?

Challenging the Selection

1. Bailey doesn't describe *how* he learned to play the drums, given the limited use of his left hand. Nor does he say anything about who gave him lessons. Are these irrelevant? Why do you think he omits this information?
2. What other details do you think Bailey might have mentioned? What questions would you ask him if you had the opportunity?

In-Class Writing Activities

1. Do you find any aspect of Bailey's experience applicable to your own life? Write a short essay in which you discuss an experience that you feel transformed your self-esteem.
2. Bailey writes that he is "complete." In a brief essay, describe what particular accomplishment would make you feel a similar sense of completion.
3. Bailey describes his drums not only as a source of pleasure but also as a means to an end: his realization of self-respect. What method, course of action, or instrument are you using to achieve a goal? Outline in five or fewer steps a plan for achieving that goal.

Discussing the Unit

Suggested Topic for Discussion

The authors in this unit all write about a negative self-image and how it affected their personal development. To what extent does our self-esteem depend on the physical image we have of ourselves? How simple is it to alter that image? One's self-image can derive from many different sources: the media, the dominant culture, gender, race, class, peers, parents, the bathroom mirror. Which source do you think plays the biggest role in determining the way you see yourself?

Preparing for Class Discussion

1. Garry Trudeau's dilemma is a common one: Even when they've changed, people seem to perceive themselves in the old ways. Overweight people who have slimmed down, for example, often say they still view themselves as overweight no matter how many pounds they've lost. But do you think a persistent inner-self image works the other way as well? Would thin people who put on a lot of weight continue — no matter how heavy they got — to see themselves as thin? Jot down a few thoughts on whether a positive self-image would persist as long as a negative one would.

2. The philosopher Arthur Schopenhauer wrote that we all proceed with people on the basis of an unspoken rule that everyone *is* as he or she *looks*. In other words, we all seem to think — despite evidence to the contrary — that we can judge people mainly by their physical appearance. Consider your own appearance and how you think it affects other people's assessment of you. Do you think others see you as you see yourself, or is there often a difference between the way you see yourself and how others see you? What might people think about the way you look that differs from how you view yourself? Do you think the way others view you has made a big difference in your life?

From Discussion to Writing

1. Which of the three essays in this unit do you think raises the most important issues about the relationship between self-image and self-esteem? In an essay, summarize the main point of the selection and explain why you find the author's ideas significant.

2. Experts debate the influences of environment and heredity on human development. All three authors in this unit cope with different genetic "destinies," and all three mention family influence. Do you think that your development has been influenced more by nature (genetics) or nurture (family influence)? Write a brief, well-supported argument for your stand on this issue. As an alternative, write a brief letter (about fifty words) to a family member who positively influenced your self-image.

3. Create a modern fairy tale of transformation in self-image. (You might want to recall Hans Christian Andersen's "The Ugly Duckling" or some other tale in which such a transformation took place.) Choose a specific audience for your tale, and keep this audience in mind as you write.

Topics for Cross-Cultural Discussion

1. Ideals of beauty differ from culture to culture. In some cultures, fat women are considered to be the most beautiful; in the United States, thin women are thought to be beautiful. Pick two cultures and compare their ideals of beauty.

2. Do you think different cultures see the connection between self-image and self-esteem differently? Do you think Americans place too great an emphasis on their physical appearance and too little on intellectual or cultural achievements? How does your own culture view the problems of a negative self-image?

3. If you are a native of a country other than America, do you think your country has a positive or negative image of itself in the "community of nations"? What are the criteria of the negative or positive image your country has of itself? Is your country's image dependent upon an economic world order or some other standard?

2

Sharing Space: Can We Learn to Live with Others?

Finding suitable living companions is one of life's constant problems. It applies not only to college — where students often complain about their roommates — but throughout our lives, as we find ourselves thrown together in the military, in travel, or in shared apartments, or as we find partners we want to live with or marry. The problem even continues into old age, as many people in retirement homes are forced to make new friends and adjust to new surroundings.

In "Take Your Shoes Off My Books," Jo McGowan describes the difficulties and rewards of sharing a life and home with a husband from another culture. Although the process of learning to live with others goes on for a lifetime, it is especially relevant to college, where most students will live away from home for the first time in their lives. In "Roommatism," Dan Zevin humorously tells new students how they can live with others without killing themselves. His detached advice is followed by the firsthand experience of a college student. Knight Stivender, from the University of Tennessee, describes in "Somewhere a Room of One's Own" her nostalgia for the cozy, private room she left at home.

JO McGOWAN

Take Your Shoes Off My Books: Negotiating a Hindu-Catholic Marriage

[COMMONWEAL / June 18, 1993]

Before You Read

Has someone with whom you shared a room or some other space ever done something that annoyed you? How did you deal with the situation?

Words to Learn

disparity (para. 1): a difference (n.)

prescribed (para. 1): dictated (adj.)

abjure (para. 1): to reject (v.)

covet (para. 2): to desire (v.)

unobtrusively (para. 4): not noticeably (adv.)

bourgeois (para. 5): concerned with conventional and materialistic values (adj.)

concede (para. 7): to agree, often grudgingly (v.)

plaintive (para. 22): sad (adj.)

enigma (para. 22): mystery (n.)

paradox (para. 23): something that seems contradictory but is nonetheless true (n.)

transgress (para. 23): to offend (v.)

sacrilege (para. 29): violation of something sacred (n.)

contempt (para. 29): dishonor (n.)

profanity (para. 29): the quality of being disrespectful or irreverent (n.)

preconceived (para. 35): formed beforehand (adj.)

fidelity (para. 36): loyalty (n.)

JO McGOWAN (b. 1958) is a frequent contributor to the U.S. Catholic Reporter, The Human Life Review, Indian Express, *the* Times of India, *and* Commonweal, *writing articles about family issues, religious values, and Indian culture. In 1996, she started a school for mentally handicapped children. A Catholic from Massachusetts, McGowan dropped out of college to get married and has lived in India with her husband and family since 1981. She is currently writing a book about India with her sister.*

When my husband, Ravi, and I married thirteen years ago, we had plenty of God-given disparities to keep us busy. I was twenty-one and he was thirty-three. I am American and he is from India. I am a Roman Catholic who attends Mass, keeps the prescribed fasts, and uses a breviary.[1] He is a Hindu who prays daily and abjures temples and idol-worship. I am a college dropout and a professional writer; he is a Ph.D. in metallurgy[2] turned environmental activist. We live in India, in the foothills of the Himalayas, on a combined yearly income of somewhat less than five thousand dollars. You would think that when we disagreed, it would be over something substantial — at any rate, something more substantial than a sofa set.

> *You would think that when we disagreed, it would be over something more substantial than a sofa set. You would be wrong.*

You would be wrong. The sofa set in question belonged to friends, a British couple who had lived in our town for eight years. They had it built their first year here and it had been heavily used by them and their two young boys, a cat, two dogs, and an endless parade of friends. It was, to be sure, an exceptionally comfortable set, deep and roomy, with just the right amounts of sink and spring to encourage leisurely reading, and conversation; but a living room containing it would not be a candidate for a *House Beautiful* award. I had, though I try not to be materialistic, coveted it since the day they announced that they were being transferred to Africa and intended to sell most of their furniture.

Without exactly discussing it with my husband, I arranged with my friends to buy it for about half what they had paid and perhaps a tenth what it would cost to buy new. When I told Ravi, he said it was up to me, but in his innocence, he assumed I was buying only the couch.

He was at work when it all arrived — an enormous couch and two large chairs which had doubled in size on the trip from my friends' large living room to our small one — and I did my best to make it fit in unobtrusively. But even I had to admit that the effect was a bit staggering. We'll get used to it, I assured him when he walked in and nearly tripped over the chair that *was* a bit too close to the door for comfort.

---

[1]*breviary:* A book of hymns and prayers.   [2]*metallurgy:* The study of metals.

Our children, at least, were delighted. They tumbled the length of   5
the couch and did headstands on the chairs, just as I had done in my
childhood. And just as my mother had, I scolded them about ruining
the springs and pointed out the heel marks on the walls. I gave that
up rather sooner than she had, however, as it suddenly occurred to
me that my concern for furniture was proof of my husband's contention that we were becoming a bourgeois, middle-class family, anxious to acquire symbols of status, eager for a life of indolence and
wealth.

Before moving to India, it had never occurred to me that a secondhand, eight-year-old sofa set could be a status symbol. But then
again, I grew up in America, where reality is very different. To me, a
refrigerator is an absolute necessity; to Ravi, pure luxury.

Over the years (we've lived in India for twelve), we've done our
share of compromising. I got the fridge on day one — even a purist
like my husband had to concede that expecting a New Englander
who wilted in Massachusetts summers to survive in temperatures of
115 degrees Fahrenheit without one was too much — but it was the
smallest model. It was I who banned a television, although Ravi
would love one (he says he needs it for "information"), and we both
agreed not to invest in a car (although I have been less enthusiastic
with each additional child; dragging all three on Indian public trans-
port isn't easy).

The discussions we had over each of these items, however, were
reasoned and logical and had to do with practical concerns: milk
spoiling, the effect of TV on family life, and the convenience of a car
vs. the expense and the pollution. We seldom got emotional and we
usually could explain ourselves.

The sofa set, on the other hand, seemed to touch both of us in a
deep and inarticulate way, stirring up images of childhood and forcing us to confront our values, both individually and as a couple.

One night not long after the sofa arrived neither of us could   10
sleep. We lay on opposite ends of the couch, our legs overlapping in
the middle (and even he had to admit it was comfortable) and talked
about living in India. Somehow this led us to the sofa set and what it
meant to each of us.

To me, a big, comfortable couch is at the center of family life. I
got quite emotional describing my memories to Ravi: the afternoon
story hours with my mother in the center of the couch and all seven
of us ranged on either side of her; the days when I would be home

sick and my mother would set me up on the couch for the day, a box of Kleenex and a bell with which to call her by my side; the times when I would see her sitting on the couch, nursing the current baby, cuddling her or him until sleep arrived. . . . "It's like a big kitchen table," I concluded. "It's essential."

Ravi found this argument quite unpersuasive, and focused first on a side issue. "You *rang a bell* for your mother?" he asked, horrified.

"Only when I was sick," I said, defensively.

"It doesn't matter how sick you were. A child never rings a bell for her mother, as if she were a servant."

"Well, unlike you," I said hotly, "we didn't grow up with servants, so the thought of treating my mother as one never occurred to me. And anyway, it was a big house. A bell was practical." 15

He just shook his head, still shocked, still unconvinced.

"But, anyway, Ravi, the point isn't the bell — it's the couch."

He, however, refused to concede anything. My comparison to the kitchen table fell flat: *He* didn't grow up with one. In his family, the children ate in a long row on the floor while the grownups took turns at the very small fold-down dining table. Family spirit did not suffer as a result.

As for the couch, although they had not one but three in their living room, there were no cuddling sessions or story hours which took place there. Children and adults operated in separate spheres and the couches were adult territory, meant for entertaining adult guests.

It was the middle-class propriety of it all which bothered him now, so many years later: the formal entertaining, the apparent desire to impress one's guests with possessions. It didn't matter, he pointed out, whether *we* thought of a sofa set as a great acquisition; everyone else most assuredly did. "My activist friends think I've sold out," he said, "I can't say what's going on in their minds, but I do know they are uncomfortable coming here now." 20

This, I had to admit, seemed true. I remembered coming home one afternoon to find Ravi sitting in one of the big chairs talking with three villagers. They were huddled close together at one end of the couch, perched awkwardly on its edge as if fearing to get it dirty, and my arrival made them even more nervous.

Obviously, this didn't make me happy. But why, I asked (in what I hoped was not too plaintive a tone) should I give up what I considered normal and ordinary to reassure people who would find me strange no matter what I did? As long as my skin remained white, my

Hindi accented, my body language Western, and my style casual, loose-limbed, and free, I was going to be an enigma and a puzzle to the average Indian villager. What difference would a sofa set make?

The discussion could have gone on and on. What we were really talking about was the paradox at the heart of every marriage: the wedding of two entirely different worlds and the constant adjustments and fine tuning required to make it all work. In a marriage like ours, however, the requirements are at times excessive. Worlds farther apart than a Hindu's India and a Catholic's America are hard to imagine, and there are times when I wonder how we ever thought our love could bridge the gap between the two. In our family lore, our favorite stories are of the times we transgressed some deeply held belief of the other's, all the while totally unconscious of having offended.

My worst mistake occurred soon after our marriage. I was tidying up our apartment in a hurry just before a weekend out of town. I had put a pair of shoes on top of a pile of books meaning to take the shoes down the hall to the closet when I left the room. In a rush to get to the train on time, however, I left them where they were. On Sunday night, we returned, tired and happy after our trip. The mood evaporated instantly when Ravi saw my shoes.

"Who did this?" he shouted, practically leaping across the room   25 to snatch them up off the books.

"Did what?" I asked, bewildered, thinking perhaps we had been robbed.

"Put these shoes on top of these *books*?" he thundered.

"Well, I guess I did. What are you so upset about?" I was still bewildered.

When he calmed down (it took awhile), he explained that what I had done was a sacrilege. Books were a representation of Saraswati, the goddess of wisdom. To put shoes, the dirtiest thing an Indian can think of, anywhere near her was contempt and profanity of the worst kind. "Please don't ever do it again," he begged me.

Needless to say, I never have and now, having lived so long in   30 India, I cannot even believe that I ever did; the idea of it shocks me as much as it did him.

His first mistake was not quite so dramatic, or perhaps it only seems less so because I have become so accustomed to Indian ways. We were married in the United States and his parents, niece, and several cousins came from India for the wedding. We spent our wedding night and the day after on Cape Cod and the next evening we drove back to our apartment, stopping on the way to pick up his parents and niece.

This seemed strange to no one but me. For the next two months (our honeymoon!) I lived as if in a foreign country. They spoke almost exclusively in Punjabi (not a word of which I could understand), cooked only Indian food, went shopping in Indian stores, and entertained Indian friends and relatives. All of it might have been bearable, but during our whole engagement I had treasured a romantic image of our first year as newlyweds: the candlelight dinners, the lazy Sunday mornings with croissants and the newspapers . . . time to get to know each other, to play house. Instead, I seemed to be constantly struggling to get a translation: By the time I could get Ravi's attention to ask what they were all in stitches about, they'd be on to the next story and he'd be too busy listening to bother with me.

What troubled me most in those days was that he didn't really understand why I was so upset. Of course, he could see that no one enjoys being left out, but he couldn't see why the timing bothered me so. "We've got our whole lives to be together," he pointed out quite logically. "We'll have our honeymoon once they leave. This is a once-in-a-lifetime trip for them."

But even while I conceded that I was being selfish and immature, I still believed there was something crucial in the fact that he didn't share my disappointment. And indeed, as I learned more about the Indian concept of marriage, I found I was right. To him, the awkward situation I was in vis-à-vis[3] his family was perfectly ordinary for a new bride in India who must adjust herself to a *family*, not, as the Western version would have it, participate in a process with her husband whereby each of them adjusts to the other.

To his credit, Ravi has proved remarkably open to *my* precon-   35
ceived ideas and has more or less gracefully accepted the fact that much is required from both of us. He has occasional relapses when we are with his family; old habits die hard. But I am no longer twenty-one, I speak the language now, and I have made my own adjustments, not the least of which has been learning to make *chapatties*.[4]

The difficulties of a cross-cultural marriage are enormous, there can be no denying. But the rewards are equally great. When I

---

[3]*vis-à-vis:* In relationship to.   [4]*chapatties:* Flat, round Indian bread.

consider Ravi's virtues as a husband, words like fidelity and devotion come to mind, old-fashioned virtues met less and less frequently in the standard American marriage. Marrying into a traditional culture where marriage is still a sacred bond and divorce still a scandal provides a security that I, for one, am grateful for. The institution is stronger than the individual couple and provides a firm and certain footing which makes it possible to take a great deal for granted.

In America, on the other hand, many couples seem to begin married life with the sense of charting unknown waters, ever mindful of the dangers of the journey and the flimsiness of their vessel. Here in India, the path is so well-worn and safe arrival so virtually assured that one hardly considers the bullock[5] cart one is traveling in. The jolts and occasional breakdowns are expected and taken in stride and there are plenty of fellow pilgrims to ask for directions. And at the end of the day there's that couch to sink into and relax on. Like our marriage, it looks like it's here to stay.

[5]*bullock:* Young bull.

Discussing Vocabulary / Using a Dictionary

1. After reviewing the definition of "unobtrusively," determine the meaning of "obtrusively." Think of a sentence using each word.

2. Review the definition of the word "paradox" and its usage in paragraph 23. Then think of at least one situation that you would describe as paradoxical.

Discussing Meaning

1. What are some of the major differences between the author and her husband? In what ways are they similar?

2. Why did the sofa set cause such a conflict in the author's marriage?

3. Why was the act of putting shoes on the books a "sacrilege" (para. 29)? In what other ways is this word commonly used?

4. Why does the author contend that there is a "paradox at the heart of every marriage" (para. 23)?

Discussing Writing

1. Skim through the essay, underlining each reference the author makes to her couch. Why does the author focus so much on the furniture? Do you think this adds to the essay or not? Explain.

2. Why does the author end the essay with a paragraph about a ride in a bullock cart?

Challenging the Selection

1. How would you describe the author's marriage based on this essay? Do you think it is a good one? Why or why not? Use evidence from the essay to support your perspective.

2. Of all the differences between husband and wife described in the essay, which did you feel was the most serious or hurtful? Explain.

3. Which person in the marriage do you think makes the most concessions? Explain.

4. Do you think the author would have had as many difficulties "sharing space" with a husband from another culture if they had set up their home in the United States instead of India? Why or why not?

In-Class Writing Activities

1. Write an essay about how you would plan to live successfully with someone from another culture.

2. Write an essay about another culture. It may be about learning a foreign language in high school or college; you might describe the first day of class or a specific incident. Or you might describe what it is like to be bilingual or from a family with representatives from two or more cultures. If you are friendly with a family from another country, you might write about how their customs differ from your family's.

DAN ZEVIN

Roommatism

[ROLLING STONE / October 20, 1994]

Before You Read

Imagine that you are about to share a room or apartment with someone you have never met. Make a list of the three things that would
worry you most about your new roommate. When you have finished
reading the selection, compare your list to the concerns raised by the
author.

Words to Learn

incompatible (para. 1): incapable of
    harmony (adj.)
genre (para. 11): type or class (n.)
nemesis (para. 15): rival or
    enemy (n.)

hermaphrodite (para. 15): a crea-
    ture that has male and female sex
    organs (n.)

The first step to mastering roommate relations is understanding
the process by which housing officials match incoming freshmen. Before school begins, colleges send out roommate questionnaires to find
out whether you are a morning or night person, whether you smoke,
whether you have ever engaged in acts of bestiality, etc. After careful
analysis, the officials then take delight in matching you with people
whose answers are the opposite of yours. Once it has been determined that the students in each pair will be entirely incompatible,
they are made roommates.

*DAN ZEVIN (b. 1964), a 1988 graduate of New York University, is the
author of* Entry-Level Life *(1994) and a comedian who lectures at colleges
about life after graduation. Zevin has contributed to such publications as*
Spy, Outside, *and* Mademoiselle *and is currently at work on a new book. He
lives in Somerville, Massachusetts.*

At this point, it may seem like the best idea is to answer each question the opposite of how you would normally respond. This is risky, because there's always that rare chance you'll be matched with someone who really *is* a peppy morning person whose hobbies include vacuuming, Bible study, and sex with livestock.

A better idea is to get matched with that one person to whom you are truly best suited: yourself.

How to Score a Single Room

To ensure a roommate-free abode, leave your survey entirely blank except for the section below:

Q: Do you have a medical condition?

A: Yes, I suffer from severe multiple-environmental-allergy syndrome. I am allergic to dust, air, sounds, and all synthetic or natural materials. That John Travolta Movie of the Week *The Boy in the Plastic Bubble* was based on my life.

What to Do if You Don't

If by some fluke the above strategy fails, resign yourself to spending the next year living in an enclosed space with a complete stranger, most likely one who does sleep in a plastic bubble. To pave the way for a smooth transition, most colleges advise contacting your designated roommate before you actually meet. This is a good idea; it allows you to ask personal, probing questions to make sure he or she is the right match for you: (1) Do you own a CD player and/or a TV? (2) A car? (3) Do you have wealthy parents who send generous care packages to share with your roommate? (4) Do you have a girlfriend or boyfriend at a nearby school, where you will spend evenings and weekends? (5) Do you require any special breathing apparatus?

> *Living together is no way to treat a friend.*

Moving Day

Of course, you've arrived early enough on moving day to take the bigger closet, the larger desk, and the unstained mattress before your roommate gets there. When he finally arrives, make him feel like a guest in your home. Show him where he'll be sleeping. Then treat him to dinner at the cafeteria to make others think you have a friend.

It is especially important to arrive early if you are placed in a triple. When you live as a threesome, it is standard practice for two to team up against the other. If you show up last, your roommates will have already bonded, and you will be outnumbered.

What if you do arrive late on moving day? Seize the opportunity   10
to snoop through your roommates' personal belongings while they are plotting against you in the cafeteria. Flee the premises at once if you come across any of the following warning signs: framed prom picture; Garfield memo board; feathered roach clip; stuffed unicorn; alarm clock; broken glass vial and hypodermic needle.

Roommate Stereotyping

In college it's possible to tell everything about a person from the type of music they like. Take some time to familiarize yourself with each genre.

(A) The Woodstock Wanna-Be: This alarmingly laid-back roommate seeks to transform your room into a patchouli-soaked commune with mattresses on the floor, tapestries on the ceiling, and the same Joni Mitchell song playing hour after hour on the stereo. Hidden payoff: gets kicked out second semester for possession and decides to follow the Dead with prep-school friends.

(B) The Grunge Guy/Gal: These hygiene-challenged roommates mark their territory with a trail of soiled undergarments, used birth-control devices, and unwieldy phlegm balls, making them ideal companions for anthropology majors.

(C) The Classic Hitter: Popular at fraternity- and sorority-infested schools, these students enjoy donning vomit-stained togas, drinking to the point of alcohol poisoning, and singing "Louie Louie" out the window by your bed until they pass out, or you push them out. Early tip-offs: guys named Chunks; girls who own pom-poms; beer-can pyramids on windowsill.

(D) The Alternative Act: Nemesis of the Classic Hitter, these ane-   15
mic, body-piercing victims get along best with desperately "different" roommates like pretentious film majors, clove-cigarette smokers, and clinically depressed hermaphrodites like themselves.

Effective Roommate Communication

Sometimes it is not possible to know everything about your roommates from the music they listen to. Often you must also talk to them. Begin by talking to them about their tendency to keep you up all night with the music they listen to — especially if it is accompanied by high-volume paper rustling, computer-keyboard banging, and yellow-Hi-Liter squeaking. Before you know it, you'll be engaged in deep, philosophical shouting matches about missed messages and unpaid phone bills.

By semester's end, you will come to know your roommate so well that words won't be necessary at all, especially since you will no longer be on speaking terms. It is at this point that you will want to make use of three roommate-communication tools:

(A) Yellow Post-It Notes: A handy way to remind roomies of the concept of yours vs. mine. Stick them on your computer, your clothes, your girlfriend or boyfriend.

(B) Resident Assistant: An objective third party trained to settle disputes and disagreements. Bribe them with alcohol and sexual favors, then ask nicely for a single.

(C) Sign Language: There is no more effective means of roommate communication than forming a fist with one's hand and extending one's middle finger in a vertical fashion. For emphasis, fold finger down and direct fist toward roommate in a rapid forward motion.

What if I Like My Roommate?

If you enjoy your roommate's company, you must move out immediately. Living together is no way to treat a friend.

Discussing Vocabulary / Using a Dictionary

1. What is the function of the prefix "in-" in "incompatible"? Name a few other things besides roommates that could be "incompatible."

2. Think of some ways to use the word "genre." How might it apply to films? What does it have in common with "gender" or "gene"?

3. Describe what having a "nemesis" means. What language does it come from? What is the origin of the term?

4. "Hermaphrodite" comes from the same language as "nemesis." How was the word formed?

Discussing Meaning

1. What does the author's title suggest? How do you interpret it?
2. Do you believe that colleges deliberately match students according to their incompatibility? What is the author's point in suggesting this fact in his opening paragraph?
3. What does the author mean in his last paragraph? Try putting his final thought into your own words.

Discussing Writing

1. How do you know when the writer is being serious or not? Can you find statements that are intended to be taken seriously?
2. Choose two statements that you find funny. Can you explain what makes them funny? Do you see any patterns in the jokes?

Challenging the Selection

1. The author offers advice throughout the selection. Consider his suggestions. Do you think that behind the humor there is useful advice for college students?
2. At times the author tries to be gender neutral, as he's offering advice to both men and women. How neutral do you think he is? Do you find that his advice is actually more appropriate to males or to females? Explain the reasons for your answer.

In-Class Writing Activities

1. You need to split the cost of an off-campus room. You don't care to live with anyone you know, so you decide to advertise for a roommate. The ad costs twelve dollars for twenty-five words, and you can't afford to pay more. Write the best advertisement you can.
2. The author breaks roommates down into four classes based on types of music each prefers. Try creating labels for four types of people you know, using a different genre — favorite movies, drinks, clothing, and so forth.

KNIGHT STIVENDER

Somewhere a Room of One's Own

[THE DAILY BEACON, UNIVERSITY OF TENNESSEE / October 23, 1995]

Before You Read

Our lives are often divided between a need for privacy and a need for company. Which need do you find more powerful and why?

Words to Learn

sibling (para. 4): brother or sister (n.)
oblivious (para. 10): unmindful, unaware (adj.)

My room at home was too small for me. I barely had room for all the little knickknacks I'd collected over the years. There were so many things I had to pack away in boxes and store in closets all over the house. Oftentimes I didn't quite remember exactly where everything was.

There were all the notes my girlfriends and I passed throughout junior high, along with all the goofy poems my first boyfriend paid his friends to write and passed along to me as his originals. I also had a separate box for rose petals collected from past birthdays, Valentine's Days, anniversaries, and proms. I kept all my pictures in neatly organized albums on the bottom shelf of my bookcase. I had jewelry that I never wore but thought I might someday need stashed away all over my room. I also saved birthday and Christmas cards, leaves that had fallen from the trees the previous fall, and medals I won for

KNIGHT STIVENDER *(b. 1977) is studying journalism and Spanish at the University of Tennessee–Knoxville, where she plans to receive her bachelor's degree in 1999. She has served as government editor at the school's* Daily Beacon *and has worked as an intern at Nashville's daily newspaper, the* Tennessean. *Stivender was a freshman when she wrote this essay.*

participating in piano recitals. On another shelf of my bookcase I even had a brick I found on the playground at my elementary school.

I'm not exactly sure why I saved everything, but I have some sort of idea. I never wanted to forget the great times I'd had growing up. I always feared I'd become one of those adults who couldn't relate to children because they simply couldn't remember having been children themselves. I wanted to remember the flowers my brother gave me when no other boy would. I wanted to someday look back at pictures of my first trip to Panama City. For some strange reason, I wanted to remember the day my playmates and I found that broken brick on the playground and thought our school was being broken into.

So I kept my life stored away in my bedroom, tucked neatly into boxes, stacked high up in my closet, on display on my bookcases, stashed discreetly away in my underwear drawer in hopes I'd never forget anything. I loved my room because it was all about me. I didn't have to share it with anyone else. My memories didn't have to mingle with a sibling's or roommate's. My room at home was just that . . . *my* room, full of *my* things.

Now that I'm away from home, enrolled in college, and sharing ten cubic feet with another girl, my old bedroom doesn't seem so small. I try my hardest to make my half of the room personal to me, but in a space so small, that proves almost impossible. Occasionally her books will find their way to my half of the desk, or her shoes will be near my closet. Sometimes crumbs from the crackers she's eating litter my half of the carpet, and every so often, her hair brush begins to hang around with mine.

Somewhere there's a bedroom that belongs strictly to me.

I don't have room for all the little memories I cherish. I only brought a handful of pictures from home, left behind all my yearbooks, as well as my dried flowers and "who loves who" notes. Perhaps the worst part about the whole ordeal is that I don't have room to start any new collections. The threat is there that I won't have anything to remind me of my college years. That's a really scary thought for me. This place where I sleep and study isn't *my* room. It's just *a* room.

404 South Carrick Hall is just a place to sleep, study, and watch my roommate watch TV. It's filled with textbooks, CD-ROMs, and dishes . . . things that aren't supposed to be in a bedroom. There's only room for one stuffed animal and three posters which have a

hard time staying on brico-block walls. I hate the fact that there's a microwave and refrigerator in the room where I sleep, and I hate that I'm responsible for filling them.

Maybe even worse than my new room's lack of personality is the lack of privacy it offers. Occasionally, and especially during Homecoming, my roommate comes in after I've gone to sleep. She doesn't mean to wake me up, but when she starts her nightly contact-removal ritual, I can't help but hear what seems like thousands of different cleaning solution bottles bumping around the sink. I've been known to bother her too. During the day when I'm trying to study, my typing interferes with her enjoyment of "The Loveboat," "Days of Our Lives," and "Another World."

My roommate is not the only one who deprives me of privacy and makes 404 a room that is not really my own. The girls next door to me see me as a back-up grammar check when their computers don't catch every mistake. I can't lock them out because it's not my room to lock. I can't say, "Go away," because they've gotten to be really good friends and I can't be rude to people I care about.

The lack of privacy thing really bothers me. Not only do I live in   10
a room that acts as a bedroom, study, kitchen, living room, and bathroom, I don't even get to be miserable in it by myself. Sometimes misery does not love company. Rather, it is created by company. If I can't decorate my room to my liking, I should at least be able to suffer in it alone. But dormitories are not for being alone — I've been told — they're about learning to get along with others. (Maybe I'll see the positive results of this nightmare when I'm giving advice to my own children when they begin college, but for the moment, I'm completely oblivious to them.)

There is some good news, however. Though she annoys me to no end, sometimes my roommate is just the person I want to see. I didn't get to know her habits so well without her taking in a few of mine. She oftentimes knows what I'm going to say even before I do, and most of the time she knows exactly when not to say anything to me at all. She's friend as well as foe, and I'd probably miss her if she left. The same sentiments apply to my neighbors. It's really quite flattering that they, even if somewhat mistakenly, consider me some sort of grammar goddess.

And perhaps most important is the next thought. While I don't live in a room that's completely mine anymore, and probably won't ever again, I do find comfort in the knowledge that somewhere there's a pink, green, and white bedroom with a brick on the book-shelf, a diary in the underwear drawer, and an air of privacy that be-longs strictly to me. It may not be my room as often as I'd like, but it will wait for me, just like I sit and wait for it.

Discussing Vocabulary / Using a Dictionary

1. Why is "sibling" a useful word? How is it related to the word "gossip"?
2. What are some things we might be "oblivious" to? How is the word related to "oblivion"?
3. The simple word "room" can mean two things. How are both meanings used in this essay?

Discussing Meaning

1. Why does the writer like to save things? What sort of things does she keep?
2. How does the writer "bother" her roommate? In what way does her explanation characterize each of them?
3. What are the two things about her dormitory room that the writer dislikes?

Discussing Writing

1. The writer provides numerous details in her opening paragraphs. What is the effect of these details? How do they add up to a sense of who she is?
2. What is the connection between the first paragraph and the last? What is the effect of the essay's conclusion?

Challenging the Selection

1. How does the writer describe her roommate and neighbors? What is your opinion of the way she characterizes them?
2. The writer worries that she won't have anything to remind her of college years. What sort of things do you think she would like to keep? Would these be different from her childhood souvenirs?

In-Class Writing Activities

1. The English writer Virginia Woolf once wrote an essay about having a "room of one's own." In a paragraph describe as clearly as you can what such a room means or would mean to you.

2. Pretend you are the writer's roommate. In two paragraphs, describe living with her based on what you know from this essay.

3. If the writer had decided to live at home and commute to college, do you think she would be happier? What are the advantages of living at home? Make a list of those advantages. In your opinion, do they outweigh the disadvantages?

Discussing the Unit

Suggested Topic for Discussion

The essays in this unit all cover the problems people encounter when they try to live together. But, as is often pointed out, every problem is really an opportunity in disguise. What benefits and opportunities come from rooming with others?

Preparing for Class Discussion

1. Zevin makes fun of the demonic ways colleges place individuals together. Yet from the university standpoint, what benefits can derive from having roommates? If your college publishes roommate guidelines, look them up. How do they differ from those offered by Zevin?

2. A good part of living together successfully involves manners. What are your feelings about good manners? Do you think they are phony? Do you think that eating with your mouth wide open or leaving a mess at your table represents the *real* you and that others should accept the way you are? Or do you believe that poor manners are a sign of disrespect for others?

3. Consider the ways that the two essays dealing with college roommates differ. Which seems more positive about roommates? Why? Which essay do you think is more honest? Which do you prefer?

From Discussion to Writing

1. Zevin and Stivender do not seem confident that there is such an individual as "the ideal roommate." Try imagining what this person would be like. Then write a five-paragraph essay in which you describe your "ideal roommate."

2. Whether you have lived with roommates or not, you have surely shared space with others. In five paragraphs or more, write an essay about your experiences living with others. It will help if you focus on a particular situation and select details carefully.

Topics for Cross-Cultural Discussion

1. Do you think that it may be easier to live with people from your own ethnic or cultural background than with Americans? What are the advantages? What are the disadvantages? (You might want to refer to McGowan's piece in particular for details.)

2. Some cultures are more concerned about personal space than others. How do you find Americans in this respect? How would you describe your own culture's attitude toward personal space? Has living in America changed some of your views?

3

How Do We Express Our Identity?

Many Americans today struggle with problems of identity. They come from a mixed ethnic, racial, or religious heritage; belong to multiple nationalities; or have lost touch with their roots and backgrounds. Others feel that gender or sexual orientation plays a large part in determining who they are. No matter how Americans define their identity, many of them declare that it is something they should be proud of. As one of the several teenagers interviewed in Nell Bernstein's "Goin' Gangsta, Choosin' Cholita" puts it, "You should be proud of what you are — every little piece and bit of what you are."

Although racial pride is also a subject of "On Honoring Blackness" by the prominent African American literary critic Henry Louis Gates, Jr., Gates wonders whether his race should be the most important thing about him. "Is that what I want on my gravestone: Here lies an African American?" he asks. Another writer proud of his identity is a student essayist from the University of Minnesota, Sean T. Wherley. In "Coming Out: A Process of Dilemmas," he discusses the "complexities" of what is called "coming out." As Wherley defines it, "coming out" is "the phrase used to encourage gay, lesbian, bisexual, and transgender people to announce their identity to friends, family members, co-workers, classmates, and neighbors." Supplementing the chapter is a strong statement about pride in gender and culture, shown in an advertisement for the American Indian College fund. It

describes Navajo women's pride in their strong identity and matriarchal society. Although all of the essays in this chapter deal centrally
with expressing an identity, they also clearly show that how we go
about this expression is not always a simple matter.

NELL BERNSTEIN

Goin' Gangsta, Choosin' Cholita

[WEST / November 13, 1994]

Before You Read

Do you think people can *choose* their ethnic or racial identity? In
what ways do you think they can? In what ways do you think they
can't?

Words to Learn

predominantly (para. 7): mostly, as
   in having the dominant share
   (adv.)
impermeable (para. 7): impossible
   to penetrate (adj.)
hybridization (para. 10): a mixing,
   as in a mixing of traits (n.)
fodder (para. 10): raw material; literally, "food" (n.)

regalia (para. 10): distinguishing
   clothing or symbols of a rank or
   order, suggesting royalty (n.)
escalate (para. 12): to increase or
   intensify (v.)
blatant (para. 30): obvious or conspicuous (adj.)
connote (para. 31): to suggest or
   hint at (v.)

NELL BERNSTEIN (b. 1965) is editor of YO! (Youth Outlook), *a bi-
monthly youth newspaper put out by Pacific News Service. A graduate of
Yale University, where she received a bachelor's degree in comparative litera-
ture, Bernstein has also contributed to* Mother Jones, Glamour, *and*
Woman's Day. *She currently lives in Marin County, California, north of San
Francisco.*

transcend (para. 35): to rise above or go beyond (v.)

scoff (para. 38): to mock or scorn (v.)

backlash (para. 43): a negative reaction to a previous action or attitude (n.)

garnish (para. 44): to add to or enhance (v.)

affectation (para. 50): fake mannerism designed to impress others (n.)

exoticism (para. 51): the condition of being exotic; that is, charming because of unfamiliar or foreign characteristics (n.)

Her lipstick is dark, the lip liner even darker, nearly black. In baggy pants, a blue plaid Pendleton, her bangs pulled back tight off her forehead, fifteen-year-old April is a perfect cholita, a Mexican gangsta girl.

But April Miller is Anglo. "And I don't like it!" she complains. "I'd rather be Mexican."

April's father wanders into the family room of their home in San Leandro, California, a suburb near Oakland. "Hey, cholita," he teases. "Go get a suntan. We'll put you in a barrio and see how much you like it."

A large, sandy-haired man with "April" tattooed on one arm and "Kelly" — the name of his older daughter — on the other, Miller spent twenty-one years working in a San Leandro glass factory that shut down and moved to Mexico a couple of years ago. He recently got a job in another factory, but he expects NAFTA[1] to swallow that one, too.

"Sooner or later we'll all get nailed," he says. "Just another stab in the back of the American middle class."   5

Later, April gets her revenge: "Hey, Mr. White Man's Last Stand," she teases. "Wait till you see how well I manage my welfare check. You'll be asking me for money."

A once almost exclusively white, now increasingly Latin and black working-class suburb, San Leandro borders on predominantly black East Oakland. For decades, the boundary was strictly policed and practically impermeable. In 1970 April Miller's hometown was

---

[1]*NAFTA:* The North American Free Trade Agreement, or NAFTA, has been in effect since 1994 and is intended to foster open trade and commerce among the United States, Canada, and Mexico. Some U.S. workers fear that NAFTA is causing the loss of American jobs to overseas workers.

97 percent white. By 1990 San Leandro was 65 percent white, 6 percent black, 15 percent Hispanic, and 13 percent Asian or Pacific Islander. With minorities moving into suburbs in growing numbers and cities becoming ever more diverse, the boundary between city and suburb is dissolving, and suburban teenagers are changing with the times.

In April's bedroom, her past and present selves lie in layers, the pink walls of girlhood almost obscured, Guns N' Roses and Pearl Jam posters overlaid by rappers Paris and Ice Cube. "I don't have a big enough attitude to be a black girl," says April, explaining her current choice of ethnic identification.

What matters is that she thinks the choice is hers. For April and her friends, identity is not a matter of where you come from, what you were born into, what color your skin is. It's what you wear, the music you listen to, the words you use — everything to which you pledge allegiance, no matter how fleetingly.

April Miller is Anglo. "And I don't like it!" she complains. "I'd rather be Mexican."

The hybridization of American teens has become talk show fodder, with "wiggers" — white kids who dress and talk "black" — appearing on TV in full gangsta regalia. In Indiana a group of white high school girls raised a national stir when they triggered an imitation race war at their virtually all white high school last fall simply by dressing "black."   10

In many parts of the country, it's television and radio, not neighbors, that introduce teens to the allure of ethnic difference. But in California, which demographers predict will be the first state with no racial majority by the year 2000, the influences are more immediate. The California public schools are the most diverse in the country: 42 percent white, 36 percent Hispanic, 9 percent black, 8 percent Asian.

Sometimes young people fight over their differences. Students at virtually any school in the Bay Area can recount the details of at least one "race riot" in which a conflict between individuals escalated into a battle between their clans. More often, though, teens would rather join than fight. Adolescence, after all, is the period when you're most inclined to mimic the power closest at hand, from stealing your older sister's clothes to copying the ruling clique at school.

White skaters and Mexican would-be gangbangers listen to gangsta rap and call each other "nigga" as a term of endearment; white girls sometimes affect Spanish accents; blond cheerleaders claim Cherokee ancestors.

"Claiming" is the central concept here. A Vietnamese teen in Hayward, another Oakland suburb, "claims" Oakland — and by implication blackness — because he lived there as a child. A law-abiding white kid "claims" a Mexican gang he says he hangs with. A brown-skinned girl with a Mexican father and a white mother "claims" her Mexican side, while her fair-skinned sister "claims" white. The word comes up over and over, as if identity were territory, the self a kind of turf.

At a restaurant in a minimall in Hayward, Nicole Huffstutler, 15 thirteen, sits with her friends and describes herself as "Indian, German, French, Welsh, and, um . . . American": "If somebody says anything like 'Yeah, you're just a peckerwood,' I'll walk up and I'll say 'white pride!' 'Cause I'm proud of my race, and I wouldn't wanna be any other race."

"Claiming" white has become a matter of principle for Heather, too, who says she's "sick of the majority looking at us like we're less than them." (Haywood schools were 51 percent white in 1990, down from 77 percent in 1980, and whites are now the minority in many schools.)

Asked if she knows that nonwhites have not traditionally been referred to as "the majority" in America, Heather gets exasperated: "I hear that all the time, every day. They say, 'Well, you guys controlled us for many years, and it's time for us to control you.' Every day."

When Jennifer Vargas — a small, brown-skinned girl in purple jeans who quietly eats her salad while Heather talks — softly announces that she's "mostly Mexican," she gets in trouble with her friends.

"No, you're not!" scolds Heather.

"I'm mostly Indian and Mexican," Jennifer continues flatly. "I'm 20 very little . . . I'm mostly . . ."

"Your mom's white!" Nicole reminds her sharply. "She has blond hair.

"That's what I mean," Nicole adds. "People think that white is a bad thing. They think that white is a bad race. So she's trying to claim more Mexican than white."

"I have very little white in me," Jennifer repeats. "I have mostly my dad's side, 'cause I look like him and stuff. And most of my friends think that me and my brother and sister aren't related, 'cause they look more like my mom."

"But you guys are all the same race, you just look different," Nicole insists. She stops eating and frowns. "OK, you're half and half each what your parents have. So you're equal as your brother and sister, you just look different. And you should be proud of what you are — every little piece and bit of what you are. Even if you were Afghan or whatever, you should be proud of it."

Will Mosley, Heather's seventeen-year-old brother, says he and   25
his friends listen to rap groups like Compton's Most Wanted, NWA, and Above the Law because they "sing about life" — that is, what happens in Oakland, Los Angeles, anyplace but where Will is sitting today, an empty Round Table Pizza in a minimall.

"No matter what race you are," Will says, "if you live like we do, then that's the kind of music you like."

And how do they live?

"We don't live bad or anything," Will admits. "We live in a pretty good neighborhood, there's no violence or crime. I was just . . . we're just city people, I guess."

Will and his friend Adolfo Garcia, sixteen, say they've outgrown trying to be something they're not. "When I was eleven or twelve," Will says, "I thought I was becoming a big gangsta and stuff. Because I liked that music, and thought it was the coolest, I wanted to become that. I wore big clothes, like you wear in jail. But then I kind of woke up. I looked at myself and thought, 'Who am I trying to be?'"

They may have outgrown blatant mimicry, but Will and his   30
friends remain convinced that they can live in a suburban tract house with a well-kept lawn on a tree-lined street in "not a bad neighborhood" and still call themselves "city" people on the basis of musical tastes. "City" for these young people means crime, graffiti, drugs. The kids are law-abiding, but these activities connote what Will admiringly calls "action." With pride in his voice, Will predicts that "in a couple of years, Hayward will be like Oakland. It's starting to get more known, because of crime and things. I think it'll be bigger, more things happening, more crime, more graffiti, stealing cars."

"That's good," chimes in fifteen-year-old Matt Jenkins, whose new beeper — an item that once connoted gangsta chic but now means little more than an active social life — goes off periodically. "More fun."

The three young men imagine with disdain life in a gangsta-free zone. "Too bland, too boring," Adolfo says. "You have to have something going on. You can't just have everyday life."

"Mowing your lawn," Matt sneers.

"Like Beaver Cleaver's house," Adolfo adds. "It's too clean out here."

Not only white kids believe that identity is a matter of choice or   35
taste, or that the power of "claiming" can transcend ethnicity. The
Manor Park Locos — a group of mostly Mexican-Americans who hang
out in San Leandro's Manor Park — say they descend from the Manor
Lords, tough white guys who ruled the neighborhood a generation ago.

They "are like our . . . uncles and dads, the older generation,"
says Jesse Martinez, fourteen. "We're what they were when they were
around, except we're Mexican."

"There's three generations," says Oso, Jesse's younger brother.
"There's Manor Lords, Manor Park Locos, and Manor Park Pee
Wees." The Pee Wees consist mainly of the Locos' younger brothers,
eager kids who circle the older boys on bikes and brag about "punk-
ing people."

Unlike Will Mosley, the Locos find little glamour in city life.
They survey the changing suburban landscape and see not "action"
or "more fun" but frightening decline. Though most of them are not
yet eighteen, the Locos are already nostalgic, longing for a Beaver
Cleaver past that white kids who mimic them would scoff at.

Walking through nearly empty Manor Park, with its eucalyptus[2]
stands, its softball diamond and tennis courts, Jesse's friend Alex, the
only Asian in the group, waves his arms in a gesture of futility. "A
few years ago, every bench was filled," he says. "Now no one comes
here. I guess it's because of everything that's going on. My parents
paid a lot for this house, and I want it to be nice for them. I just hope
this doesn't turn into Oakland."

Glancing across the park at April Miller's street, Jesse says he   40
knows what the white cholitas are about. "It's not a racial thing," he
explains. "It's just all the most popular people out here are Mexican.
We're just the gangstas that everyone knows. I guess those girls
wanna be known."

Not every young Californian embraces the new racial hybridism.
Andrea Jones, twenty, an African American who grew up in the Bay
Area suburbs of Union City and Hayward, is unimpressed by what
she sees mainly as shallow mimicry. "It's full of posers out here," she
says. "When *Boyz N the Hood* came out on video, it was sold out for

---

[2]*eucalyptus:* Tall trees with fragrant leaves, common in California.

weeks. The boys all wanna be black, the girls all wanna be Mexican. It's the glamour."

Driving down the quiet, shaded streets of her old neighborhood in Union City, Andrea spots two white preteen boys in Raiders jackets and hugely baggy pants strutting erratically down the empty sidewalk. "Look at them," she says. "Dislocated."

She knows why. "In a lot of these schools out here, it's hard being white," she says. "I don't think these kids were prepared for the backlash that is going on, all the pride now in people of color's ethnicity, and our boldness with it. They have nothing like that, no identity, nothing they can say they're proud of.

"So they latch onto their great-grandmother who's a Cherokee, or they take on the most stereotypical aspects of being black or Mexican. It's beautiful to appreciate different aspects of other people's culture — that's like the dream of what the twenty-first century should be. But to garnish yourself with pop culture stereotypes just to blend — that's really sad."

Roland Krevocheza, eighteen, graduated last year from Arroyo High School in San Leandro. He is Mexican on his mother's side, Eastern European on his father's. In the new hierarchies, it may be mixed kids like Roland who have the hardest time finding their place, even as their numbers grow. (One in five marriages in California is between people of different races.) They can always be called "wannabes," no matter what they claim.

"I'll state all my nationalities," Roland says. But he takes a greater interest in his father's side, his Ukrainian, Romanian, and Czech ancestors. "It's more unique," he explains. "Mexican culture is all around me. We eat Mexican food all the time, I hear stories from my grandmother. I see the low-riders and stuff. I'm already part of it. I'm not trying to be; I am."

His darker-skinned brother "says he's not proud to be white," Roland adds. "He calls me 'Mr. Nazi.'" In the room the two share, the American flags and the reproduction of the Bill of Rights are Roland's; the Public Enemy poster belongs to his brother.

Roland has good reason to mistrust gangsta attitudes. In his junior year in high school, he was one of several Arroyo students who were beaten up outside the school at lunchtime by a group of Samoans who came in cars from Oakland. Roland wound up with a split lip, a concussion, and a broken tailbone. Later he was told that the assault was "gang-related" — that the Samoans were beating up anyone wearing red.

"Rappers, I don't like them," Roland says. "I think they're a bad influence on kids. It makes kids think they're all tough and bad."

Those who, like Roland, dismiss the gangsta and cholo styles as 50 affectations can point to the fact that several companies market over-priced knockoffs of "ghetto wear" targeted at teens.

But there's also something going on out here that transcends adolescent faddishness and pop culture exoticism. When white kids call their parents "racist" for nagging them about their baggy pants; when they learn Spanish to talk to their boyfriends; when Mexican American boys feel themselves descended in spirit from white "uncles"; when children of mixed marriages insist that they are whatever race they say they are, all of them are more than just confused.

They're inching toward what Andrea Jones calls "the dream of what the twenty-first century should be." In the ever more diverse communities of Northern California, they're also facing the compli-cated reality of what their twenty-first century will be.

Meanwhile, in the living room of the Miller family's San Leandro home, the argument continues unabated. "You don't know what you are," April's father has told her more than once. But she just keeps on telling him he doesn't know what time it is.

Discussing Vocabulary / Using a Dictionary

1. In paragraph 10, the author speaks of the "hybridization" of American teens. What does the word mean? What is a "hybrid" and what does the word usually refer to? How does it apply to American teenagers?

2. Some teenagers dismiss gangsta and cholo styles as "affecta-tions." What does it mean to call something an "affectation"? Give some examples of an "affectation." Is the word used posi-tively or negatively?

3. How does one "connote" something? How does "connote" dif-fer from "denote"?

4. When we call something "exotic" what do we mean? Is it a fa-vorable or unfavorable comment? Where does the word come from?

Discussing Meaning

1. How does April Miller express an identity? How does it differ from the way people usually express their identities?

2. What is "claiming" an identity? Give a few examples of "claiming."

3. What social changes are seen as contributing to white teenagers' attraction to other identities?

4. One teen believes "It's beautiful to appreciate different aspects of other people's culture — that's like the dream of what the twenty-first century should be" (para. 44). Can this dream, realistically, be fulfilled? How?

Discussing Writing

1. What do the opening paragraphs and final paragraph have in common? Why do you think the author organized her material in this way?

2. Notice how the author provides concrete examples for general statements. Find such a statement and the examples she gives to back it up. How convincing do you find her examples? Are you confused by the use of multiple examples and details, or do you think such examples clarify the author's statements?

3. What words from the teenagers are new to you? Were you able to guess at meanings for them?

4. The selection depends very heavily on interviews. Can you tell the difference between the author's language and that of the teenagers she speaks with? Which ideas in the essay seem derived from the teenagers? Which ideas seem to be the author's?

Challenging the Selection

1. We often hear that in America minorities are treated with disrespect. News stories commonly describe acts of racism and prejudice. Does that condition seem to be the case in this selection? If there is a disadvantage in being a racial or ethnic minority, why would whites want to resemble people from these groups? Explain how you think the reasoning works.

2. Most of the white California teenagers interviewed for this article feel that they would rather be black or Mexican. If that is true, then future racial and ethnic conflict in California is unlikely. True or false? (Explain the reason for your answer.)

3. Do you think the selection provides an accurate or a distorted view of American teenage life? Explain the reasons for your opinion.

In-Class Writing Activities

1. Imagine that you have to meet a total stranger at the airport and need to describe yourself to him or her over the phone. Write a brief description (about fifty words) of yourself for a phone dialogue. Would you include your race? How else would you identify yourself?

2. If you were to "claim" an identity, what would it be? In a two-paragraph essay, describe the identity you would like to have and then explain why.

3. Analyze the dialogue and actions of one of the teens in this article. Include at least five details that support your view of the teen's identity. In your opinion, is the teen totally confused or realistic about his or her identity? Are family and peers influencing the teen's identity? If so, is this influence positive or negative?

4. During adolescence, peer pressure has an especially strong influence on a person's identity. Interpret the effects of peer pressure on you in the development of your identity. Do you view the California teens' experiences as similar or dissimilar to your own adolescent experiences?

HENRY LOUIS GATES, JR.

On Honoring Blackness

[THE AMERICAN ENTERPRISE / September–October 1995]

Before You Read

Each of us possesses several identities — for example, our gender, race, ethnic background, religion, and group affiliations. Which one of your identities do you put first? Why is it the most important to you?

Words to Learn

implicate (para. 3): to connect to a crime or another misdeed (v.)

recrimination (para. 3): a counter-charge or accusation (n.)

repertoire (para. 6): a group of songs, stories, or other pieces

that someone is ready to perform or to read (n.)

elective (para. 7): subject to choice or election; optional (adj.)

affinity (para. 7): attraction (n.)

I was once walking in Washington, D.C., with my two young daughters, heading for the National Zoo, when one asked if I knew the man to whom I had just spoken. I said no. My daughter Liza volunteered that she found it embarrassing that I would speak to a complete stranger on the street. It called to mind a trip I'd made to Pittsburgh with my father. On the way, I heard Daddy speak to a colored

---

Scholar and writer HENRY LOUIS GATES, JR. (b. 1950) is W. E. B. Du Bois Professor of the Humanities at Harvard University. In addition to editing works by African American writers, Gates has contributed articles to numerous publications, including Harper's, The New Yorker, *and the* Village Voice. *He has written several books, including* The Signifying Monkey *(1988), winner of a National Book Award;* Loose Canons: Notes on the Culture Wars *(1992);* Colored People *(1994), a memoir; and, with Cornel West,* The Future of the Race *(1996).*

man, then saw him tip his hat to the man's wife. It's just something that you do, he said, when I asked him if he had known those people and why had he spoken to them.

Last summer, I sat at a sidewalk café in Italy, and three or four "black" Italians walked casually by, as well as a dozen or more blacker Africans. Each nodded his head slightly or acknowledged me by a glance, ever so subtly. When I was growing up, we always did this with each other, passing boats in a sea of white folk.

Some Negroes distrust this reflex — the nod, the glance, the murmured greeting. One reason is a resentment at being lumped together with thirty million African Americans whom they don't know and most of whom they never will know. Completely by the accident of racism we have been bound together with people we may or may not have something in common with, just because we are "black." Thirty million is a lot of people. One day you wonder: What do the misdeeds of a Mike Tyson have to do with me? So why do I feel implicated? And how can I not feel racial recrimination when I can feel racial pride?

> *I enjoy the unselfconscious moments of shared cultural intimacy . . . when no white people are around.*

Then, too, there are Negroes who are embarrassed about *being* Negroes, who didn't want to be bothered with race and with other black people. One of the more painful things about being colored is being colored in public around other colored people who are embarrassed to be colored and embarrassed that we *both* are colored and in public together. I used to reserve my special scorn for those Negroes, but have gradually stopped trying to tell others how to be black.

I wonder if my children will remember when their mother and I woke them up early on a Sunday morning, just to watch Nelson Mandela walk out of prison, and how it took a couple of hours for him to emerge, and how they both wanted to go back to bed and, then, to watch cartoons? And how we began to worry that something bad had happened to him on the way out, because the delay was so long? And how, when he finally walked out of that prison, we were so excited and teary-eyed at Mandela's nobility, his princeliness, his straight back and unbowed head? I think I felt that there walked the Negro, as Pop might have said; there walked the whole of the African people, as regal as any king. And that feeling I had, that gooseflesh sense of identity that I felt at seeing Nelson Mandela, listening to

5

Mahalia Jackson sing, watching Muhammad Ali fight, or hearing Martin Luther King speak, is part of what I mean by being colored. I realize the sentiment may not be logical, but I want to have my cake and eat it too. Which is why I still nod or speak to black people on the street and why it felt so good to be acknowledged by the Afro-Italians who passed my table at the café in Milan.

I want to be able to take special pride in a Jessye Norman aria, a Michael Jordan dunk, a Spike Lee movie, a Thurgood Marshall opinion, a Toni Morrison novel, James Brown's Camel Walk. I enjoy the unselfconscious moments of shared cultural intimacy, whatever form it takes, when no white people are around. Like Joe Louis's fights, which my father still talks about as part of a fixed repertoire of stories. His eyes shine as he describes how Louis hit Max Schmeling so many times and so hard, and how some reporter asked him, after the fight: "Joe, what would you have done if that last punch hadn't knocked Schmeling out?" And how ole Joe responded, without missing a beat: "I'da run around behind him to see what was holdin' him up!"

Even so, I rebel at the notion that I can't be part of other groups, that I can't construct identities through elective affinity, that race must be the most important thing about me. Is that what I want on my gravestone: Here lies an African American? So I'm divided. I want to be black, to know black, to luxuriate in whatever I might be calling blackness at any particular time — but to do so in order to come out the other side, to experience a humanity that is neither colorless nor reducible to color. Bach *and* James Brown. Sushi *and* fried catfish. Part of me admires those people who can say with a straight face that they have transcended any attachment to a particular community or group . . . but I always want to run around behind them to see what holds them up.

Discussing Vocabulary / Using a Dictionary

1. What does it mean to be "implicated" in a criminal case? How can one be "implicated" within one's race?

2. In paragraph 3, Gates opposes racial pride to racial "recrimination." What are some synonyms for "recrimination"? In what way could it be contrasted to pride?

3. What does it mean to "luxuriate" in something? How is "luxuriate" related to "luxury"? Give some other examples of things we luxuriate in.

Discussing Meaning

1. What is the main point of Gates's first two paragraphs? How are they related to the topic of identity?

2. What do you think Gates means by a "gooseflesh sense of identity" (para. 5)? Can you describe more fully what this sense might feel like?

3. In paragraph 7, what does Gates mean by "Bach *and* James Brown. Sushi *and* fried catfish"? How do these examples illustrate his desire to "have my cake and eat it too" (para. 5)? What is he referring to?

4. Two important phrases Gates uses are "shared cultural intimacy" (para. 6) and "elective affinity" (para. 7). Why are these processes so important to Gates or to anyone who wants to define or clarify his or her identity?

Discussing Writing

1. Note the list of examples Gates provides in paragraphs 5 and 6 of prominent African Americans. What do they have in common? What does the list tell us about Gates himself?

2. Writers often end essays with a catchy quotation. How does Gates prepare us for his final sentence, an allusion to the quotation at the end of paragraph 6? How does the quotation change its meaning when he uses it the second time?

3. Gates uses personal narrative to support his views. Select the examples you think support his thesis vividly.

Challenging the Selection

1. Note that Gates uses the words "colored," "Negro," "black," and "African American" to describe the group to which he belongs. Do all of these words mean the same thing, or are they different? Would you use all of these words yourself? Do you think Gates uses them interchangeably? Why do you think he doesn't stick to one? How do other people use these terms?

2. Why does Gates say in his final paragraph: "I rebel at the notion that I can't be part of other groups, that I can't construct identities through elective affinity, that race must be the most important

thing about me"? Who might restrict Gates's ability to have multiple identities or roles?

In-Class Writing Activities

1. In his conclusion Gates wonders, "Is this what I want on my gravestone: Here lies an African American?" What identity would you like inscribed on your own gravestone? Write an inscription you think would be fitting.

2. Gates considers himself "divided" (para. 7). In a few paragraphs describe a division you feel exists between two parts of yourself.

3. In a small group of three to five students, produce a list of commonly accepted criteria for identifying people as male or female, minority or majority, native or non-native, or as belonging to some other varying categories. Have someone in your group summarize your group's findings for the rest of the class. Then briefly summarize the findings of the class as a whole.

Advertisement

The Navajo is a matriarchal society. It is the Navajo woman who owns the land and the houses, and she brings to her marriage a flock of sheep that she has tended since childhood, contributions which form the basis of the couple's wealth. When Navajos meet they introduce themselves by their mother's clan name first, and then their father's, and if a Navajo woman wants her husband to go away she has only to put his saddle in front of the door and he will do just that. Navajo women have always had at least as much power and respect as Navajo men; their folk tales abound with resourceful heroines, and so do their immediate families. Generation after generation of Navajo girls are brought up guided by strong, smart women who don't raise their voices because they don't need to, and who have never had to fight for equality because they have never been without it.

I'LL NEVER FIGHT FOR WOMEN'S RIGHTS.

AMERICAN
INDIAN
COLLEGE
FUND

Help save a culture that could save ours
by giving to the American Indian College Fund, Dept. PN,
21 West 68th St., New York, NY 10023. 1-800-776-FUND.
We would like to give a special thanks
to US West for all their concern and support.

Photo: Tina Begay, Tribal College Student

53

SEAN T. WHERLEY

Coming Out: A Process of Dilemmas

[THE MINNESOTA DAILY, UNIVERSITY OF MINNESOTA / October 9, 1995]

Before You Read

Consider what you find hardest to tell the truth about and how you would go about telling this information to others. Are there some truths that you will always keep secret?

Words to Learn

advocate (para. 1): someone who supports or defends (n.)

accommodate (para. 1): to include or make room for (v.)

transgender (para. 2): changed to another sex (adj.)

forge (para. 2): to make or form (v.)

deplorable (para. 3): bad; worthy of scorn (adj.)

pinnacle (para. 6): the height or peak of something (n.)

incorporate (para. 7): to include (v.)

rambunctious (para. 11): disorderly (adj.)

badger (para. 16): to pester (v.)

My sister Colleen is a college graduate and an aspiring liberal who needs time to understand the complexities of my being a gay man. I do not intend to single out Colleen because she is one of my strongest advocates. She regularly accompanies me to a family support group for lesbians and gay men, and willingly discusses issues related to my being a minority. But her attitude is probably reflective of many people who choose not to get too involved. For example, she

---

SEAN T. WHERLEY (b. 1973), a 1996 graduate of the University of Minnesota, is currently living and studying in Tanzania. Wherley wrote this essay during National Coming Out Week, "an event intended to encourage gay, lesbian, bisexual, and transgender people to 'come out' to friends, family, co-workers, and classmates."

compared my "coming out" process to a wedding. She noted the similarities of exhaustive planning, accommodating people's feelings, and recovering from the draining day. While I do appreciate comparing the "celebratory" aspect of both events, coming out is clearly no wedding.

Therefore, with Colleen's perspective as a basis, I want to clarify the coming out process. Coming out is the phrase used to encourage gay, lesbian, bisexual, and transgender people to announce their identity to friends, family members, co-workers, classmates, and neighbors. People are encouraged to come out in order to increase their visibility in the larger community, and to forge stronger relationships with those closest to them. To highlight this process, National Coming Out Day is celebrated each October 11 to commemorate the first Washington, D.C., march for gay and lesbian rights in 1987.

With that in mind, let us return to the comparison of a wedding and coming out. Although a wedding is filled with happiness, it is deplorable to compare it to the coming out process. A wedding lasts one day. It usually includes a gathering of friends and family to mark the momentous occasion. Support of the union is rarely solicited and often overflowing. Guests are eager to attend and lavish the couple with gifts. Sometimes the event entails months of planning to determine a site, date, and accessories. Thousands of dollars are spent on invitations, meals, and entertainment. After the day ends, the couple begins life as a legally recognized couple. A smattering of conversation will follow the gala-filled day, but for the most part the day and its related discussion have concluded.

> *The process of coming out never ends.*

Meanwhile, coming out as a gay man also entails months of planning. Dilemmas include: "Do I tell both parents simultaneously? Where should I tell them? Dare I consider coming out to co-workers?"

Some money may be spent returning to hometowns to tell parents or friends, but otherwise the costs of coming out are psychological, not financial.

After those examples, however, the similarities between a wedding and coming out end. Where weddings last one day, the process of coming out never ends. The coming out pinnacle of the year may occur on National Coming Out Day, but it does not serve as the only time to come out. As much as I wish that one day could suffice in announcing my sexual orientation to everyone, that is far from a reality. National Coming Out Day does not account for the other 364 days and the events endured during that time. It is during those other 364 days that the joys of coming out are experienced. Situations continuously arise where I can choose to withhold my identity or speak proudly.

As a student, I am faced with coming out each quarter to classmates and professors. This does not mean announcing to them, "I'm gay." Rather, it means incorporating gay issues into class discussions or making reference to my group involvement and my partner (as straight students constantly do).

The workplace is another environment I must confront. As a prospective employee, I contemplate asking if the company's non-discrimination policy includes sexual orientation, or if the benefits package is extended to same-sex domestic partners. After being hired, I could come out one day, but new employees are always arriving, thus rendering some unaware of my identity.

As a son and brother, I can tell my parents and siblings that I am gay, but what about grandparents, aunts, uncles, and cousins? I cannot tell them all on one day; that is impossible with the geographic distance separating us. And once the family members know I am gay, will they be accepting if I bring my partner to family gatherings?

Thankfully, my family was more supportive than most families   10
when I came out; however, this is not the norm. Gay, lesbian, bisexual, and transgender people incessantly worry that parents will reject them upon learning of their identity, and sadly, some parents do.

In addition to the major settings of life (school, work, and family), coming out occurs in fleeting and casual situations. For example, last October I bought some flowers for my then-boyfriend, whom I had been dating for one month. While grasping the flowers and waiting to board the bus to his house, four rambunctious teenagers approached me. One of the teenagers turned to comment on my assortment of flowers.

"Your flowers are pretty, sir," he said.

"Thank you," I replied.

"Are they for your mom?" he asked.

"No," I said, growing restless and craning my neck for the next   15
bus.

He continued badgering: "Are they for your girlfriend?"

My body immediately froze and I began sweating. I debated the risk of telling him the truth and possibly being harassed after we boarded the bus together.

"Yeah," I said in a whisper. "They're for my girlfriend."

Now, if coming out was a one-time event (like a wedding), I would have had no qualms about telling the boy who the recipient of my flowers was. That is a circumstance, however, enjoyed only in dreams. And if coming out was a celebration (like a wedding), my family members would be delighted that I am at peace with myself. They would insist upon telling friends and family, and holding a party.

That, too, however, is a dream, as my parents were outraged that   20
I told my aunt before them.

Discussing Vocabulary / Using a Dictionary

1. The writer calls his sister one of his strongest "advocates" (para. 1). What is an advocate? In what different ways is the word used?

2. What does "transgender" (para. 2) imply? Does the word have a positive, negative, or neutral sense?

3. "Deplorable" (para. 3) is a strong word. What is its root? What are some synonyms?

4. How is the "pinnacle" of a mountain related to the way the author uses the word when he refers to the "coming out pinnacle of the year" (para. 6)?

Discussing Meaning

1. Why does the writer call his sister an "aspiring liberal" (para. 1)? Is he being complimentary?

2. According to the writer, what are the main difficulties of "coming out"? Expand upon the author's definition.

3. Why do you think the writer's sister compared his "coming out" to a wedding? Why a wedding and not some other celebration? Write at least three reasons why the author disagrees with his sister's analogy.

4. Why does the author lie to the teenagers about the flowers? Why is he caught in such a dilemma when he writes that he has "come out"?

Discussing Writing

1. Why do you think the author begins his essay with a reference to his sister? Do you really think she accepts him *unconditionally* as her gay brother? Find subtle hints that she does or doesn't.

2. Many writers base essays on a central comparison or contrast. Does the writer use this form effectively?

Challenging the Selection

1. How does the writer explain his lie about the flowers? Do you accept his explanation? Can you think of other explanations he might have offered? What might have happened if he had explained the flowers differently?
2. What sense do you make of the writer's final sentence? Are his parents "outraged" that he is gay?

In-Class Writing Activities

1. The writer doesn't think that "coming out" can be realistically compared to a "wedding." In a paragraph, offer another comparison that you think would be more appropriate.
2. Make a list of the things you would find hardest to tell your parents.
3. Some people think that "homophobia," the fear or hatred of gay men and lesbians, is one of the worst prejudices in our society. Imagine that you have just been told that a close friend or family member is gay. Do you think that your reaction would be homophobic or accepting? If you would be accepting of the news, how would you help friends or family members who are not as understanding accept it? If you would have trouble accepting the news, outline a plan for overcoming your objections, or at least explain your objections.

Discussing the Unit

Suggested Topic for Discussion

One of the teenagers interviewed in "Goin' Gangsta, Choosin' Cholita" says, "You should be proud of what you are — every little piece and bit of what you are" (para. 24). Consider her comment. In what ways can people be "proud" of some aspect of their identity (like their race) that they had nothing to do with? Should we take pride in our ethnic identities in the same way that we take pride in our personal achievements, like high grades, athletic awards, musical accomplishments, community honors, and courageous actions? What are your opinions of racial, ethnic, or group pride?

Preparing for Class Discussion

1. Consider "pride" in general. What does the word mean? Does a person earn pride or acquire it? Is pride considered a good attribute, or is it ever sinful or wrong? In Catholicism it is one of the "Seven Deadly Sins." Why do you think this is the case? Can someone, for example, be proud for the wrong reasons? List a few examples of different kinds of pride.

2. Do you think gay or lesbian pride is similar to or different from ethnic, racial, or national pride? What other kinds of group "pride" can you think of? (You might refer to the advertisement on p. 53.)

From Discussion to Writing

1. Write an essay in which you describe what you are most proud of about yourself. Is it your identification with a group, a public achievement, or a private accomplishment? Be sure to explain why you feel the way you do.

2. Henry Louis Gates, Jr., wonders if we must identify not only with positive racial and ethnic accomplishments but also with negative actions of people in our group. Does identification work in only positive directions?

Topics for Cross-Cultural Discussion

1. Of what importance is group identity in your culture? Which aspect of one's identity — religion, gender, class, ethnicity, and so forth — is most important?

2. Do you find that in America you have the identity you would like to have? Do Americans identify you properly? Do they make mistakes about who or what you are? In what ways?

4

What Are We Afraid Of?

Franklin D. Roosevelt famously proclaimed that "the only thing we have to fear is fear itself." Yet for many Americans, fear pervades daily life. On the one hand, we no longer live under the shadow of a possible nuclear holocaust, and modern medicine has come up with cures for many of the illnesses that ended our grandparents' lives prematurely. On the other hand, the world seems faster, more dangerous, and more unpredictable than it used to. Do we have good reasons to be afraid, or is fear just an irrational emotion we cling to?

The essays in this chapter address three contemporary fears. Meghan Daum discusses the threat of AIDS from the perspective of a young, educated, heterosexual woman. She highlights the fear of her generation toward AIDS and explains how young people arm themselves against this fear. (Following Daum's piece is the controversial Benetton ad on AIDS that she refers to.) Lawyer Debra Dickerson tells the horrifying story of her nephew — shot in a senseless, random encounter on the street in front of his home — and examines stereotypes of the black, urban, violent male. In the final selection, Wake Forest University student Brian Brady comments on the rash of antigovernment sentiment in the past several years and wonders whether we have any real cause to fear that the federal government is usurping our civil liberties.

MEGHAN DAUM

Safe-Sex Lies

[THE NEW YORK TIMES MAGAZINE / January 21, 1996]

Before You Read

"Safe sex" became a common expression in the 1980s, as the AIDS virus spread to epidemic proportions. But according to Meghan Daum, an understanding of the facts about AIDS doesn't always lead to more careful behavior. Compare your own knowledge about the subject with your actions: Have you ever taken a risk you knew you shouldn't have?

Words to Learn

retrospect (para. 1): looking back on something; reflecting (adj.)

demographic (para. 1): pertaining to the study of characteristics of particular human populations (adj.)

incumbent (para. 1): characterized by duty or obligation (adj.)

entitlement (para. 2): a rightful claim to something (n.)

cynical (para. 3): scornful or mistrustful (adj.)

mantra (para. 4): a sacred chant or formula believed to have magical powers (n.)

naïveté (para. 4): the quality of lacking worldliness and sophistication (n.)

onus (para. 6): an unpleasant responsibility (n.)

subsume (para. 7): to include under a more general category (v.)

collage (para. 7): a picture made up of smaller pictures or other fragments that have been pasted onto a surface (n.)

tousled (para. 7): messy; in disarray (adj.)

specter (para. 10): a ghostly presence (n.)

MEGHAN DAUM (b. 1970) received a bachelor's degree in English from Vassar in 1992 and a master's degree in nonfiction writing from Columbia University in 1996. She has worked as an assistant editor at Columbia University Press and has contributed articles to the New York Times, *the* New York Times Book Review, *and* GQ. *Daum currently lives in New York City.*

vigilant (para. 11): alert or watchful   *corrosion* (para. 11): the act of
   (adj.)   wearing away or rusting (n.)

I have been tested for HIV three times. I've gone to clinics and stuck my arm out for those disposable needles, each time forgetting the fear and nausea that descend upon me before the results come back, those minutes spent in a publicly financed waiting room staring at a video loop about "living with" this thing that kills you. These tests have taken place over five years, and the results have always been negative — not surprisingly in retrospect, since I am not a member of a "high-risk group," don't sleep around, and don't take pity on heroin-addicted bass players by going to bed with them in the hopes of being thanked in the liner notes of their first major independent release. Still, getting tested always seemed like the thing to do. Despite my demographic profile, despite the fact that I grew up middle class, attended an elite college, and do not personally know any women or straight men within that demographic profile who have the AIDS virus, I am terrified of this disease. I went to a college where condoms and dental dams lay in baskets in dormitory lobbies, where it seemed incumbent on health service counselors to give us the straight talk, to tell us never, ever to have sex without condoms unless we wanted to die; that's right, *die,* shrivel overnight, vomit up our futures, pose a threat to others. (And they'd seen it happen, oh, yes, they had.) They gave us pamphlets, didn't quite explain how to use dental dams, told us where we could get tested, threw us more fistfuls of condoms (even some glow-in-the-dark brands, just for variety). This can actually be fun, they said, if only we'd adopt a better attitude.

> *Despite the fact that I grew up middle class, attended an elite college, and do not personally know any women or straight men within that demographic profile who have the AIDS virus, I am terrified of this disease.*

We're told we can get this disease and we believe it and vow to protect ourselves, and intend (really, truly) to stick by this rule, until we don't because we just can't, because it's just not fair, because our sense of entitlement exceeds our sense of vulnerability. So we blow off precaution again and again, and then we get scared and get tested, and when it comes out OK, we run out of the clinic, pamphlets in hand, eyes cast upward, promising ourselves we'll never be stupid again. But of course we are stupid, again and again. And the testing is always for the same reasons and with the same results, and soon it becomes more like fibbing about S.A.T. scores ten years after the fact than lying about whether we practice unsafe sex, a lie that sounds like such a breach of contract with ourselves that we might as well be talking about putting a loaded gun under our pillow every night.

Still, I've gone into more than a few relationships with the safest of intentions and discarded them after the fourth or fifth encounter. Perhaps this is a shocking admission, but my hunch is that I'm not the only one doing it. My suspicion is, in fact, that very few of us — "us" being the demographic profile frequently charged with thinking we're immortal, the population accused of being cynical and lazy and weak — have really responded to the AIDS crisis the way the Federal Government and educators would like us to believe. My guess is that we're all but ignoring it and that almost anyone who claims otherwise is lying.

It seems there is a lot of lying going around. One of the main tenets of the safe-sex message is that ageless mantra "you don't know where he's been," meaning that everyone is a potential threat, that we're all either scoundrels or ignoramuses. "He didn't tell me he was shooting drugs," says an HIV-positive woman on a public-service advertisement. Safe-sex "documentaries" on MTV and call-in radio shows on pop stations give us woman after woman whose boyfriend "claimed he loved me but was sleeping around." The message we receive is that trusting anyone is itself an irresponsible act, that having faith in an intimate partner, particularly women in relation to men, is a symptom of such profound naïveté that we're obviously not mature enough to be having sex anyway.

I find this reasoning almost more troubling than the disease itself. 5 It flies in the face of the social order from which I, as someone born in 1970, was supposed to benefit. That this reasoning runs counter to almost any feminist ideology — the ideology that proclaimed, at least back in the seventies that women should feel free to ask men on dates and wear jeans and have orgasms — is an admission that no AIDS-concerned citizen is willing to make. Two decades after *The Joy of Sex* made sexual pleasure permissible for both sexes and three decades after the pill put a government-approved stamp on premarital sex, we're still told not to trust each other. We've entered a period where mistrust equals responsibility, where fear signifies health.

Since I spent all of the seventies under the age of ten, I've never known a significantly different sexual and social climate. Supposedly this makes it easier to live with the AIDS crisis. Health educators and AIDS activists like to think that people of my generation can be made to unlearn what we never knew, to break the reckless habits we didn't actually form. But what we have learned thoroughly is how not to enjoy ourselves. Just like our mothers, whose adolescences were haunted by the abstract taboo against being "bad" girls, my contemporaries and I are discouraged from doing what feels good. As it did with our mothers, the onus falls largely on the women. We know that it's much easier for women to contract HIV from a man than the other way around. We know that an "unsafe" man generally means someone who has shot drugs or slept with other men, or possibly slept with prostitutes. We find ourselves wondering about these things over dinner dates. We look for any hints of homosexual tendencies, any references to a hypodermic moment. We try to catch him in the lie we've been told he'll tell.

What could be sadder? We're not allowed to believe anyone anymore. And the reason we're not isn't so much because of AIDS but because of the anxiety that ripples around the disease. The information about AIDS that is supposed to produce "awareness" has been subsumed into the aura of style. AIDS awareness has become so much a part of the pop culture that not only is it barely noticeable, it is largely ineffectual. MTV runs programs about safe sex that are barely distinguishable from documentaries about Madonna. A print advertisement for Benetton features a collage of hundreds of tiny photographs of young people, some of whom are shaded with the word "AIDS" written across their faces. Many are white and blond and have the tousled, moneyed look common to more traditional fashion spreads or even yearbooks from colleges like the one I attended. There is no text other than the company's slogan. There is no explanation of how these faces were chosen, no public statement of whether these people actually have the disease or not. I called Benetton for clarification and was told that the photographs were supposed to represent people from all over the world and that no one was known to be HIV-positive — just as I suspected. The advertisement was a work of art, which meant I could interpret the image any way I liked. This is how the deliverers of the safe-sex message shoot themselves in the foot. Confronted with arty effects instead of actual information, people like me are going to believe what we want to believe, which, of course, is whatever isn't too scary. So we turn the page.

Since I am pretty sure I do not sleep with bisexual men or IV-drug users, my main personal concern about AIDS is that men can get the virus from women and subsequently pass it on to other women. According to the Centers for Disease Control's National AIDS Clearinghouse surveillance report, less than three-quarters of 1 percent of white non-Hispanic men with HIV infection contracted the virus through heterosexual sex with a non-IV-drug-using woman. (Interestingly, the C.D.C. labels this category as "risk not specified.") But this statistic seems too dry for MTV and campus health brochures, whose eye-catching "sex kills" rhetoric tells us nothing other than to ignore what we don't feel like thinking about. Obviously, there are still too many cases of HIV; there is a deadly risk in certain kinds of sexual behavior and therefore reason to take precautions. But until more people appear on television, look into the camera, and tell me that they contracted HIV through heterosexual sex with someone who had no risk factors, I will continue to disregard the message.

Besides, the very sophistication that allows people like me to filter out much of the hype behind music videos, fashion magazines, and television talk shows is what we use to block out the safe-sex message. We are not a population that makes personal decisions based on the public service work of a rock star. We're not going to sacrifice the thing we believe we deserve, the experiences we waited for, because Levi Strauss is a major sponsor of MTV's coverage of World AIDS Day.

So the inconsistent behavior continues, as do the confessions   10
among friends and the lies to health care providers during routine exams, because we just can't bear the terrifying lectures that ensue when we confess to not always protecting ourselves. Life in your twenties is fraught not only with financial and professional uncertainty, but also with a specter of death that floats above the pursuit of a sex life. And there is no solution, only the conclusion that invariably finishes the hushed conversations: The whole thing simply "sucks." It's a bummer on a grand scale.

Heterosexuals are receiving vague signals. We're told that if we are sufficiently vigilant, we will probably be all right. We're being told to assume the worst and to not invite disaster by hoping for the best. We're being encouraged to keep our fantasies on a tight rein, otherwise we'll lose control of the whole buggy, and no one can say we weren't warned. So for us AIDS remains a private hell, smoldering beneath intimate conversations among friends and surfacing on those occasional sleepless nights when it occurs to us to wonder about it, upon which that dark hysteria sets in, and those catalogues of whom we've done it with and whom they might have done it with and oh-my-God-I'll-surely-die seem to project themselves onto the ceiling, the way fanged monsters did when we were children. But we fall asleep and then we wake up. And nothing has changed except our willingness to forget about it, which has become the ultimate survival mechanism. What my peers and I are left with is a generalized anxiety, a low-grade fear and anger that resides at the core of everything we do. Our attitudes have been affected by the disease by leaving us scared, but our behavior has stayed largely the same. One result is a corrosion of the soul, a chronic dishonesty and fear that will most likely damage us more than the disease itself. In this world, peace of mind is a utopian concept.

Discussing Vocabulary / Using a Dictionary

1. Daum mentions her "demographic" profile several times. What kind of details does such a profile reveal about a person? What does a demographer do?

2. In paragraph 1 Daum writes, "It seemed incumbent on health service counselors to give us the straight talk." When political office holders are running for re-election, they are also called "incumbents." How are the word's two meanings related?

3. Daum describes the saying "you don't know where he's been" as an "ageless mantra" (para. 4). What are some synonyms for the word "mantra"? What connotations of the word are relevant in this context?

4. A "specter" of death "floats above" life for those in their twenties, according to Daum (para. 10). What images does the word "specter" bring to mind for you? Can you think of other words with the same root?

Discussing Meaning

1. What reasons does Daum give for saying that her negative HIV test results were "not surprising"?

2. In paragraph 2, Daum explains that her generation can't stick by safe-sex rules because "we just can't, because it's just not fair." Is her attitude toward sexual freedom realistic or "rose-colored"?

3. According to Daum, the feminist ideology of the 1970s formed her generation's attitudes toward sex. Would feminists of the 1990s guide her toward a different sexual philosophy? In what ways?

4. What does Daum say is her "main personal concern" about AIDS?

5. What is Daum's "hunch" about the sexual behavior of her heterosexual peers? What has become their "ultimate survival mechanisms" against the fear of AIDS?

Discussing Writing

1. Why does Daum begin the essay with her personal experience of being tested for HIV? Does her description of the process add or detract from her credibility?

2. Daum frequently uses the first-person plural subject "we" to state beliefs, opinions, and attitudes. For whom is she speaking besides herself?

3. How does Daum convey the intensity of her fear of AIDS? Point to particular words and images that indicate her powerful emotions.

Challenging the Selection

1. Consider Daum's description of the Benetton ad, which is reprinted on page 69. Do you think it's legitimate for her to generalize about "deliverers of the safe-sex message" from the example of a print advertisement? What is your response to the ad?

2. In paragraph 5, Daum says she finds current mistrustful attitudes "almost more troubling than the disease itself" and asks "what could be sadder" than not being able to trust one's sexual partner. Do you agree that this mistrust is the most terrible effect of the AIDS epidemic?

3. Daum compares the current fear of AIDS to the "taboo" against being a "bad" girl that her mother's generation faced. Does this comparison seem valid to you?

In-Class Writing Activities

1. Daum suggests that the burden of AIDS strikes her as unfair, in part, because an earlier generation led her to believe that her generation would reap the benefits of freedom; instead it is threatened with a fatal disease. Think of another fear or problem that you and your friends face today that your parents did not. How do you deal with the problem without their example?

2. Even honest people sometimes tell lies — to friends, to strangers, even to themselves. Describe one instance in which you put yourself in danger by telling a lie. Why did you do it? Did anyone notice? What was the result?

3. Daum writes that her generation's unsafe sex practices are like "putting a loaded gun under our pillow every night" (para. 2). Analyze another situation in which someone gambles with a risk. What motivates one to go against the odds? You can also consider the positive side of risks, where someone might take a risk to reap a greater benefit.

4. Why have young people, according to Daum, not heeded the messages of the safe-sex campaign? Is there too much "hype" in the campaign? Survey your peers in class to determine how effective they think the campaign has been. Then, as a class (or in groups of three to five students), outline a realistic public relations campaign for "safe sex" that takes into account Daum's views and those of the class.

Advertisement

AIDS Faces. United Colors of Benetton.
Concept: O. Toscani. Fall–Winter 1994.

DEBRA DICKERSON

Who Shot Johnny?

[THE NEW REPUBLIC / January 1, 1996]

Before You Read

When asked what they most fear, many Americans put violent crime high up on their list. Are you afraid of violent crime? Before reading the following essay, consider how you would react if you, a relative, or a loved one were permanently disabled as the result of criminal violence.

Words to Learn

prism (para. 1): something that filters or processes; literally, a glass instrument that breaks light down into a color spectrum (n.)

flag (para. 1): to wane or decrease (v.)

brandish (para. 2): to wave threateningly (v.)

divulge (para. 3): to reveal (v.)

corroborate (para. 3): to support or attest to (v.)

syncopate (para. 5): to provide a beat for, as in music (v.)

catheterize (para. 6): to drain with a catheter (tube) (v.)

masticate (para. 8): to chew (v.)

demur (para. 8): objection (n.)

dirge (para. 9): a somber hymn played at a funeral (n.)

raucously (para. 14): noisily; boisterously (adv.)

nihilism (para. 14): nothingness (n.)

anomalous (para. 15): abnormal; out of the ordinary (adj.)

DEBRA DICKERSON (b. 1959), a graduate of Harvard Law School, worked as a lawyer for the NAACP before leaving that organization to write full time. A regular contributor to The Nation, Dickerson has also written for such publications as the Christian Science Monitor, the Boston Review, and Good Housekeeping. She currently lives in Arlington, Virginia.

Given my level of political awareness, it was inevitable that I would come to view the everyday events of my life through the prism of politics and the national discourse. I read the *Washington Post*, *The New Republic*, *The New Yorker*, *Harper's*, *The Atlantic Monthly*, *The Nation*, *National Review*, *Black Enterprise*, and *Essence* and wrote a weekly column for the *Harvard Law School Record* during my three years just ended there. I do this because I know that those of us who are not well-fed white guys in suits must not yield the debate to them, however well-intentioned or well-informed they may be. Accordingly, I am unrepentant and vocal about having gained admittance to Harvard through affirmative action; I am a feminist, stoic about my marriage chances as a well-educated, thirty-six-year-old black woman who won't pretend to need help taking care of herself. My strength flags, though, in the face of the latest role assigned to my family in the national drama. On July 27, 1995, my sixteen-year-old nephew was shot and paralyzed.

Talking with friends in front of his home, Johnny saw a car he thought he recognized. He waved boisterously — his trademark — throwing both arms in the air in a full-bodied, hip-hop Y. When he got no response, he and his friends sauntered down the walk to join a group loitering in front of an apartment building. The car followed. The driver got out, brandished a revolver and fired into the air. Everyone scattered. Then he took aim and shot my running nephew in the back.

> We know him. We've known and feared him all our lives.

Johnny never lost consciousness. He lay in the road, trying to understand what had happened to him, why he couldn't get up. Emotionlessly, he told the story again and again on demand, remaining apologetically firm against all demands to divulge the missing details that would make sense of the shooting but obviously cast him in a bad light. Being black, male, and shot, he must, apparently, be gang- or drug-involved. Probably both. Witnesses corroborate his version of events.

Nearly six months have passed since that phone call in the night and my nightmarish, headlong drive from Boston to Charlotte. After twenty hours behind the wheel, I arrived haggard enough to reduce my mother to fresh tears and to find my nephew reassuring well-wishers with an eerie sangfroid.[1]

---

[1]*sangfroid*: Composure; literally "cold-bloodedness" (French).

I take the day shift in his hospital room; his mother and grand-   5
mother, a clerk and cafeteria worker, respectively, alternate nights
there on a cot. They don their uniforms the next day, gaunt after
hours spent listening to Johnny moan in his sleep. How often must
his subconscious replay those events and curse its host for saying
hello without permission, for being carefree and young while a
would-be murderer hefted the weight of his uselessness and failure
like Jacob Marley's[2] chains? How often must he watch himself lying
stubbornly immobile on the pavement of his nightmares while the
sound of running feet syncopate his attacker's taunts?

I spend these days beating him at gin rummy and Scrabble, holding a basin while he coughs up phlegm, and crying in the corridor
while he catheterizes himself. There are children here much worse off
than he. I should be grateful. The doctors can't, or won't, say
whether he'll walk again.

I am at once repulsed and fascinated by the bullet, which remains
lodged in his spine (having done all the damage it can do, the doctors
say). The wound is undramatic — small, neat, and perfectly centered
— an impossibly pink pit surrounded by an otherwise undisturbed
expanse of mahogany. Johnny has asked me several times to describe
it but politely declines to look in the mirror I hold for him.

Here on the pediatric rehab ward, Johnny speaks little, never
cries, never complains, works diligently to become independent. He
does whatever he is told; if two hours remain until the next pain pill,
he waits quietly. Eyes bloodshot, hands gripping the bed rails. During
the week of his intravenous feeding when he was tormented by the
primal need to masticate, he never asked for food. He just listened
while we counted down the days for him and planned his favorite
meals. Now required to dress himself unassisted, he does so without
demur, rolling himself back and forth valiantly on the bed and shiver-
ing afterwards, exhausted. He "ma'am"s and "sir"s everyone politely. Before his "accident," a simple request to take out the trash
could provoke a firestorm of teenage attitude. We, the women who
have raised him, have changed as well; we've finally come to appreciate those boxer-baring, oversized pants we used to hate — it would
be much more difficult to fit properly sized pants over his diaper.

He spends a lot of time tethered to rap music still loud enough to
break my concentration as I read my many magazines. I hear him try

---

[2]*Jacob Marley:* Doomed, chain-dragging spirit in Charles Dickens's *A Christmas
Carol.*

to soundlessly mouth the obligatory "mothafuckers" overlaying the funereal dirge of the music tracks. I do not normally tolerate disrespectful music in my or my mother's presence, but if it distracts him now . . .

"Johnny," I ask later, "do you still like gangster rap?" During the long pause I hear him think loudly, *I'm paralyzed Auntie, not stupid.* "I mostly just listen to hip hop," he says evasively into his *Sports Illustrated.*

Miserable though it is, time passes quickly here. We always seem to be jerking awake in our chairs just in time for the next pill, his every-other-night bowel program, the doctor's rounds. Harvard feels a galaxy away — the world revolves around Family Members Living With Spinal Cord Injury class, Johnny's urine output, and strategizing with my sister to find affordable, accessible housing. There is always another long-distance uncle in need of an update, another church member wanting to pray with us, or Johnny's little brother in need of some attention.

We Dickerson women are so constant a presence the ward nurses and cleaning staff call us by name and join us for cafeteria meals and cigarette breaks. At Johnny's birthday pizza party, they crack jokes and make fun of each other's husbands (there are no men here). I pass slices around and try not to think, "Seventeen with a bullet."

Oddly, we feel little curiosity or specific anger toward the man who shot him. We have to remind ourselves to check in with the police. Even so, it feels pro forma,[3] like sending in those $2 rebate forms that come with new pantyhose: You know your request will fall into a deep, dark hole somewhere but, still, it's your duty to try. We push for an arrest because we owe it to Johnny and to ourselves as citizens. We don't think about it otherwise — our low expectations are too ingrained. A Harvard aunt notwithstanding, for people like Johnny, Marvin Gaye was right that only three things are sure: taxes, death, and trouble. At least it wasn't the second.

We rarely wonder about or discuss the brother who shot him because we already know everything about him. When the call came, my first thought was the same one I'd had when I'd heard about Rosa Parks's beating: A brother did it. A non-job-having, middle-of-the-day malt-liquor-drinking, crotch-clutching, loud-talking brother with

10

---

[3]*pro forma:* Done according to predetermined rules or custom; literally, "according to form" (Latin).

many neglected children born of many forgotten women. He lives in his mother's basement with furniture rented at an astronomical interest rate, the exact amount of which he does not know. He has a car phone, an $80 monthly cable bill, and every possible phone feature but no savings. He steals social security numbers from unsuspecting relatives and assumes their identities to acquire large TV sets for which he will never pay. On the slim chance that he is brought to justice, he will have a colorful criminal history and no coherent explanation to offer for this act. His family will raucously defend him and cry cover-up. Some liberal lawyer just like me will help him plea bargain his way to yet another short stay in a prison pesthouse that will serve only to add another layer to the brother's sociopathology[4] and formless, mindless nihilism. We know him. We've known and feared him all our lives.

As a teenager, he called, "Hey, baby, gimme somma that boodie!" at us from car windows. Indignant at our lack of response, he followed up with, "Fuck you, then, 'ho!" He called me a "white-boy lovin' nigger bitch oreo" for being in the gifted program and loving it. At twenty-seven, he got my seventeen-year-old sister pregnant with Johnny and lost interest without ever informing her that he was married. He snatched my widowed mother's purse as she waited in pre-dawn darkness for the bus to work and then broke into our house while she soldered on an assembly line. He chased all the small entrepreneurs from our neighborhood with his violent thievery, and put bars on our windows. He kept us from sitting on our own front porch after dark and laid the foundation for our periodic bouts of self-hating anger and racial embarrassment. He made our neighborhood a ghetto. He is the poster fool behind the maddening community knowledge that there are still some black mothers who raise their daughters but merely love their sons. He and his cancerous carbon copies eclipse that vast majority of us who are not sociopaths and render us invisible. He is the Siamese twin who has died but cannot be separated from his living, vibrant sibling; which of us must attract more notice? We despise and disown this anomalous loser but, for many, he *is* black America. We know him, we know that he is outside the fold, and we know that he will only get worse. What we didn't know is that, because of him, my little sister would one day be the latest hysterical black mother wailing over a fallen child on TV.

[4]*sociopathology:* Quality of being a sociopath: one who acts without regard to, or against, the rules of society.

Alone, lying in the road bleeding and paralyzed but hideously conscious, Johnny had laid helpless as he watched his would-be murderer come to stand over him and offer this prophecy: "Betch'ou won't be doin' nomo' wavin', motha'fucker."

Fuck you, asshole. He's fine from the waist up. You just can't do anything right, can you?

Discussing Vocabulary / Using a Dictionary

1. Dickerson calls herself "unrepentant" (para. 1). What is the root of this word? In what other contexts have you seen this root form of the word?

2. What does it mean to "corroborate" someone's version of events? In what situations are people typically called upon to do this?

3. Consider the relation between the word "nihilism" (para. 14) and the word "nil." What other words ending in "ism" describe beliefs or political views?

4. What is an "anomaly"? How is the attacker an "anomalous" loser in his culture (para. 15)?

Discussing Meaning

1. What did Johnny do that prompted his attacker to shoot him?

2. How has the "accident" changed Johnny's behavior toward his family?

3. How does Dickerson describe the lawyer whom she imagines will defend her nephew's attacker?

4. What, according to Dickerson, is the "maddening community knowledge" about black mothers' relationships with their children?

Discussing Writing

1. Dickerson begins her essay with what rhetoricians call an "ethical" appeal: She tells the reader not about her subject but about herself, as a way of establishing her authority and good sense. What do you learn about Dickerson from the publications she reads, the school she attends, and the attitude she has toward politics?

2. In paragraphs 14 and 15 Dickerson provides a long description of the man who shot her nephew. Is she saying that the same man did all these things? What does she mean when she compares the figure she describes to a "carbon copy" and a "Siamese twin"?

3. Some periodicals might have refused to print the obscenity with which Dickerson ends her piece. Could she have achieved the same effect without it? Try to come up with another ending that you feel is equally powerful.

Challenging the Selection

1. At several points, Dickerson emphasizes her education and demonstrates her clear distaste for "disrespectful" music and language. Yet she ends her essay with an obscenity directed at her nephew's attacker. Does such language harm or benefit her argument? Why do you think she uses obscenity?

2. Dickerson's description of the man who shot Johnny is a catalog of negative stereotypes about black males. Do you think Dickerson believes these stereotypes? Are you bothered by her presentation of them? Why or why not? Do you see any connection between Johnny's father and his attacker?

3. Dickerson tells the story from her perspective as a concerned aunt and focuses largely on the reactions of her sister and mother to the shooting. How do you think her account would differ if she were Johnny's uncle or another male relative?

In-Class Writing Activities

1. Many people claim that urban life is more dangerous today largely because young people have access to guns. Do you agree? Write several paragraphs discussing your opinion on gun control and possession. Would this situation have been different if Johnny's attacker had had a knife instead? What if Johnny had had a gun?

2. To what extent should fear of crime influence our behavior? Does such fear make us better prepared or just anxious about something we can't control?

3. Reflect on the title "Who Shot Johnny?" and try to answer the question it poses. Is just the attacker responsible? Is an entire society responsible? Is a segment of society responsible? Be sure to explain your answer.

BRIAN BRADY

America's Real Fear

[OLD GOLD AND BLACK, WAKE FOREST UNIVERSITY / September 14, 1995]

Before You Read

This selection deals with the issue of what the federal government's role should be in a democracy. Does the government have a positive or negative influence on our lives for the most part? Are there areas of life that should definitely be off-limits to governmental involvement?

Words to Learn

zealous (para. 1): extremely devoted to a cause (adj.)
audacity (para. 2): offensive boldness (n.)
scapegoat (para. 7): a person, group, or institution bearing the blame for others' wrongdoings (n.)
venomous (para. 7): poisonous; malicious (adj.)

BRIAN BRADY *(b. 1973) received a bachelor's degree in history from Wake Forest University in 1996 and plans to pursue a master's degree in mass communications and broadcast journalism. In 1992 he received a W. David Stedman Merit Scholarship at Wake Forest. Brady currently lives in Winston-Salem, North Carolina.*

The key word in American society today when it comes to government is fear. Countless times we have heard of the fear of an over-reaching, zealous federal government. Check the headlines of any major newspaper and you will be sure to find an article or editorial dealing with the topic.

The summer of 1995 provided a stomping ground for the "fear" of government. Attorney General Janet Reno was grilled over the Federal Bureau of Investigation's role and actions in Waco, Texas, with the Branch Davidians. In early September, white separatist Randy Weaver testified in front of a congressional judiciary committee that the federal government unjustly cornered him at his home in Ruby Ridge, Idaho. The tragic Oklahoma City bombing has been construed as a warning from the growing militia movement in the heartland of America that the federal government should back off. Even more outrageous, militia members from Michigan appeared in front of the Senate and had the audacity to suggest that the federal government itself was responsible for blowing up the federal building in Oklahoma City, as well as for the poisonous-gas attack in a Tokyo subway in the spring of 1995.

> *The key word in American society today when it comes to government is fear.*

What is generating this tidal wave of fear of government? Is Washington overstepping its bounds, or is our nation producing an unusual amount of crazies whose extremist attitudes are a threat to the safety of all Americans?

Popular opinion has shifted this fear onto the federal government, with Capitol Hill and federal authorities carrying the burden like Atlas did the earth. It is true that government should play a very limited role in the private lives of Americans. It is also true that when government enters into the private affairs of citizens that basic civil rights can be stepped upon. But one must realize that these incidents are few and far between. Sometimes government and authorities are expected to step in, and while these times in the past have been limited, they are occurring at a disturbingly higher rate today.

Some actions by groups or individuals warrant a response from   5
federal authorities, and the incidents at Ruby Ridge, Waco, and the growing militia movement are such examples. In a country where the majority rules, minorities — in this case, unsafe and vigilant minorities — should not be allowed to be an exception.

Some will undoubtedly argue that the federal government needs a reality check, that it has crossed the line of governance by entering our private lives in a dramatic fashion. To what extent this assumption is true is debatable. The federal government has made mistakes, but for the most part federal authorities have executed their job well — protecting the rights and safety of American citizens who otherwise would be subject to the radical and unsafe ideas and opinions of extremist groups, whose doctrines attempt to poison America.

The fact is that government has become a scapegoat for right- and left-wing extremist actions. As a group, we holler for Washington to help us when a man like Branch Davidian leader David Koresh threatens society and our well-being, then condemn the authorities after they put the situation to rest. It is this hypocrisy that is creating the tension that resides within America today. While hasty or unjust actions by federal authorities must be questioned, we cannot stand by and let small, radical factions with venomous agendas continue to grow and fester across this nation. For it is these individuals and these groups who generate the real fear in America.

Discussing Vocabulary / Using a Dictionary

1. Brady suggests that people fear a "zealous" federal government. When is it a compliment to be "zealous"? When is it a derogatory statement?

2. Brady concludes his essay with several examples of highly metaphoric language. In paragraph 7, what kind of image does he suggest by describing the agendas of radical groups as "venomous"? What is he comparing such groups to in saying that they cannot be allowed to "fester" across the nation?

Discussing Meaning

1. In comparing the federal government to the mythical figure Atlas, the Titan who held up the heavens, what is Brady saying about the "burden" of fear?

2. In Brady's view, what types of actions warrant a federal response? Does he view the government's actions favorably or unfavorably for the most part?

3. Who is responsible for creating the real fear in America, according to Brady?

Discussing Writing

1. In paragraph 1, Brady writes that one can "check the headlines of any major newspaper and you will be sure to find an article" dealing with the topic of fear. He then cites several 1995 news stories. What effect do these examples have on you as a reader? How do they help to establish Brady's authority to speak on his topic?

2. Effective writers sometimes address opposing arguments in the course of making their own argument. Can you find an example of this tactic in paragraphs 4 and 6 of Brady's essay? Do you find Brady's rebuttal of the opposing arguments convincing?

Challenging the Selection

1. Is Brady justified in saying that the Waco, Oklahoma City, and Ruby Ridge incidents represent a "tidal wave" of fear of government? Are the people you know more afraid of the government than they used to be? Do you think most people supported or opposed the government's handling of these incidents?

2. Do you agree with Brady that America is "a country where the majority rules"? What protections does our political system offer to minorities?

3. In paragraph 6, Brady states that the job of the federal government is to protect citizens from the "radical and unsafe ideas and opinions of extremist groups, whose doctrines attempt to poison America." Do you believe this?

In-Class Writing Activities

1. List five examples of government services that you believe are appropriate and necessary. Can you also think of areas in which the government goes too far into or unnecessarily intrudes upon people's lives?

2. Conservatives generally speak negatively about the threat of "big government," whereas most liberals say that government helps improve people's lives. Which view do you hold? Explain the reasons for your position in a short essay.

Discussing the Unit

Suggested Topic for Discussion

Fear is usually considered a negative emotion, something to avoid. When we call someone "fearless," we typically mean it as a compliment. But if fear is so terrible, why do people go to horror movies, ride roller coasters, and read scary novels by Stephen King? How is the fear of a monster on the screen different from the fear of losing one's job? How is fear for our own safety, as described in "Safe-Sex Lies," different from the fear we have for our loved ones, as in "Who Shot Johnny?"? What's the scariest thing you can think of?

Preparing for Class Discussion

1. Each selection in this chapter deals with a specific fear in modern life: AIDS, crime, government oppression. Make a list of some other fears. Consider how our fears change as we get older. What things were you afraid of as a child? What things do you think your parents and grandparents are afraid of?

2. Compare Daum's description of herself with Dickerson's. What assumptions do the two authors make about how their education and background have prepared them for their present predicament?

3. Compare Brady's attitude toward the government with Daum's attitude toward educators and other sources of information about AIDS. How does each author respond to the idea that the government is acting for his or her own good?

From Discussion to Writing

1. For Meghan Daum, fear of AIDS is a "private hell, smoldering beneath intimate conversations among friends." What fears do you and your friends have? How do you share them? Write a one-page dialogue, based on either a real or an imaginary conversation, in which you and a friend discuss something you both are afraid of.

2. Describe a particular occasion when you were afraid of some-
    thing. How did you react to the fear? Looking back now, was
    your fear justified?

Topics for Cross-Cultural Discussion

1. People are often scared in situations where they do not feel at
    home, or where they don't quite know what to expect. For this
    reason, moving to a foreign country can be a very frightening ex-
    perience. How did you deal with your fears of America when you
    arrived? What differences about this country (language, food,
    people, and so forth) did you find most frightening at first?

2. Do you feel that life in America is more or less frightening than
    life in your native country? Explain your reasoning using specific
    examples from both places.

3. In your culture, would the Benetton advertisement on page 69 be
    considered art, effective advertising, or an offensive statement?
    Why?

5

Can We Resist Stereotypes?

America has often been called a "melting pot," a place where hundreds of cultures mingle together. But how well do Americans actually know one another? Is our understanding of other cultures only skin deep? In this section we take a look at stereotypes — the standard beliefs (sometimes justified, often not) that people hold about those different from themselves.

In the first selection, Eric Kim describes how he deals with the stereotypes of Asian men, which range from kung fu wizard to geek. Born in Korea, where he felt comfortable with the way he looked, Kim found that his confidence suffered when he moved to the United States for college. Next, Herbert J. Gans shows how stereotypes are often used to make poor people scapegoats for social problems. These problems, he argues, are the result of economic factors, not the moral failings of the poor. Finally, Northwestern University student Maggie Bandur tackles high heels, Diet Cokes, and the Victoria's Secret catalog in examining why women often play male-defined roles, even when the roles they might choose for themselves are quite different.

ERIC KIM

Have You Ever Met an Asian Man You Thought Was Sexy?

[GLAMOUR / March 1995]

Before You Read

This piece was written by a Korean. Think of some stereotypes of Asian men you have seen in movies and on television. Keep these in mind as you read Kim's essay.

Words to Learn

affront (para. 3): insult (n.)
chauvinist (para. 4): characterized by the belief that one's own group is superior (adj.)
diatribe (para. 5): abusive criticism (n.)

nonentity (para. 6): something that is nonexistent or unimportant (n.)
waylay (para. 7): to attack unexpectedly (v.)

"Yo, Bruce Lee! Hey, whatzaah happening?" That's what a group of teenage guys shouted at me a couple of years ago as I walked down the street with a friend. They followed that up with a series of yelps and shrieks that I took to be their attempts at kung fu sounds. As I was about to turn and respond, my friend quickly pointed out that it would be better, and safer, to ignore these guys.

In retrospect, though, I wonder if rising above it was the best response. Sometimes I don't believe I can change people's stereotypes about Asians without confronting them. At least Bruce Lee, the late

---

ERIC KIM (b. 1970) grew up in Raleigh, North Carolina, and Seoul, Korea, where he attended Seoul International High School. He received a bachelor's degree in English literature from the University of Pennsylvania in 1993, and he now works for a film production company in New York City.

martial arts expert, is at the macho end of the spectrum, along with the stereotype of the greedy, wealthy businessmen who are invading America. At the other end of the spectrum, Asian men in America are seen as geeks — short, nerdy, passive, and somewhat asexual "Orientals."

As a six-foot, 180-pound, Korean American guy, I always hated that people would assume I was a wimpy bookworm who couldn't play sports. It pleased me to see how upset non-Asians would get after a few Asian friends and I whipped them in a game of full-court basketball. Before we hit the court, the other guys would snicker and assume we'd be easy to beat. Afterward, they'd act as if being outdone in sports by an Asian was an affront to their masculinity.

It's different for Asian women, who are usually stereotyped as exotic, passive, sensual, the ultimate chauvinist fantasy. The reality of these stereotypes is played out on the street: Look around and you'll see an Asian woman with a Caucasian man a lot sooner than you'll see a white woman with an Asian date. Even Asian women sometimes shun Asian men as being either too wimpy or too dominating. I was born and grew up in Seoul, South Korea, and went to an international high school there. The student body was about 80 percent Asian and 20 percent Caucasian. I think being in the majority gave me a certain social confidence. I never thought twice about dating or flirting with non-Asian girls. If I felt nervous or awkward, it was because I was shy, not because I wasn't white.

> *As a six-foot, 180-pound Korean American guy, I always hated that people would assume I was a wimpy bookworm who couldn't play sports.*

When I started college in the United States, I promised myself   5
that I'd meet people of all races, since most of my friends in Seoul had been Asian. Yet when I arrived here, for the first time in my life I felt like a minority. For the first time in my life, I was told to "go back home" and had to listen to strangers on the bus give me their diatribes on Vietnam and Korea. Feeling I was a minority affected how I approached other people.

Even though there were a lot of attractive non-Asian women at school, I hesitated to approach them, because I imagined that they were only interested in Caucasian guys. I assumed that non-Asian women bought the Asian stereotypes and saw me as a nonentity. It wasn't that I kept trying and getting shot down; I simply assumed they would never consider me. The frustrating mix of my own pride and the fear of getting rejected always managed to keep me from approaching a non-Asian woman I was attracted to.

My girlfriend now is Asian American. There are many things I love about her, and it strengthens our relationship that we have a cultural bond. Relationships are about trust, vulnerability, and a willingness to open up. That can be hard for an Asian man to achieve with a non-Asian woman; though he may find her attractive, his emotions may be blocked by fear, waylaid by the caricatures of Asian men as paranoid deli owners, Confucius[1]-spewing detectives, or kung fu fighters with fists of fury.

These images say little about what it means to be a twenty-four-year-old Asian man. These images don't reflect our athleticism, our love of rap, or our possible addiction to ESPN. Because of these images, Asian men are rarely seen for what we are — and so we may look at a non-Asian woman with interest, then tuck that interest away.

It's not easy to confess that I know many women don't find me attractive. But for me, the very process of facing down Asian stereotypes makes them less meaningful. Most of all, I try to keep a sense of humor about it. After all, when my friends and I whip some unsuspecting non-Asians on the basketball court, *they* are the ones who are victims of the stereotypes, not us.

---

[1]*Confucius:* Ancient Chinese philosopher (551–479 B.C.) known for his wise sayings.

Discussing Vocabulary / Using a Dictionary

1. Explain the difference between a "caricature" (para. 7) and a "stereotype" (paras. 2, 4, 6, and 9). In what ways are the two words related?

2. The stereotype of Asian women is "the ultimate chauvinist fantasy," Kim writes (para. 4). What do chauvinists believe about themselves and the group to which they belong? Which meaning of the word do you think Kim intends here?

3. Kim writes about being made to listen to "diatribes" by strangers on the bus (para. 5). What type of speech is he describing? Does the word have a positive or negative meaning?

Discussing Meaning

1. What are some of the stereotypes Kim presents of Asian men? How are they different from those of Asian women?

2. Why does Kim feel that white men date Asian women more often than Asian men date white women? What prevented Kim from approaching non-Asian women in college?

3. Is Kim himself helping to perpetuate any stereotypes by refusing to approach non-Asian women?

4. What are some of the things about Asian men not reflected in typical images, according to Kim?

Discussing Writing

1. Kim begins his essay by quoting a phrase shouted at him by strangers on the street. What effect does this opening have? Why do you think Kim chooses to start with other people's words instead of his own?

2. How does the contrast Kim draws between his high school and college experiences (paras. 4–6) strengthen his argument about stereotypes?

3. Consider Kim's audience: the readers of *Glamour,* a magazine designed primarily for young women. In what way might his essay have been different if he had written it for a men's magazine like *Playboy* or *Esquire*?

Challenging the Selection

1. Kim says that he ignored the teenagers who shouted at him but then later wondered if that was the best response (paras. 1 and 2). What do you think? Should he have confronted them? Why or why not?

2. Do you believe Kim when he says, "After all, when my friends and I whip some unsuspecting non-Asians on the basketball court, they are the ones who are victims of the stereotypes, not us" (para. 9)? In what ways are the losers "victims"? Why doesn't Kim want to be seen as a "victim" of stereotypes?

In-Class Writing Activities

1. Have you ever been attracted to someone who you were afraid wouldn't be interested in you? Write an essay describing how you dealt with the situation.

2. Kim says that it's important to maintain a sense of humor about stereotypes. Do you agree? Should we laugh at stereotypes or take them seriously? Write a paragraph stating your view.

3. Do you think you have ever been the victim of a stereotype? If so, how did the experience make you feel? How did you deal with it?

HERBERT J. GANS

Fitting the Poor into the Economy

[TECHNOLOGY REVIEW / October 1995]

Before You Read

In this essay, Herbert J. Gans argues that we need a more generous welfare system, among other things, to help the poor. What images do you think of when you read the word "poor"? Do you think that these images arise from uninformed stereotypes of the poor or from facts?

HERBERT J. GANS (b. 1927) is Robert S. Lynd Professor of Sociology at Columbia University. Gans, who holds a doctorate in planning and sociology from the University of Pennsylvania, has published several books—most recently The War against the Poor: The Underclass and Antipoverty Policy (1995)—and his scholarly articles have appeared in numerous publications, including Commonweal, Dissent, The Nation, The New Republic, the New York Times Magazine, and the Partisan Review.

Words to Learn

subsistence (para. 1): the minimum necessary to survive (adj.)

onus (para. 2): an unpleasant responsibility (n.)

antidote (para. 4): something that counteracts negative effects (n.)

infrastructure (para. 4): the basic structural needs or equipment

of a community or organization (n.)

inroad (para. 6): an advance or encroachment (n.)

paltry (para. 7): pathetically small or insignificant (adj.)

dereliction (para. 8): neglect of duty; irresponsibility (n.)

The notion of the poor as too lazy or morally deficient to deserve assistance seems to be indestructible. Public policies limit poor people to substandard services and incomes below the subsistence level, and Congress and state legislatures are tightening up even on these miserly allocations — holding those in the "underclass" responsible for their own sorry state. Indeed, labeling the poor as undeserving has lately become politically useful as a justification for the effort to eliminate much of the antipoverty safety net and permit tax cuts for the affluent people who do most of the voting.

Such misplaced blame offers mainstream society a convenient evasion of its own responsibility. Blaming poor men and women for not working, for example, takes the onus off both private enterprise and government for failing to supply employment. It is easier to charge poor unmarried mothers with lacking family values than to make sure that there are jobs for them and for the young men who are not marriageable because they are unable to support families. Indeed, the poor make excellent scapegoats for a range of social problems, such as street crime and drug and alcohol addiction. Never mind the reversal of cause and effect that underlies this point of view — for centuries crime, alcoholism, and single motherhood have risen whenever there has not been enough work and income to go around.

> *The poor make excellent scapegoats for a range of social problems.*

The undeserving underclass is also a useful notion for employers as the economy appears to be entering a period of long-term stagnation. Jobs are disappearing — some displaced by labor-saving technologies, others exported to newly industrializing, low-wage countries, others lost as companies "downsize" to face tougher global competition. Indeed, the true rate of unemployment — which includes involuntary part-time workers and long-term "discouraged" workers who have dropped out of the job market altogether — has remained in double digits for more than a generation and no longer seems to drop during times of economic strength. Labeling poor people as lacking the needed work ethic is a politically simple way of shedding them from a labor market that will most likely never need them again.

The most efficient antidote to poverty is not welfare but full employment. In the short run, therefore, today's war against the poor should be replaced with efforts to create jobs for now-surplus workers. New Deal[1]-style programs of large-scale governmental employment, for example, can jump-start a slow economy. Besides being the fastest way to put people to work, a public-works program can improve the country's infrastructure, including highways, buildings, parks, and computer databases.

In addition, private enterprise and government should aim to   5
stimulate the most promising labor-intensive economic activities and stop encouraging new technology that will further destroy jobs — reviving, for example, the practice of making cars and appliances partly by hand. A parallel policy would tax companies for their use of labor-saving technology; the revenues from this tax would pay for alternative jobs for people in occupations that technology renders obsolete. This idea makes good business as well as social sense: Human workers are needed as customers for the goods that machines now produce.

To distribute the jobs that do exist among more people, employers could shorten the work day, week, or year. Several large manufacturing companies in Western Europe already use worksharing to create a thirty-five-hour week. Making significant inroads on U.S. joblessness may require reducing the work week to thirty hours.

Finding Solutions, Not Scapegoats

A more generous welfare system would go a long way toward solving the problems of the remainder: those who cannot work or cannot find jobs. By persisting in the belief that poor people deserve their fate, society can easily justify a paltry and demeaning welfare system that pays recipients only about one-quarter of the median income. A system that paid closer to half the median income, by contrast, would enable those without work to remain full members of

---

[1]*New Deal:* Broad program of economic relief instituted by former U.S. President Franklin D. Roosevelt between 1933 and 1939.

society and thus minimize the despair, anger, and various illnesses, as well as premature mortality, distinctive to the poor.

For such antipoverty policies to gain acceptance, mainstream America will have to unlearn the stereotype of poor people as immoral. Most of the poor are just as law-abiding as everyone else. (While a minority of poor people cheat on their welfare applications, an even larger minority of affluent people cheat on their tax returns — yet the notion of undeservingness is never applied to the middle or upper classes.) In admitting that the phenomena now explained as moral dereliction are actually traceable to poverty, Americans will force themselves to find solutions, not scapegoats, to the country's problems.

Most of the people assigned to today's undeserving underclass are the first victims of what is already being called the future "jobless economy." In the long run, if the cancer of joblessness spreads more widely among the population, large numbers of the present middle class will have to adapt to the reality that eventually most workers may no longer be employed full time. In that case, more drastic job-creation policies will be needed, including a ban on additional job-destroying technology and the establishment of permanent public employment modeled on the kind now associated with military spending. Worksharing would most likely be based on a twenty-four-hour week.

At that point, everyone would in fact be working part-time by today's standards, and new ways to maintain standards of living would have to be found. One approach, already being discussed in Europe, is a universal, subsistence-level income grant. This "demogrant," a twenty-first-century version of the $1,000-per-person allotment that presidential candidate George McGovern proposed in 1972, would be taxed away from people still working full time. In any case, private and government agencies should begin now to study what policies might be needed to preserve the American way of life when the full-time job will no longer be around to pay for the American Dream.

It is possible, of course, that new sources of economic growth will suddenly develop to revive the full employment and prosperity of the post–World War II decades. And some labor-saving technologies may, in the long run, create more jobs than they destroy; that may well be the case for computers, which have spawned a large sector of the economy. Such happy outcomes cannot be counted on to materialize, however, and there remains the danger that the war on the poor will continue as the politically most convenient path. We will undoubtedly find that when the economy begins to threaten the descendants of today's middle and even affluent classes with becoming poor, and then "undeserving," policies that today seem utopian will be demanded, and quickly.

Discussing Vocabulary / Using a Dictionary

1. Consider the meaning of the noun "onus" (para. 2) and its adjective form, "onerous." What are some more common synonyms for these words?

2. Does "affluent" (para. 1) mean the same thing as rich? Consider the word's relation to other words with the same root — for instance, "influence."

3. What does it mean to say that the economy is entering a period of "stagnation" (para. 3)?

4. Gans suggests that full employment is an "antidote" (para. 4) to poverty. In what other contexts have you seen this word used?

5. From what source does the word "utopian" (para. 11) derive? Provide some different definitions of this word.

Discussing Meaning

1. Why, according to Gans, does mainstream society blame poor people for its problems?

2. What does Gans argue are the real sources of crime, alcoholism, and single motherhood?

3. In addition to providing employment, how, in Gans's view, do large-scale public-works programs benefit the country?

4. What does Gans think will have to happen before antipoverty policies gain acceptance in America?

Discussing Writing

1. Gans addresses both our society's policies and its attitudes toward the poor. In what ways does he show the two things as connected?

2. How would you describe Gans's tone when he writes that the poor "make excellent scapegoats for a range of social problems" (para. 2)? Does he seem to approve or disapprove of poor people being used as scapegoats? How can you tell?

3. Is the tone in this essay harsh or gentle? aggressive or passive? formal or casual? Can you note instances where Gans uses sarcasm or irony (saying one thing but meaning another)? How do these devices contribute to his overall tone?

Challenging the Selection

1. Gans suggests that with the economy slowing down, people may have to work fewer hours and receive less pay in order to ensure that everyone has a job. Would you prefer a high-paying job with little leisure time or a lower-paying one with ample time off? Which do you think most Americans would choose?

2. In paragraph 9, Gans says that joblessness is a "cancer" and suggests that it may spread more widely through the population in the future. Do you think the comparison of an economic trend to a disease makes sense? Why or why not?

3. Gans mentions the possibility of taxing people who work full time. Could such a tax be counterproductive? Could it diminish the notion of the American work ethic? Why or why not?

In-Class Writing Activities

1. Gans suggests that poor people are blamed for social problems because politicians find them to be a convenient scapegoat. Describe an incident in which you were made a scapegoat for something that wasn't your fault. What were you blamed for, and who blamed you? How did it feel?

2. Imagine that you are a politician who wants to help the poor. Write a short speech in which you propose one idea from Gans's essay (or, if you prefer, an idea of your own). Remember to address the benefits the plan will have for your voters, and try to anticipate any objections to the plan they (or your election opponent) might have.

3. "Automation" is the process by which machines replace humans

in the production of goods and services. What are some positive and negative effects of automation, according to this essay? Think of some others on your own.

MAGGIE BANDUR

Women Play the Roles Men Want to See

[THE DAILY NORTHWESTERN, NORTHWESTERN UNIVERSITY / January 23, 1996)

Before You Read

Why is it that we can be aware of harmful stereotypes and yet still allow them to influence our behavior? Why do we strive to conform to standards that don't make us happy? Do we try to convince ourselves that these standards do indeed make us happy? Do we value pleasing others more than pleasing ourselves?

Words to Learn

antiquated (para. 2): so old as to be outdated, no longer useful (adj.)
ogling (para. 3): staring in a lustful manner (n.)
credence (para. 5): trustworthiness (n.)

A favorite assignment of media courses is to have students analyze advertisements. Without fail, some boy will bring in a picture from the Victoria's Secret catalog as an example of the objectification of women. Does it objectify women? Considering how many sex-starved, male dorm residents steal the mailroom's copies to check out

In 1996 MAGGIE BANDUR (b. 1974) received a bachelor's degree in speech from Northwestern University, where she studied radio, television, and film. While at Northwestern, Bandur was a contestant in the college tournament of the television quiz show Jeopardy! *She currently lives in Chicago.*

the scantily clad women wearing submissive, come-hither looks, I would have to say "yes." The male-dominated society's lack of respect for women is alive and well!

What is not always pointed out, but should be, is that the catalog is marketed to women. And this type of marketing apparently works. The women are just as excited as the men on the day it arrives. Many antiquated attitudes and stereotypes of women persist because men still have a lot of power. But what makes it hard to destroy the stereotypes is that some women still go along with them.

Sometimes, I'm one of those women. As much as I hate the fact that men think girls are stupid, I have on occasion played dumb to get male assistance. As much as I am offended by male ogling, there have been times when I have worn tight clothing and endured the agony of heels so that boys would pay attention to me. (Keep in mind, of course, that attention is not synonymous with being touched.) As saddened as I am at how many girls will let men treat them horribly, I haven't fared much better. As much as I try not to give in to all the stereotypes and societal expectations, I sometimes do, but I don't think that I am alone.

Every woman who embraces a stereotype is giving that stereotype more credence.

In high school, when my friends and I would go out to dinner, none of the girls would want the guys to see us actually eating. Ordering anything more than a salad and a Diet Coke would supposedly insure that all the boys would think you were a cow. Every once in a while, the other girls and I would agree that this was ridiculous, that we were hungry, and that we would order whatever we darn well pleased. We'd get to the table and I, like a fool, would order first. "Hamburger and a chocolate milk shake, please." And then those traitors would all order salads and Diet Cokes. If four or five girls can't work together on a trip to a restaurant, can all womankind join together to defy male expectations? If everyone dressed comfortably, let themselves reach the weight their bodies wanted, and stubbornly refused to give men the time of day until they treated women with the respect they deserved, men would come around a whole helluva lot faster. But there is always someone who is going to order that Diet Coke.

Sometimes it's easier to play along, and some people always will; but in the long run it's better for all women if you don't. Every woman who embraces a stereotype — even if it is as a tool to get

5

ahead in a world that men have made harder for women — is giving that stereotype more credence.

It may take a while before I have the strength to resist every dictate of male society, but I am trying. I have almost accepted the fact that I will always be forty to fifty pounds heavier than supermodels my height, and I can almost get through a large meal with a boy without apologizing for eating. Small victories, I will admit, but at least it's a start.

Discussing Vocabulary / Using a Dictionary

1. In paragraph 1, Bandur says that the Victoria's Secret catalog is used as an example of the "objectification of women." What does it mean to "objectify" someone?

2. What is Bandur saying about certain attitudes toward women by describing them as "antiquated" (para. 2)? Explain the difference between "antiquated" and "antique."

Discussing Meaning

1. According to Bandur, what factor is often overlooked in discussing the way women are portrayed in Victoria's Secret catalogs?

2. Why would Bandur's friends only order salads and Diet Cokes when they went out to dinner?

3. What steps, in Bandur's view, could women take to make men treat them with more respect?

Discussing Writing

1. Police detectives typically use deductive reasoning: They gather up all the clues, then piece them together to figure out what happened. Inductive reasoning takes the opposite approach: It makes a statement about human behavior in general based on a particular example. Which form of reasoning does Bandur use in this essay? Can you find an example of her method?

2. In paragraph 5, Bandur suddenly addresses the reader with the second-person pronoun "you": "In the long run, it's better for

all women if you don't." Who is Bandur addressing? What effect does this direct form of address have on you as a reader?

Challenging the Selection

1. If Bandur thinks that men's stereotypes of women are unhealthy, why does she admit that she has occasionally played such roles herself? Would you find her essay more or less convincing if she claimed that she had never conformed to a stereotype? Why?

2. In paragraph 3, Bandur mentions hating the fact that "men think girls are stupid." How do you react to her use of "men" and "girls" in the same sentence? Does the use of these words undercut her argument?

3. Bandur mentions the influence of "male expectations" on the way she thinks about herself. In what ways are men influenced by "female expectations" of how they should look or dress? Do you think that men "play roles" too? What kinds? Are men harmed by these expectations as much as women are? Why or why not?

4. Many of Bandur's terms (for example, "victories," "traitors," and "defy") imply that she thinks a battle of the sexes is necessary to achieve female empowerment. Is cooperation between men and women in order to achieve equality of the sexes an unrealistic goal? Why or why not?

In-Class Writing Activities

1. Have you ever been in a situation where you had to "play a role" you didn't feel comfortable with? Write a few paragraphs describing the incident and how you felt. Why did you act the way you did? Would you act differently if you were in the same situation today?

2. Bandur takes a class discussion as the starting point for her essay. Write a similar essay in which you analyze something that happened in one of your classes and then discuss its larger relevance.

Discussing the Unit

Suggested Topic for Discussion

The selections in this section deal with three different forms of stereotypes — those based on race (that Asian men are nerdy), class (that poor people are lazy), and gender (that women should not act smart or eat a lot). What do the authors say is the appeal of such stereotypes? How are they damaging?

Preparing for Class Discussion

1. Consider the words "generalization" and "stereotype." How are they different? What do you feel is the intention behind each? Write two statements — one a generalization and the other a stereotype — that people might use to describe Asian men, poor people, and women.

2. Have you ever made assumptions about a person, based on his or her race, class, or gender, only to discover later that your assumptions were wrong? Where did you get your initial ideas about the person? What made you change your mind?

From Discussion to Writing

1. Although stereotypes, by nature, are distorted, they sometimes contain a small element of truth. For example, while it's not true that all African American men are good basketball players, it is true that the majority of players in the NBA are African American. In several paragraphs discuss a stereotype about a group with which you are familiar, addressing both the aspects of the stereotype that have some basis in truth and those that are false or misleading.

2. Some people consider certain stereotypes (for example, that Asians are excellent students) to be positive. Write a comparison/contrast paper in which you address both positive and negative stereotypes. Consider whether you think that all stereotypes, both those seen as positive and those seen as negative, are ultimately harmful.

3. Bandur writes that stereotypes about women "persist because men still have a lot of power." Why do you think stereotypes in general persist? Who benefits from them? Write an essay stating your view.

Topics for Cross-Cultural Discussion

1. In your opinion, are Americans more or less likely to believe stereotypes about others than are people in your native country? Why?

2. What stereotypes do people in America have about your racial or cultural group? What stereotypes about Americans did you or your parents have when you came to this country?

6

Can Interracial Relationships Succeed?

Choosing a romantic partner is one of the most private and personal issues that we confront in life. But what happens when the person we are attracted to is of a different race, and we face opposition from family, friends, and even strangers? Can we overcome both our own differences and the objections of others?

In the first essay, Viet D. Dinh wonders why race remains acceptable as a factor in judging relationships, when similar judgments are considered racist in other areas of life. Then Valerie Richard, a white college student, contributes a detailed account of the struggle for acceptance she and her black boyfriend faced when they started dating. The section concludes with a wide-ranging collection of opinions and perspectives on this issue from African American students.

VIET D. DINH

Single White Female

[RECONSTRUCTION / Vol. 2, No. 3, 1994]

Before You Read

Walking down the street one day, you see a couple, an Asian man and a white woman, approaching. How do you react? Or what do you think to yourself? Why do you think that interracial dating is still widely perceived as a social taboo?

Words to Learn

surreptitiously (para. 12): secretly (adj.)

inexplicably (para. 12): without explanation or incapable of being explained (adv.)

bohemian (para. 15): an unconventional, artistic person (n.)

opprobrium (para. 16): disgrace or shame (n.)

innocuous (para. 17): harmless (adj.)

proxy (para. 18): a substitute; someone standing in or acting for someone else (n.)

succumb (para. 18): to yield to; to be overcome by (v.)

talisman (para. 21): a magical object believed to protect its possessor (n.)

bequeath (para. 21): to pass on; to will (v.)

unrequitedly (para. 21): without hope of having something returned or repaid (adv.)

absolve (para. 23): to free from blame or responsibility (v.)

conflagration (para. 23): a big fire (n.)

husbandry (para. 23): management or breeding (n.)

VIET D. DINH *is an associate professor of law at Georgetown University Law Center.*

Mary and I met in my senior year of high school at a weekend speech and debate tournament in northern California. By chance, I stopped at an afternoon storytelling competition and listened to her recite passages from *Jonathan Livingston Seagull.* We fell in love — quickly, foolishly. Each day after watching each other compete, we'd sneak into San Francisco for dinner in Chinatown (my choice) or Ghiradelli Square (hers) and a stroll through North Beach to Coit Tower.

About a week later, Mary's mother asked about her new boyfriend on the drive to school.

"I hear you've met a new boy."

"Yes."

"Is he Catholic?"   5

"Yes."

"College?"

"Yes, he's going to Harvard."

Her mother smiled, "Well, good. What's his name?"

"Viet," Mary answered, wittily adding a pronunciation tip, "as   10
in Vietnam."

"I'm sorry, Mary, tell him you can't see him anymore."

That was the end. I saw Mary only a few times after she told me this story, mostly to talk about what happened. She wondered why we didn't continue surreptitiously; I tried to understand what motivated her mother's response. Mary offered (inexplicably) that her mother was from Indiana, and argued that she really was not racist, that if I were to apply for a job at her real estate office she probably would hire me.

I met Mary's mother once, years later. I worked as a real estate developer and wanted to buy some land in the area. More as an excuse than out of necessity, I called up to schedule a tour of her listings. She never placed me, and after an hour in her car, I began to accept that Mary was right. Her mother was not a racist — at least not in the sense that I had imagined in high school. She was comfortable with me. Nothing in her manner betrayed nervousness or artificial cordiality.

That revelation only made my question harder to answer. What motivates an otherwise intelligent person to inflict such pain on such a seemingly irrational basis? She is not racist, yet cannot tolerate her daughter dating an Asian. Why is love, or sex, so special?

The question presents itself frequently. Open any magazine to the   15
personal ads and one finds exposed on every page the impulse that

Mary's mother displayed. Single White Female seeking same; Divorced Black Male, professional, seeking compatible companion; Gay White Male seeking mate; Asian Woman seeking a gentleman. The open invitation to judge based on race extends shamelessly across all social barriers, from *New York Review of Books* intellectuals to *Village Voice* bohemians to *Washingtonian* power brokers.

Such open reliance on racial qualifications is hard to reconcile with moral and social opprobrium accorded to racism and the suspicion of racial classifications in the post-Civil Rights era. In most cases, race cannot legally be a factor in hiring or firing, in buying or selling, in admission or rejection. Even an acknowledgment that one's friends or associates are only of a particular race gives pause and sometimes has derailed otherwise promising public careers. Yet romantic race-typing persists, explicitly and pervasively, not noticed and hardly questioned.

> *She feared that in searching for an American, I would stop being Vietnamese.*

Maybe the designation of one's race in a personal ad is innocuous. The ad, after all, attempts to convey a full (maybe even inflated) picture of its owner, and race is simply part of the picture, like a glimpse of someone walking down the street or eating in a restaurant. But to offer race as part of that verbal picture is to recognize, and approve, that race matters when one judges a stranger for compatibility and attraction. Why?

For one thing, the racial designation may be shorthand for a number of cultural and ethnic traits that cannot be fully captured in a short ad or a quick glimpse. But to accept race as proxy for personal characteristics is to succumb to exactly the impulse that one finds reprehensible in racism: the blind acceptance of generalized biases without regard to individual qualities. It is not justifiable (both factually and morally) to assume that a black man likes jazz or that an Asian woman is petite any more than to say that black men are muggers or Asian women are submissive.

Moreover, race is just one arbitrary level of generalization. If it is a "package" of personal characteristics that one is looking for, that mix need not be determined by race. Asian Male describes very little of who I am, the differences among Asian cultures being large. Southeast Asian is closer, but then why not Vietnamese, or South Vietnamese? Better yet, why not simply Male?

When I told my sister that I don't discriminate in my romantic   20
decisions, she replied, "Maybe you're just not very discriminating."
Race-typing, she argued, flows from the natural desire to preserve
one's culture in a pluralistic society. She feared that in searching for
an American, I would stop being Vietnamese.

But this argument assumes that culture is something timeless, a
never-changing talisman that has been begotten and bequeathed and is
to be passed on forever. That is hardly the case. Any immigrant who
returns to his native country can readily observe the chasm that only a
few years' absence has forged between him and the culture that he had
nostalgically and unrequitedly loved. People change, traditions evolve,
and institutions adapt. To assume that one's "culture" could remain
unchanged is to ignore that what defines culture is simply a dynamic
and complex process of human and natural interaction.

I do not deny that I am Vietnamese, that I have a distinct cultural
heritage in which to take pride. It is precisely that pride which makes
me willing to share my culture, not to lock it away in a tower of
racial chastity. Whatever is lost in authenticity I hope is gained dou-
bly in wider acceptance and deeper appreciation.

Perhaps romantic race-typing can be absolved as a Darwinian[1]
strategy to perpetuate one's genetic longevity. A friend confesses to
having felt a tinge of alarm when her then-fiancé casually remarked
that their children would look like him, since his Jamaican genes
would dominate her recessive white ones. Such a reaction, natural as
it may be, is only valid if the animating desire for racial purity is itself
justifiable. At another time or in a different place, racial homogeneity
may have been an effective means of preservation and survival. But in
America's multiracial 1990s, where the danger is not of racial extinc-
tion but of ethnic conflagration, racial husbandry is as unwise as it is
indefensible.

After my relationship with a Vietnamese woman ended when we
could find little in common, I recently began seeing someone new, a
white woman. Often when we walk hand in hand down Capitol Hill
or through the Boston Common, we smile at the people who hold us
in their stares. I think I will stop wondering about Mary's mother
when I can be confident that the heads that turn do so because of my
girlfriend's beauty or our apparent happiness together.

---

[1] *Darwinian:* A reference to the English naturalist Charles Darwin (1809–1882), who
proposed the evolutionary theory of "natural selection" holding that species inherit the
most beneficial physical traits from previous generations.

Discussing Vocabulary / Using a Dictionary

1. Mary "wondered why we didn't continue surreptitiously," Dinh writes (para. 12). What are some synonyms for the word "surreptitious"?

2. Dinh writes of the "opprobrium accorded to racism" today (para. 16). What is the meaning of "opprobrium"? Can one person accord opprobrium? Does the word indicate a private or a public reaction to something?

3. Dinh wonders whether specifying race in a personal ad is "innocuous" (para. 17). Doctors sometimes give people shots to "innoculate" them against diseases. How are these words related?

4. How is "discriminating" used in paragraph 20? In what other ways is this word used?

5. The word "conflagration" (para. 23) has many definitions and subtle shades of meaning. Why is Dinh's use of the word especially appropriate?

Discussing Meaning

1. What reasons did Mary give Dinh for her mother's objection to him? Did she see her mother as racist? Does Dinh think Mary's mother was racist? How so and how not?

2. What are some of the areas of life, according to Dinh, in which it is no longer acceptable to use race as a factor?

3. Why do people include race in personal ads, according to Dinh? What things does he say that race is a "shorthand" for? Does he approve of this use of racial categorization? Why or why not?

4. How does Dinh's sister respond to his views on interracial dating? How does she defend discrimination in choosing a romantic partner?

5. What does Dinh say makes him willing to share his culture with a non-Vietnamese woman? What does he see as the advantages of doing so?

Discussing Writing

1. How does Dinh's presentation of the scene between Mary and her mother strengthen his argument about interracial dating?

What significance is there in his being Catholic and going to Harvard?

2. In paragraph 14 Dinh asks, "Why is love, or sex, so special?" Find several other instances in which Dinh asks the reader a question. What effect do these questions have? Does Dinh seem to know the answers?

3. Why do you think Dinh chooses to begin and end his essay with a description of him and his girlfriend walking in public? Did you react differently to the second scene than you did to the first? How effective is the ending?

Challenging the Selection

1. Dinh discusses at some length the idea of race as an indicator of cultural views but does not specifically address the issue of physical attraction. Do you believe that people can (or should) find others attractive regardless of their race? What do you think Dinh would say? Is it racist for a person to say that he or she is not attracted to members of a particular group?

2. Would Mary's mother have been justified in objecting to Dinh if he wasn't Catholic, or if he wasn't going to college? What role should parents play in influencing who their children can date?

3. Dinh says that race cannot legally be a factor in many areas of corporate and collegiate America. Considering affirmative action's role in society, do you agree with Dinh on this point?

In-Class Writing Activities

1. Have you ever had a close friend or romantic interest who was quite different from yourself racially, culturally, or in some other way? In a short essay, discuss some of the ways in which you were different. What did you like about the person? How did your family and friends react to your interest in him or her? Describe some of the difficulties you had overcoming your differences and what you learned from the experience.

2. Write a twenty-five-word ad that you might place in the personals section of your local newspaper. In the ad reveal both something about yourself and the qualities you look for in a romantic partner. Try to be specific without resorting to the kinds of

"shorthand" Dinh describes. Then, write a brief postscript addressing these questions: If you decided to include your race or
specify the race of your desired partner, why did you do this? If
you left out race, what were your reasons?

VALERIE RICHARD

Love Sees No Color

[ROCK WRITING, SLIPPERY ROCK UNIVERSITY / 1994–1995]

Before You Read

Do you think that black-white couples face more discrimination than
black-Hispanic, Asian-white, or other mixed-race couples, or do you
think there is no difference?

Words to Learn

disown (para. 3): to deny any relationship to (v.)
prestigious (para. 5): prominent or of high status (adj.)
snide (para. 6): sarcastic or malicious (adj.)

"Nigger lover," "Sellout," "Once you go black, you never come
back": These are just some of the many ignorant comments I have encountered since I started dating my boyfriend, Jamar, eight months
ago.

VALERIE RICHARD *(b. 1976) has completed her first semester at Slippery
Rock University in Pennsylvania. Richard says that in writing this essay, "I
wanted people to realize how difficult it is to have an interracial relationship.
I also wanted to make people understand that love is hard in the first place,
even without outside pressure, and it's not anyone's place to judge any relationship."*

I never set out to date a black guy. It just happened. Just like the sun setting and like the wind blowing, it just happened. We met at a dance club and our relationship blossomed.

My parents and three out of my four siblings are fine with this idea. The big conflict in my family comes from my twenty-seven-year-old brother, Rodney. Racism and hate flow steadily through his veins. To him, being black means to be jobless, feeble-minded, a gang member, or any other negative stereotypes placed on blacks. He never was racist when he was younger because he was never raised to be so. Rodney had a nasty addiction to drugs starting at age eighteen until he was twenty-two. His drug dealer was a black guy from New Castle [Pennsylvania]. Hatred toward blacks started the first day that drug dealer sold him drugs because Rodney felt that his addiction wasn't his fault but the "monkey" drug dealer's. Rodney has informed me that if I ever married a black guy, he would disown me. I really love Rodney, and it tears me apart that he has this attitude because we were very close at one time.

Why is there so much narrow-mindedness toward black-white relationships?

This harsh treatment is not only pressed on me by my brother, but also by my friends and their families. My best friend Brandy started dating Jamar's best friend Quiad. They introduced Jamar and me. Brandy's parents are very racist and would kill her if they ever found out she was dating a black guy. Well, they did find out about, as they called it, Brandy's "evil" relationship. I was blamed for her behavior because I was dating a black guy. The funny thing about her parents blaming me is that her sister is married to a black guy. They were always accepting of that relationship. Also, her parents believed that their perfect daughter would never dare date a black man of her own free will. No responsibility was placed on Brandy. She is no longer allowed to speak to me because I am such a bad influence.

Another hardship comes from society in general. My neighborhood, I thought, was pretty cool and it seemed very open-minded. But to assume something is to make an ass of yourself. The entire summer the hardworking cops of my town stopped Jamar and me numerous times. Let it be known that we were walking, not driving, when we were stopped. We weren't breaking any pedestrian laws like jaywalking. We even looked both ways when we crossed the road. Each time they asked *me* if I was all right, as if the only reason I would dare be with a black man would be if he forced me. My mom

5

is friends with one of these prestigious cops, and he informed me that more than ten different neighbors called the police station numerous times to tell them that a black guy was staying at my house. Jamar was just staying, not partying, selling drugs, or playing loud rap music — no, just staying with me. This is why the cops were harassing Jamar and me.

But by far, the worst case of harassment stems from the black women. When Jamar and I are walking in public, they make it a point to give us a snide remark. They say things like what a shame it is for one of their black men to be with a white girl or what a sell-out Jamar is for betraying his race. They have even gone as far as to find out where I lived and came to my house to confront me about Jamar. These girls were from Pittsburgh. That means they drove one hour to tell me how angry they were about my situation.

Despite all of this, I love Jamar regardless of color. I can't say I ignore the fact that he is black because to do that would disrespect something that is important to him. Neither would I want him to overlook the fact that I'm white. Our differences in culture and race add flavor to our relationship.

The United States is supposed to be a melting pot, but that melting pot is boiling over with racism, prejudice, intolerance, and ignorance. We live in a country that accepts German-Italian, Japanese-Irish, and even black-Hispanic relationships, so why is there so much narrow-mindedness toward black-white relationships? Society needs to start worrying about things that are really important in the United States such as gangs, AIDS, and homelessness, not whether someone dates within his/her race. We as a society need to realize that love sees no color.

Discussing Vocabulary / Using a Dictionary

1. What are some antonyms for the word "prestigious" (para. 5)?

2. Richard states that black women make snide remarks about her when she walks in public with Jamar (para. 6). Come up with several similar words she could have used to describe their comments.

3. Richard uses the word "stereotypes" (para. 3) and "prejudice" (para. 8). What do these two words mean and how are they different?

Discussing Meaning

1. What stereotypes about black men does Richard's brother be-
    lieve? What, according to Richard, has caused him to hold such
    negative views?
2. What does Richard find funny or ironic about being blamed for
    her friend's dating a black man?
3. What do black women say to Richard and Jamar when they are
    walking together in public?
4. What problems does Richard see with the notion of the United
    States as a "melting pot" (para. 8)?

Discussing Writing

1. Consider the way in which Richard starts her essay, by simply
    quoting three angry comments. Do you find this opening star-
    tling? Offensive? Why or why not? How does it set the tone for
    the rest of Richard's essay?
2. In paragraph 2, why does Richard state that she "never set out to
    date a black guy," that "it just happened"? Does this statement
    influence the way you read her essay? Would you react differ-
    ently to her account if she said she had been interested in dating
    black men even before she met Jamar?
3. Is Richard being serious in paragraph 5 when she describes the
    police in her town as "hardworking" and "prestigious"? How
    would you describe her tone in this paragraph?

Challenging the Selection

1. For most of the essay, Richard focuses solely on opposition to
    her relationship with Jamar. Yet she concludes with a paragraph
    about racial tensions and societal problems in the United States
    as a whole. Does her personal experience back up her claims at
    the end? How effective is this conclusion?
2. How do you react to Richard's description of harassment by
    "black women" (para. 6)? Do you think Richard is fair in judg-
    ing the reactions of black women based on the behavior of the
    few who drove to her house?

3. Do you think it's really true that "love sees no color"? Does Richard's writing support her title?

In-Class Writing Activities

1. Richard describes the problems she and Jamar face in dealing with family, friends, the authorities, neighbors, and even strangers. Write about a time when you did something for which you were widely criticized. Where did the criticism come from? How did you respond? Why did you think you were right and everybody else was wrong?

2. Write a brief essay in which you use a thought-provoking quotation, comment, or observation to begin a discussion of a serious issue, as Richard does in this selection.

Interracial Dating: Yes or No?

[THE BLACK COLLEGIAN / March–April 1993]

Before You Read

Is dating people of other races a sign of tolerance or of self-hatred? Does it make us lose our identity or help us to know ourselves better? Should we date within our own race as a show of cultural pride or date other races as a way of combating racism and moving closer to equality?

Words to Learn

righteous (para. 5): those who uphold what is morally right(n.)
intraracial (para. 24): within one's own race (adj.)
chastise (para. 25): to criticize (v.)

The students who contributed to this piece took part in a forum sponsored and published by the Black Collegian, *a publication of New Orleans–based Black Collegiate Services, Inc.*

Sha-Sha Allen
Brooklyn, New York

As an African American woman, I don't have a problem with a person dating people of other ethnic groups. I believe dating is just one of many ways of socializing. It is through socializing with different people that we learn about who we are.

However, I do have a problem with a person dating solely outside of his or her own ethnic group. I believe if one allows a few bad people to spoil his or her perception of his or her own people, then he or she is giving in to generalizations. I don't think one is being fair to oneself to allow generalizations to stop him or her from dating within his or her own ethnic group. If a person does give in, he or she is preventing himself or herself from learning about what we are, as a people, as well as who he or she is, as an individual.

Gregory Clark
Louisiana College, Lecompte, Louisiana

Yes, I believe that people should start using the content of one's character to find a date. Rejection on the basis of race is an unfair practice that deprives us of the opportunity to explore the personalities of people of other races. The more open we become to others, the more likely we are to find the "right" match and eliminate prejudices and hostilities toward other ethnic groups.

The Holy Scriptures declare that we are all created from one blood and are therefore the same within. Picking dates by their race is discrimination in the wake of an America that desires change and equality. Shouldn't we live in harmony?

Kermit A. Franklin
Graduate — West Bank Technical Institute,
Southern University of New Orleans,
Marrero, Louisiana

Yes, although many people disagree based on their own prejudices against other races. But it is ordained by God that we are all one race of human beings, with no differences except between the righteous and the sinners.   5

It is a person's God-given right to date or choose whomever he or she wants as long as they are good persons who bring out the best in the other.

Regardless of what some men and women may feel or what is "outlawed" in society, people are going to date, marry, and reproduce interracially, and have done so since the beginning and will until the end. Everyone needs to live and let live. We should focus on making ourselves and our lives better.

Kyle C. Gibson
Florida African American Student Association,
Florida Atlantic University,
Boca Raton, Florida

This is a very good question, and very difficult to answer in so few words. As a proud male of African descent, I feel that we, as Pan-Africans,[1] should keep intimate relationships within our own Nubian[2] circle. I believe interracial dating is o.k. as long as it is kept at the level of friend. But before we Pan-Africans become seriously involved and fall in love with members of other ethnic groups, we should first learn to love ourselves. After we master the art of loving our own Pan-African sisters and brothers, we can love anybody we want to. But love of self should come first.

Becky Goodwin
Senior, Coppin State College,
Aberdeen, Maryland

Movies like *Jungle Fever* and *The Bodyguard* have appeared to focus on interracial dating as mainstream while African Americans continue to struggle against the increasing undercurrent of racism and bigotry within our country, which is partly due to an economic recession. Fortunately, the Clinton administration's theme embraces unity, prosperity, and equality through diversity.

> *Interracial dating can be healthy if it is not pursued as a form of self-hatred.*
>
> *— Becky Goodwin*

Interracial dating can be healthy if it   10
is not pursued as a form of self-hatred. It is important to learn, understand, and respect other cultures. This can be achieved through interracial dating in some instances. However, it is equally important and perhaps more so that we African Americans attempt to heal our hurting relationships.

---

[1]*Pan-Africans:* A union of people sharing African heritage; literally "all Africans."
[2]*Nubian:* Refers, literally, to an ancient region in northeastern Africa.

History will teach us, if we are willing to learn. Historically, before the Jews were persecuted, the relationships and marriages between Jews and non-Jews had grown to an all-time high. Quoting Maya Angelou, "History, despite its wrenching pain, cannot be unlived, but if faced with courage, need not be lived again."

Nana Baffour Gyewu
Lawrence University,
Appleton, Wisconsin

I think interracial dating should be encouraged. To me, it's about the only way that the ideas of racial superiority or inferiority can be erased to bring about equality. Because if there are a lot of interracial relationships, we can expect a lot of "colored" children. Thus, a time might come in this society when "colored" folks would be the majority and non-colored, the minority. Thus, the tables would be turned, and with an experience of what it is like to be a minority, people will appreciate equality all the more.

> *I think interracial dating should be encouraged.*
> *— Nana Baffour Gyewu*

Kharis Jones
West Georgia College,
Carrolton, Georgia

It seems that today there is an unusually high rise in the number of interracial relationships. However, the rise is not because of our black sisters dating white men, but because of our so-called "strong" black brothers who are eagerly crossing the tracks.

I might understand it if our black men were going after the "top notch" white females, but they aren't. It seems as if they are only dating those on the other side because of their color, not because of their intellect. And it seems that the black men are some of our finest — for example, Sidney Poitier, James Earl Jones, Arsenio Hall, and Supreme Court Justice Clarence Thomas.

How can we as blacks serve as role models for our youth if we continue to relate with others in this manner? Black brothers, take note: We black women are a most precious gift from God. We come in all different shapes, sizes, and COLORS. Black men, be strong and cross the tracks back to your roots!

15

Chris McCain
Journalism Major,
University of South Carolina, Aiken

This is a great question, one for which no definite answer can be given. If the question is asking if interracial dating should be allowed, then the answer is yes. Race should not be a factor when one considers whom he/she will date. A dating relationship is based in love, respect, honesty, and trust. More serious relationships include a degree of intimacy and commitment.

The fact that someone is dating interracially should not affect the relationship of the couple or relationships that members of the couple are a part of (friends, parents, relatives).

I have dated interracially ever since I have known the definition of the concept. There should never have been a problem with dating a person of a different race in the first place. The goal of a relationship is for two partners to learn from each other while sharing and pursuing the couple's lifetime dream.

Jay U. Odunukwe
Boston, Massachusetts

Many people are feeding into the negative and misguided stereotypes about interracial dating/relationships. People should be allowed to choose whom they like to date and share their lives with and not be bogged down by societal reprimands. Everybody has his/her own ideas of what is attractive.

That someone is dating outside of his/her own race does not   20
mean the person is in denial or is ashamed of his/her race. In this day and age, you are blessed if you can get a partner who is "gonna treat you right." There is nothing slick or hip about being ignorant or prejudiced.

All segments/races of this society have to come together and establish common ground. Peace, understanding, mutual trust, and respect can exist only when all are treated as equals.

What is the color of love?

Tiauna C. Phillips
Central Missouri State University,
Warrensburg, Missouri

Dating interracially is a matter of personal preference. Those who choose to date outside their race should have some sense of who they are and where they come from. In some instances, a person who has had a few bad experiences will decide to explore other ethnicities. By supporting one another and treating each other with respect, we will, hopefully, eliminate the desire, among these who are unhappy with themselves or with our people, to date outside our race.

Patience Rockymore
University of Georgia,
Athens, Georgia

All relationships should include trust, love, and devotion, and these feelings should be the key components to the relationship — not race. Although race is a significant factor, it should not be the only factor. Interracial relationships, just like intraracial relationships, should be entered into for sincere, heartfelt reasons.

I agree with the need for racial and ethnic groups to want to   25
strengthen their communities through intraracial marriage, especially when the group finds itself in the minority in a society, but also I believe that love is love (whether society agrees or not), and is not always easily redirected. Instead of chastising people in interracial relationships, I think we should congratulate them on finding love.

Discussing Vocabulary / Using a Dictionary

1. What is the biblical meaning of the word "righteous" (para. 5)? What does it mean to say that someone is "self-righteous"?

2. Patience Rockymore suggests people should not "chastise" those who choose interracial relationships (para. 25). What are several synonyms for "chastise"? What other words can you think of with the same root?

Discussing Meaning

1. Find three opinions expressed in favor of interracial dating and three opposed to it.

2. What bothers Kharis Jones about black men dating white women? Why does she specifically object to black celebrities dating outside their race?

3. What, according to Chris McCain, are the key factors in a romantic relationship? Is race important in comparison with these?

Discussing Writing

1. Gregory Clark writes that we should use "the content of one's character" in deciding whom to date (para. 3). This is a famous phrase from Martin Luther King's "I Have a Dream" speech, in which King stated, "I have a dream my four little children will one day live in a nation where they will not be judged by the color of their skin but by the content of their character." Why do you think Clark chooses to invoke King's speech in defense of interracial dating?

2. Find several instances in which the students quoted here use God in support of their arguments. Which do you find most convincing? Why?

3. "Interracial dating can be healthy if it is not pursued as a form of self-hatred," Becky Goodwin says (para. 10). What does she mean by this? Why might people who are unhappy with themselves choose to date people of a different race? What is the solution to this tendency, according to Tiauna Phillips? How might Sha-Sha Allen respond?

4. This article provides short clips of various opinions on a single topic. What do you think of this format? Does it encourage adequate development of ideas, or does it place too much of a limit on the arguments of individual students?

Challenging the Selection

1. Kyle Gibson states that interracial dating is acceptable if kept at the level of friendship (para. 8). Is this a realistic view? Do you agree that people should have one attitude toward friends of a different race and another toward romantic partners? Why or why not?

2. "Picking dates by their race is discrimination," Gregory Clark argues (para. 4). Do you agree? Is it possible to avoid discrimination in romantic matters?

In-Class Writing Activities

1. Write your own short essay explaining your views on interracial dating. Be sure to include any relevant personal experience or knowledge you have about the topic. Do you believe that love

can overcome cultural and racial differences? Are people justified in wanting to date exclusively within their own race?

2.   Some writers in this selection believe that people lose their identity through dating outside their race, while others hold that interracial dating can help people better learn who they are and where they come from. Which of these arguments corresponds more with your own beliefs? Explain your position in a well-argued paragraph.

Discussing the Unit

Suggested Topic for Discussion

"Society needs to start worrying about things that are really important in the United States such as gangs, AIDS, and homelessness," Valerie Richard argues, "not whether or not someone dates within his/her race." Drawing on the opinions expressed in this section, as well as your own views, discuss why people "worry" about interracial dating. Do you agree with Richard that it is not an important issue for the country? Why does the topic stir up such strong emotions? Consider what you know about the history of America, including such factors as slavery and immigration.

Preparing for Class Discussion

1.   How does interracial dating and marrying differ from other types of taboo relationships, such as those between people of different religions or social classes, or between people of the same sex? Society has always frowned on certain forms of love: After all, forbidden love is the theme of Shakespeare's *Romeo and Juliet*. Why does society attempt to dictate who should be with whom?

2.   We live in a country that appears to be growing more multicultural all the time, and in a world that technology is continually making smaller. Do you foresee a day when racial and cultural differences no longer matter in dating? Why or why not?

From Discussion to Writing

1.   Write an imaginary debate between Valerie Richard and Kharis Jones (or one of the other writers from the third selection). Try

not to focus solely on their differences; see if you can find some common ground — points they might agree on.

2. Try writing on this topic from two perspectives. First, imagine that you are a parent opposed to your child's interracial relationship and write a paragraph explaining your objections. Then imagine that you are the son or daughter and write another paragraph defending the relationship.

3. Based on the articles in this unit, your personal experiences, and class discussion, do you see a trend in America's attitudes toward interracial relationships? Do you think Americans are becoming more, or less, accepting? Explain your position in a well-supported essay.

Topics for Cross-Cultural Discussion

1. How do dating customs in your homeland differ from those in America?

2. What relationships in your country are considered taboo or practically forbidden? What happens if a couple dates despite the popular belief that their relationship is wrong?

7

Do Gender Differences Really Exist?

When it was published in 1990, Deborah Tannen's controversial best-seller *You Just Don't Understand* opened a new round of debate on a subject that has been discussed for centuries: Do men and women really think differently? And if so, how and why? Tannen argued that men are conditioned to use conversation as a way of competing with others, whereas women try to make connections with others instead. By learning how men and women typically look at things, she suggested, people could eliminate many misunderstandings in dealing with spouses, friends, and co-workers.

This chapter looks at the idea of gender difference in three areas: using computers, making public policy, and speaking in class. Tannen begins the chapter, updating her earlier work with an essay on how e-mail and new technology inspire different responses from men and women. Next, the well-known newspaper columnist Ellen Goodman ponders the very different audiences of talk radio shows (such as Rush Limbaugh's) and talk television shows (such as Sally Jessy Raphael's). The final piece, by University of Michigan student Kate Epstein, investigates the dynamics of class participation: Are women getting their fair share of classroom speaking time?

DEBORAH TANNEN

Gender Gap in Cyberspace

[NEWSWEEK / May 16, 1994]

Before You Read

Is there a typically "male" or "female" way of using computers? Do you think you have any advantages or disadvantages in understanding computers because of your gender?

Words to Learn

paradox (para. 1): something that seems contradictory but is nonetheless true (n.)

maven (para. 2): an expert (n.)

obliqueness (para. 6): indirectness (n.)

balk (para. 7): to refuse abruptly (v.)

incite (para. 7): to provoke (v.)

defiance (para. 7): resistance to authority or opposition (n.)

anonymity (para. 10): the quality of being anonymous; that is, having an unknown name or identity (n.)

vituperative (para. 10): abusive (adj.)

rapport (para. 12): a good relationship, mutual understanding (n.)

begrudge (para. 13): to be reluctant to give over (v.)

chivalry (para. 14): the qualities believed to be embodied in knights; for instance, courage, honor, and care of those who are weaker (n.)

damsel (para. 14): a girl or young woman; a maiden (n.)

knave (para. 14): an unprincipled or uncivilized person (n.)

Linguist and author DEBORAH TANNEN *(b. 1945) has written best-selling books about how men and women communicate:* That's Not What I Meant! *(1986),* You Just Don't Understand *(1990), and* Talking 9 to 5 *(1994). Tannen, who has lectured widely on language and communication, has taught linguistics at Georgetown University since 1979.*

I was a computer pioneer, but I'm still something of a novice. That paradox is telling.

I was the second person on my block to get a computer. The first was my colleague Ralph. It was 1980. Ralph got a Radio Shack TRS-80; I got a used Apple II + . He helped me get started and went on to become a maven, reading computer magazines, hungering for the new technology he read about, and buying and mastering it as quickly as he could afford. I hung on to old equipment far too long because I dislike giving up what I'm used to, fear making the wrong decision about what to buy, and resent the time it takes to install and learn a new system.

My first Apple came with videogames; I gave them away. Playing games on the computer didn't interest me. If I had free time I'd spend it talking on the telephone to friends.

Ralph got hooked. His wife was often annoyed by the hours he spent at his computer and the money he spent upgrading it. My marriage had no such strains — until I discovered e-mail. Then I got hooked. E-mail draws me the same way the phone does: It's a souped-up conversation.

On college campuses, as soon as women students log on, they are bombarded by references to sex.

E-mail deepened my friendship with Ralph. Though his office was next to mine, we rarely had extended conversation because he is shy. Face-to-face he mumbled so, I could barely tell he was speaking. But when we both got e-mail, I started receiving long, self-revealing messages; we poured our hearts out to each other. A friend discovered that e-mail opened up that kind of communication with her father. He would never talk much on the phone (as her mother would), but they have become close since they both got on-line.

Why, I wondered, would some men find it easier to open up on e-mail? It's a combination of the technology (which they enjoy) and the obliqueness of the written word, just as many men will reveal feelings in dribs and drabs while riding in the car or doing something, which they'd never talk about sitting face-to-face. It's too intense, too bearing-down on them, and once you start you have to keep going. With a computer in between, it's safer.

It was on e-mail, in fact, that I described to Ralph how boys in groups often struggle to get the upper hand whereas girls tend to maintain an appearance of cooperation. And he pointed out that this explained why boys are more likely to be captivated by computers than girls are. Boys are typically motivated by a social structure that says if you don't dominate you will be dominated. Computers, by their nature, balk; you type a perfectly appropriate command and it refuses to do what it should. Many boys and men are incited by this defiance: "I'm going to whip this into line and teach it who's boss! I'll get it to do what I say!" (and if they work hard enough, they always can). Girls and women are more likely to respond, "This thing won't cooperate. Get it away from me!"

Although no one wants to think of herself as "typical" — how much nicer to be *sui generis*[1] — my relationship to my computer is — gulp — fairly typical for a woman. Most women (with plenty of exceptions) aren't excited by tinkering with the technology, grappling with the challenge of eliminating bugs, or getting the biggest and best computer. These dynamics appeal to many men's interest in making sure they're on the top side of the inevitable who's-up-who's-down struggle that life is for them. E-mail appeals to my view of life as a contest for connections to others. When I see that I have fifteen messages, I feel loved.

I once posted a technical question on a computer network for linguists and was flooded with long dispositions, some pages long. I was staggered by the generosity and the expertise, but wondered where these guys found the time — and why all the answers I got were from men.

Like coed classrooms and meetings, discussions on e-mail networks tend to be dominated by the male voices, unless they're specifically women-only, like single-sex schools. On-line, women don't have to worry about getting the floor (you just send a message when you feel like it), but, according to linguists Susan Herring and Laurel Sutton, who have studied this, they have the usual problems of having their messages ignored or attacked. The anonymity of public networks frees a small number of men to send long, vituperative, sarcastic messages that many other men either can tolerate or actually enjoy, but that turn most women off.

The anonymity of networks leads to another sad part of the e-mail story: There are men who deluge women with questions about their appearance and invitations to sex. On college campuses, as soon as women students log on, they are bombarded by references to sex, like going to work and finding pornographic posters adorning the walls.

10

---

[1]*Sui generis:* "Of its own kind," "unique" (Latin).

Most women want one thing from a computer — to work. This is significant counterevidence to the claim that men want to focus on information while women are interested in rapport. That claim I found was often true in casual conversation, in which there is no particular information to be conveyed. But with computers, it is often women who are more focused on information, because they don't respond to the challenge of getting equipment to submit.

Once I had learned the basics, my interest in computers waned. I use it to write books (though I never mastered having it do bibliographies or tables of contents) and write checks (but not balance my checkbook). Much as I'd like to use it to do more, I begrudge the time it would take to learn.

Ralph's computer expertise costs him a lot of time. Chivalry requires that he rescue novices in need, and he is called upon by damsel novices far more often than knaves. More men would rather study the instruction booklet than ask directions, as it were, from another person. "When I do help men," Ralph wrote (on e-mail, of course), "they want to be more involved. I once installed a hard drive for a guy, and he wanted to be there with me, wielding the screwdriver and giving his own advice where he could." Women, he finds, usually are not interested in what he's doing; they just want him to get the computer to the point where they can do what they want.

Which pretty much explains how I managed to be a pioneer   15 without becoming an expert.

Discussing Vocabulary / Using a Dictionary

1. Tannen titles her essay "Gender Gap in Cyberspace," but the word "gender" never actually appears in it. What is "gender," and how is it different from "sex"? Which meaning of the word do you think Tannen intends in her title?

2. Her friend Ralph became a computer "maven," Tannen writes in paragraph 2. Can you come up with several synonyms for the word "maven"? What examples does Tannen give of Ralph being a maven?

3. What does Tannen mean when she says that boys and men are "incited" by the challenge computers present (para. 7)? Consider how "incited" relates to other words with similar roots, like "excite" or "citation."

4. In what era did the word "chivalry" (para. 14) originate? How does Tannen's use of the words "damsel" and "knaves" (both in para. 14) fit in with modern-day chivalry in cyberspace?

Discussing Meaning

1. Why does Tannen hang on to old computer equipment rather than trade it in? Which aspects of computers does she find interesting and which not?

2. How did e-mail change Tannen's relationship with her friend Ralph? Why, according to Tannen, do some men find it easier to talk via e-mail?

3. How does Tannen say men and women react differently to computer problems? What factors motivate their different responses?

4. Why, according to Tannen, are discussions on e-mail networks dominated by men?

Discussing Writing

1. Tannen uses many comparisons in her essay. Find several instances in which she compares men's behavior to women's. How do these comparisons strengthen the points she is trying to make?

2. Reread Tannen's short first and last paragraphs. How effective are they, in your opinion? How well does her essay explain the "paradox" of how she became a "pioneer without becoming an expert"?

Challenging the Selection

1. Although Tannen is a professor of linguistics (the study of languages), her essay is very informal, even personal, in tone; she cites only one "expert" source. Do you find her approach persuasive? Why do you think Tannen chose to use just two examples — Ralph and herself — rather than gathering stories from a wider range of men and women? Would you trust her authority more or less if she had relied on academic research rather than her own experiences to prove her point?

2. Tannen writes that e-mail draws her "the same way the phone does: It's a souped-up conversation" (para. 4) and that her relationship to computers is "fairly typical for a woman" (para. 8). But she also states that "most women want one thing from a computer — to work" (para. 12). How does Tannen try to reconcile these contradictory statements? Does her explanation make sense?

In-Class Writing Activities

1. Write a short essay in which you describe how you and a friend do a particular thing differently. Explain why you think each of you behaves the way you do: How much are you influenced by societal pressures, and how much by your own individual personalities? Do you believe that you and your friend are representative of people in general? Can you draw any conclusions about human behavior from your differences?

2. Tannen's essay examines how a development in technology — the invention of e-mail — has changed relations between men and women. Can you think of another innovation that has changed the way people interact with one another? Write several paragraphs in which you consider how things were different before and after some development in modern life. Pay particular attention to how people have adapted their behavior to deal with the changing circumstances.

3. Now that you've read Tannen's essay (and based on your own experience), do you think that men and women use computers differently? Write a few paragraphs stating your position.

ELLEN GOODMAN

When Mars Eclipses Venus

[THE BOSTON GLOBE / March 12, 1995]

Before You Read

"You've come a long way, baby," says the cigarette ad. But how far have we come from the days when women stayed at home and only men were involved in public affairs? In studying how men and women might think differently, are we learning to understand one another better or only building up the same old barriers that divide us?

Words to Learn

resegregation (para. 10): a reseparation (n.)
testosterone (para. 11): male sex hormone (n.)
cacophony (para. 17): an inharmonious sound (n.)

I think this is where I came in. Only when I was a kid we didn't need books to tell us that men were from Mars and women were from Venus. We could see that they inhabited different worlds.

Women were at home; men in the office. Women wore the skirts; men wore the pants in the family. She raised the kids; he ran the world.

Now, after thirty years of emphasizing what we have in common, we're back to focusing on the differences between the sexes. The more similar our real lives, the more we seem to focus on the separateness of our emotional workings and biological wirings.

Longtime Boston Globe *columnist* ELLEN GOODMAN *(b. 1941) has received numerous awards for her writing, including a Pulitzer Prize for commentary in 1980. An associate editor of the* Globe, *Goodman has also published several books, including* Turning Points *(1979) and* Making Sense *(1989).*

The pop talk now is all about the different languages we speak, the different ways our brains work, the difference in our feelings. We scan the latest research looking for evidence of gender gaps rather than common ground.

Deborah Tannen's work, *You Just Don't Understand*, has become proof that men and women can't communicate, even though her point was that we can. The complex new brain research has been reduced to a similar shorthand pronouncement that men and women "think differently."

We've become hooked again on notions of natural differences. But we should be more concerned with ways we are again nurturing differences.

The Yale researcher, Dr. Sally Shaywitz, who watched men and women sounding out words under a magnetic resonance imaging machine,[1] was struck by the alternate paths the male and female brain took to get to the same place. But today we're directing men and women to separate places.

> *Talk radio has become largely a guy thing; talk television is largely a gal thing.*

You don't need an MRI to see that in the world I work in. Newspapers once put men and women into single-sex spheres. The male world was public affairs — by and for men. The female world was private matters — by and for women. It took time to break down the print barriers, to have women reporting the news, and to have "women's subjects" — from breast cancer to child care — leading the news.

Many of us who believe the old women's movement slogan — the personal is political — still struggle to connect private life and public policy.

But in enclaves of new media, we are facing a resegregation of men and women. It's not just ESPN for the boys and Lifetime for the girls. Not just the Internet, though it has chat groups that most resemble fraternities. The most glaring examples are the talk shows.

Talk radio has become largely a guy thing. It's not only moved to the right, but to the testosterone. The powerful hosts are mostly male, so are the callers, and so are the listeners. It's become the turf of the angry white man.

---

[1]*magnetic resonance imaging machine:* A devise used to make detailed images of the inside of the body.

Talk television, on the other hand, is largely a gal thing. The hosts may be more equally divided by gender — Ricki Lake and Montel Williams, Rolonda and Geraldo, Sally Jessy Raphael and Maury Povich — but the viewers are mostly female.

The sexes are split and so are the subjects. Male talk radio is about political life. Female talk television is about personal life. The hot topics of the radio week are the balanced budget, food stamps, Congress. The hot topics of the television week are "man-stealers," "meddling mothers-in-law," "obese women."

I don't think that men naturally "evolved" from hunting mammoths to attacking Congress. Nor did the fittest of the female species survive gathering berries to be obsessed with man-stealing.

But the right-wing talk radio folk deliberately point their followers to the world, the arena of public policy, while the no-wing talk television hosts direct their audience to the home, the drama of private life. One sex gets marching orders, the other gets hankies.

In the end, keeping either men or women in single-sex slots may be equally destructive. But in the current rush of policymaking and unmaking, it's most troubling that the public voice is overwhelmingly male. These men are arguing, faxing, and forming what we call "public" opinion, while the women are talking personally in the traditional living room of relationships. Men are told to worry about laws and women about their in-laws.

In the cacophony of loud broadcast voices, women are uncomfortable in a shouting match. They're drowned out when speaking in their own voice. Indeed the year of the angry white man, typified by the sound of the talk radio, may not signify a male backlash as much as it does a female retreat.

But public policy is not a boy thing. Whether you believe in nature or nurture, governing is not done in one part of the brain or for one half of the population.

Don't tell me that men are from Mars and women are from Venus. The last time I looked we were living here, together.

Discussing Vocabulary / Using a Dictionary

1. What does Goodman mean when she says in paragraph 10 that "we are facing a resegregation of women and men" in the media? What is the opposite of "segregation"?

2. What is Goodman implying about the content of talk radio by referring to a male hormone, "testosterone" (para. 11), to describe it?

3. Find two synonyms and two antonyms for the word "cacophony" (para. 17). What is Goodman implying about the world of broadcasting by using this word?

Discussing Meaning

1. What kind of thinking about gender, according to Goodman, has Deborah Tannen's work led to? What effect has this had?

2. Which subjects does Goodman say were acceptable for male reporters to write about in the past? Which subjects did women cover? How have things changed?

3. In what ways, in Goodman's view, are talk radio and talk television different?

4. What is most troubling to Goodman about the way that public policy is being made?

Discussing Writing

1. The title of Goodman's essay is an allusion, or implied reference, to a popular book called *Men Are from Mars, Women Are from Venus*, which argues that men and women act as though they are from different planets. How does Goodman play on the book's title? In what ways does her title suggest the point of the essay?

2. Goodman makes frequent use of a figure of speech known as "metonymy," which means using one thing as a symbol for something else. (For example, if we say that "The White House today announced a plan to create new jobs," we are using metonymy, substituting a symbol for the president in place of the man himself.) Find an example of metonymy in Goodman's essay, and then analyze how it works.

3. One of the underlying themes in Goodman's essay is the debate often labeled "nature versus nurture." Are we shaped more by our biology or by our environment? How does Goodman respond to this ongoing debate? Which side is she on? What evidence of her position can you find?

Challenging the Selection

1. Do you agree with Goodman that women in America are being told to focus on their personal lives rather than on public policy? Which area does Goodman seem to think is more important? Do you agree? How influential do you think talk radio and talk television are in shaping roles for men and women?

2. Goodman displays some irritation at the idea that men and women should live in separate worlds, but she also writes that because of all the "loud broadcast voices, women are uncomfortable in a shouting match" (para. 17). Does this seem contradictory to you? Do you agree that women "retreat" from the kind of debate that is aired on talk radio? Why or why not?

In-Class Writing Activities

1. Imagine that you are the host of a television talk show and want to schedule a program discussing the points that Goodman raises. Make a list of five to six questions that you would ask Goodman if she were a guest on your show. What other kinds of guests would you invite to participate in the program with Goodman?

2. Goodman suggests, in paragraph 4, that we spend too much time "looking for evidence of gender gaps" when we should be searching for "common ground" between men and women. Where do you think we might find such common ground? Write an essay in which you discuss some issues or professions that require both an understanding of private life and a knowledge of public affairs. What things can each gender learn from the other?

KATE EPSTEIN

The Classroom Gender Balance: Who Speaks More, Men or Women?

[THE MICHIGAN DAILY, UNIVERSITY OF MICHIGAN / March 25, 1996]

Before You Read

Have you ever wanted to speak more in a class but didn't because you were intimidated? Or have you ever felt you were the only one speaking and wondered why others didn't contribute as well? Reflect on your own classroom experiences as you read the following essay.

Words to Learn

tallying (para. 2): counting (n.)
adverse (para. 3): negative or in-
    hospitable (adj.)
disproportionately (para. 5): not
    proportionally; unevenly (adv.)

posit (para. 6): to propose (v.)
rigorous (para. 8): difficult or chal-
    lenging (adj.)

It took a class with gender-imbalanced enrollment for me to no-tice gender imbalance in class participation.

My Feminist Film Theory class has fewer than half as many men as women, but over several different days of tallying I have found that approximately half of the comments in class come from men. Several of the men in the class frequently speak twice during a single class period — a lot in an eighty-minute period, when nearly eighty students share the floor.

KATE EPSTEIN (b. 1974) *was a senior at the University of Michigan when she wrote this essay, which, she later noted, "did not have any effect on how much women spoke up in class." Epstein, who received a* Wagner Award *for excellence in academic writing, graduated with a bachelor's de-gree in English in 1996.*

The gender imbalance does not stem from adverse classroom conditions. Professor Rebecca Egger does not belittle or demean comments from students of either sex. The students in the class are also respectful of one another. The professor is a woman, living proof that gender identity cannot stop a woman from having authority about the class's subject matter. The subject matter, feminist theory about cinema, lends itself to female empowerment, not female silence. If anything, I would expect the men in the class to be too quiet.

The men in the class, of course, are not a random sample. The fact that the class's title has the word "feminist" in it biases the sample. In my experience, almost no men sign up for classes with "feminist," "woman," or "women" in the title. The men who do are not the ones who find feminist subject matter intimidating, especially not in 400-level classes like Feminist Film Theory. Self-selection makes it unsurprising that men do not speak less than women in such classes.

Their scarcity may actually encourage the men in my class to participate. The importance of personal experience of gender has never been articulated in class discussion, but in discussions about gender politics it doesn't need to be. The few men in the room bear the responsibility of representing male experience. They may be compensating for the lack of men present, although they speak so disproportionately often that this cannot entirely explain what's happening. It also cannot explain the imbalance in other large classes, including those that apparently have nothing to do with gender.   5

Women are schooled to listen to men; men are schooled to impart their wisdom to women.

The best-selling book by linguist Deborah Tannen, *You Just Don't Understand*, posits an explanation for gender-imbalanced class participation based solely on gender difference. In Tannen's argument, owing to their conditioning, men use language to compete, and women use language to make emotional connections. This difference gives women less practice and, therefore, less confidence in speaking in competitive situations like large lecture classes.

But gender relations respond to more than difference. They respond to the difference in power between men and women. The situation Tannen describes in her book stems partly from the fact that Western society presumes men have more intellectual authority than women. Women are schooled to listen to men; men are schooled to impart their wisdom to women. Even while studying feminist theory, the men and women in my class are unable as a group to break out of this schooling. The fact that a woman teaches the class and women produced much of the material we study has been insufficient to cause such a change.

The men in my class may also be subtly challenging the threat feminist theory poses to the pattern of men dominating classroom discussions. Feminist theory identifies male privilege, that is, it points a finger at the unearned fringe benefits of having a Y chromosome.[1] One of these benefits is that men are widely considered smarter than women, especially about rigorous subjects like the ones studied in Feminist Film Theory, and therefore, better entitled to take up class time by sharing their thoughts. The mere act of pointing out that this benefit is unearned threatens it. In taking up a disproportionate amount of class time, the men in my class are reasserting their entitlement.

The men in my class would protest that the women who never or rarely participate in class do not permit men to lay down the privilege of nearly dominating class discussion. But they rush into the void too easily not to bear some of the responsibility for the gender imbalance in class discussion. Privilege has been given to them like a birthright. It has immense staying power, in part because it is so normal that it's hard to see. It will never change until everyone, male and female, takes responsibility.

[1]Y *chromosome:* The chromosome that determines the development of male sex characteristics.

Discussing Vocabulary / Using a Dictionary

1. What does Epstein mean in paragraph 5 when she says that the men speak "disproportionately" often in her class?

2. Deborah Tannen's book "posits an explanation," Epstein writes in paragraph 6. How is the definition of "posit" related to other words with the same root, like "position" and "positive"?

Discussing Meaning

1. How does Epstein describe the conditions in her classroom? Does she feel that her professor discourages women from talking? Why or why not?

2. Does Epstein consider the men in her class typical male students? In what ways are they biased as a sample group?

3. What factors, besides differences in conditioning, help explain why, in Epstein's view, men speak often in class? Why does she believe male privilege has such staying power?

Discussing Writing

1. What message do you think Epstein meant readers to take away from her essay? Who is her intended audience? Does she just want the men in her class to speak less and the women to speak up more, or does she have a larger point to make?

2. Consider Epstein's use of the terms "balance" and "imbalance." How would you respond to her essay differently if she merely complained that "the men spoke too much" in class? How does the idea of "balance" strengthen her argument?

3. Good writers often make their arguments more convincing by anticipating the opposition: They state a view contrary to their own and then show why the opposing view is false or misguided. Can you find an example of this tactic in Epstein's essay? How does her rebuttal of the opposing view help her case?

Challenging the Selection

1. Do you think that more women would participate in Epstein's class if the men did not speak so much? Should the burden be on men to limit their class participation, or should women be more assertive with their contributions? How realistic is it to expect that men will ever be less vocal in class?

2. Do you think that a course's subject should be a factor in determining which students participate in class? Suppose Epstein's course were on male film theorists instead: Would it be more acceptable for the discussion in that course to be dominated by men? Why or why not?

In-Class Writing Activities

1. Imagine that you are a male student who contributes often in Epstein's Feminist Film Theory course. Write a paragraph in which you defend your class participation. How would you respond to Epstein's claim that you speak out as a way of asserting your "entitlement" (para. 8) as a man?

2. Describe an occasion when a student in one of your classes spoke more often than anyone else. How did the professor deal with it? How did the class react to the person? Why do you think the person felt entitled to participate so much?

Discussing the Unit

Suggested Topic for Discussion

Do you believe that men and women are essentially different or basically the same? What do you think are the reasons they often act differently? Are perceived gender differences always harmful for women and men, or can they also be an advantage?

Preparing for Class Discussion

1. How do you think Ellen Goodman would respond to Deborah Tannen's essay in this chapter? Would Goodman accept Tannen's suggestion that women do not typically have the right temperament to become experts with computers? What might Goodman argue is wrong with such a view?

2. All three authors in this chapter deal with gender difference in what could be called privileged environments: They discuss people who have a high enough income to buy a computer or a high enough level of education to understand feminist film theory. How do you think gender difference affects people without a college degree, an interest in public policy, or an e-mail account? In what other areas of life are you aware of gender difference?

3. What behavior do you personally find most difficult to understand about "the opposite sex"? Have you ever had a fight with someone over something you thought should be perfectly clear, but that he or she simply could not comprehend? How did you resolve your disagreement? What did you learn from doing so?

From Discussion to Writing

1. In this chapter you've read essays on gender difference in three separate areas of life. Now, using these pieces as a model, write

your own essay examining the typical behavior of men and women in some area you know well.

2. Write several paragraphs about the people whom you believe have most helped in shaping your attitudes about gender. Take into account the influence of parents, siblings, relatives, friends, celebrities, historical figures, and so forth. Did you grow up wanting to be a man like Arnold Schwarzenegger or a woman like Eleanor Roosevelt? What qualities about your influences most impressed you? How have your ideas about manhood or womanhood changed with age?

3. If you believe there are major differences in the way that men and women behave, what do you think causes such differences? Are the differences natural or something that society creates? Consider these questions in a brief essay.

Topics for Cross-Cultural Discussion

1. How are gender roles different in your homeland? Are there tasks considered "women's work" in America that men do in your native country? Are there tasks that are exclusively "a man's job" here that women commonly do there?

2. Compare the beliefs about gender difference held by Americans to those held by people in your native country. Are differences between men and women considered more or less important here? Did you or your parents have any difficulties adjusting to ideas about gender in America?

8

Can We Just Say "No" to Addictions?

"Just say no," public officials told kids in the 1980s: The best way to avoid getting hooked on drugs is not to start in the first place. But what about other kinds of addictions? And what do we do if we're already hooked?

This section examines just a few of the many activities that people engage in excessively, despite their best instincts. Linda Chavez looks at how not just people but now whole states are getting addicted to the lottery. Ed Carson takes us to the University of Oregon to find out who's drinking on campus, how much, and why. Rene Sanchez reveals the consequences for students who just can't leave their computer monitors. And, finally, Kirk Hoffman delivers a tribute to the enduring appeal of those cancer-causing — but cool — cigarettes.

LINDA CHAVEZ

There's No Future in Lady Luck

[USA TODAY / September 13, 1995]

Before You Read

Statisticians say a person has a far better chance of getting hit by lightening than of winning the jackpot in a lottery. So why do people keep playing? And why are so many states trying to make it easier for them to do so?

Words to Learn

adrenaline (para. 5): a hormone that stimulates nerve activity (n.)
compulsive (para. 5): acting on an uncontrollable impulse (adj.)

con (para. 12): to cheat or defraud through deception (v.)
gullible (para. 12): easily fooled (adj.)

Remember when the American dream meant becoming a millionaire through talent, hard work, and thrift?

No longer.

Now it's hitting the lottery, with state governments spending millions of dollars a year to promote luck as the key to success.

In 1995, New York expanded the frontier of legalized gambling by offering a new, casino-style game called Quick Draw. Now, instead of a daily lottery, the state draws winning numbers every five minutes, thirteen hours a day, in bars and restaurants around the state.

Writer and commentator LINDA CHAVEZ *(b. 1947) was the executive director of the U.S. Commission on Civil Rights under the Reagan administration, serving from 1983 to 1985. Currently, she writes and speaks widely on civil rights and public policy issues, and her articles have appeared in such publications as* Fortune, The New Republic, *the* Wall Street Journal, *and the* Los Angeles Times. *Chavez's book* Out of the Barrio: Toward a New Politics of Hispanic Assimilation *was published in 1991.*

It's a constant adrenaline rush for compulsive gamblers.   5

As one woman explained to the *New York Times,* "I play the daily number, but you have to wait until 7:30 P.M. to know. This is quicker — five minutes — it's like being in Atlantic City."

This same woman, interviewed at a Staten Island, N.Y., shopping center, had come into the place to buy milk and diapers. She won $1 in half an hour — and lost $7. "I have no more money for the diapers and the milk, but I had fun," she said in the interview.

Yeah, well what about her baby? What fun will Junior have sitting in wet diapers all day, crying from hunger?

This woman isn't alone — in fact, she's typical of state lottery players.

If you doubt it, spend some time in any   10 convenience store in an inner city in one of the thirty-seven states or the District of Columbia that sell state lottery tickets. The lines of men and women waiting to play their lucky numbers are filled with poor people, many of them no doubt refunding to the state cash from welfare checks paid out for the care of dependent children.

> *The lines of men and women waiting to play their lucky numbers are filled with poor people.*

In 1994, states sold $34 billion in lottery tickets. Lottery defenders — most prominently the state officials who oversee the games — claim this money brings in needed revenue for everything from education to health care.

But the fact is, the money is conned from the least educated, most gullible segment of the population.

Joshua Wolf Shenk, writing in the *Washington Monthly* magazine, notes that state lotteries clearly target the poor as their best customers. He quotes an Iowa lottery media plan "to target our message demographically against those that we know to be heavy users."

According to several studies on the subject, that means blacks, Hispanics, and poor whites.

It's bad enough that the state sponsors lotteries, but what is   15 worse is the huge state investment in promoting ticket sales. New York spends $30 million a year in advertising.

And lottery ads are slick.

Virginia's Lady Luck commercials are among the most appealing on television. But their message is no different from all the other lottery ads. You've got to play to win, which means playing every week, every day — or, as now in New York, every hour.

And adults who are legally permitted to buy tickets aren't the only targets of the ad campaigns. Kids are tomorrow's customers.

Recently, I went riding in Potomac, Md., with a little boy who visits me each summer from New York where he lives in a housing project. He had never seen houses like the huge homes that dot the affluent Washington suburb.

"Is that where people who win the lottery live?" he asked. No, I   20 explained, most of the people in those houses are lawyers, doctors, or other professionals who had studied hard, gone to college, and worked many years before they could buy such homes.

Of course, my little New Yorker isn't likely to ever buy a house such as the ones he saw — nor am I, for that matter.

But his chances of owning any house are certainly improved if he heeds my message rather than his own state government's.

Reprinted by permission from Linda Chavez, © 1995.

Discussing Vocabulary / Using a Dictionary

1. Look up the word "revenue" (para. 11). What is its root? What language is the word derived from?

2. What are several synonyms for the word "conned" (para. 12)? What does a "con man" do? Why does Chavez use this word to describe how the lottery raises money?

3. In paragraph 12, Chavez writes of the "least educated, most gullible segment of the population." What is the relation between the words "educated" and "gullible"? Can someone be both?

Discussing Meaning

1. How is the Quick Draw game offered in New York different from the old daily lottery? What does the Staten Island woman quoted by Chavez say she likes about the new game (para. 6)?

2. How do state officials defend the sale of lottery tickets?

3. What is the message of the Virginia lottery commercials? Who, according to Chavez, is the target audience for such advertising?

Discussing Writing

1. How does Chavez use the example of the Staten Island woman to support her general argument about people who play the lottery?

2. Consider Chavez's use of stories about children in the essay. How does she portray the children? How do you think she expects readers to react to such stories? How would you react differently to her essay if she focused only on statistics, or only on adults?

Challenging the Selection

1. Chavez suggests that many of the poor people who play the lottery do so with money from "welfare checks paid out for the care of dependent children" (para. 10). What evidence does she provide to back up this assertion?

2. Do you believe Chavez's claim, in paragraph 20, that affluent suburban residents got their houses because they had "studied hard, gone to college, and worked many years" to afford them? What factors might she be leaving out? Why do you think she says that the little boy "isn't likely to ever buy" such a house (para. 21)?

In-Class Writing Activities

1. Have you ever played the lottery? Why or why not?

2. In seventy-five words or fewer, write the text for a newspaper advertisement that tries to convince people that playing the lottery is a waste of money. Feel free to adapt Chavez's arguments, or invent totally new ones if you like. What images would you use to accompany the text of your ad?

3. Is "the American dream" only a dream? Or is it really possible to become a millionaire through "talent, hard work, and thrift"? Write several paragraphs stating your view.

ED CARSON

Purging Bingeing

[REASON / December 1995]

Before You Read

Is heavy drinking as much a part of college life as late-night studying and final exams? And who bears the blame for rowdy, drunken behavior: Is it the beer, the bar, or the bingers?

Words to Learn

repercussion (para. 5): an effect — usually indirect — of an action (n.)
uninhibited (para. 14): unrestrained (adj.)
compulsion (para. 15): an uncontrollable impulse (n.)

pharmacology (para. 16): the science of drugs (n.)
boorish (para. 19): offensive or rude (adj.)

Erin and Jason don't think they drink excessively. "When I think of bingeing, I think of people drinking until they puke," says Erin, a twenty-year-old sophomore at the University of Oregon, adding that she usually stops at six drinks when she goes out on the weekend.

"I think drinking to get really drunk is stupid," says Jason, a twenty-one-year-old junior. So what is a reasonable amount? "I usually have seven or eight beers," he says as he takes a gulp from his sixth glass.

ED CARSON *(b. 1971) is a reporter for* Reason, *a magazine of social and political commentary published by the Reason Foundation, a public-policy research organization. At* Reason, *Carson has covered a wide range of issues, including free speech, popular culture, property rights, and taxation. He holds a bachelor's degree in economics from the University of Oregon.*

But the public health establishment says both Erin and Jason are binge drinkers, defined as anyone who has had at least five drinks (sometimes four drinks for women) in one sitting during the previous two weeks. College drinking has attracted a lot of attention recently with the release of several studies reporting that some two-fifths of college students are binge drinkers. The studies say virtually all binge drinkers admit suffering some negative consequences, ranging from hangovers to sexual assaults. And they don't hurt just themselves. In a 1994 study by the Harvard School of Public Health, 82 percent of non–binge drinkers living in dorms, fraternities, or sororities said they had experienced "secondhand binge effects." As Selena, an eighteen-year-old Oregon freshman, puts it, "You always know when they come back from bars at four A.M. screaming their heads off."

So last year, when the Center on Addiction and Substance Abuse at Columbia University (CASA) claimed the percentage of college women drinking to get drunk had more than tripled during the previous fifteen years, the news media were quick to hype the finding that drinking on campus had reached "epidemic proportions." But as Kathy McNamara-Meis revealed in the Winter 1995 *Forbes Media-Critic,* CASA's conclusions were based on a misleading comparison of results from a 1977 survey of all college women and a 1992 survey of freshman women. Since freshmen drink more than any other class, such a comparison would suggest an increase in drunkenness even if nothing had changed. In fact, says David Hanson, a professor of sociology at the State University of New York at Potsdam who has studied alcohol use on campus for more than twenty years, "the evidence shows that the actual trend is as flat as your little sister's chest."

As this episode suggests, the problems associated with college drinking are overstated and misunderstood. Since college students have limited responsibilities, they can usually drink heavily without serious repercussions. Drunken college students do sometimes get into trouble, of course. But this is not a drinking problem; it is a drinking *behavior* problem.   5

For neoprohibitionists,[1] alcohol itself is the problem. In their eyes, college students are children — children who can vote and serve in the military, but still children — who must be shielded from the

---

[1] *neoprohibitionists:* Those who would reinstitute the prohibition of the manufacture and sale of alcohol. The original Prohibition lasted from 1920 to 1933.

pernicious effects of drinking. According to the federal Office for Substance Abuse Prevention, "for kids under twenty-one, there is no difference between alcohol or other drug use and abuse." Yet most college students under twenty-one don't think they are doing anything wrong by drinking. "I'm not hurting anyone," says Derek, a twenty-year-old sophomore. "I'm just having a good time." Many college administrators say the twenty-one-year purchase age just makes drinking more attractive.

"The twenty-one law makes alcohol a forbidden fruit and encourages underage students to drink," says Carl Wartenburg, dean of admissions at Swarthmore College. A 1994 survey by the CORE Institute at Southern Illinois University found that students under twenty-one drink more, and more often, than older students.

> *The principle that people are responsible for their behavior even when drinking should be drilled into young people's heads.*

Underage students at the University of Oregon have little trouble obtaining alcohol. Most dorms have a no-use policy, but resident assistants just try to crack down on partying and encourage students to drink off campus. Fake IDs are everywhere. If they don't have IDs, students usually can find a party off campus or get someone older to buy for them.

Students may drink to let off steam, or drink to get drunk, or boast about how much they can drink without puking. But college drinking, by and large, remains social drinking. UO students could buy a half-rack of Henry Weinhard's Ale and drink at home. But instead they pay a lot more to drink at Rennie's or Max's because they want to be around other people.

Drinking isn't only something to do — it's something everyone 10 can do together. It's how many freshmen begin meeting people. "You don't know anybody, and then somebody hands you a beer and pretty soon you're hanging out with a bunch of guys," says Eric, a nineteen-year-old sophomore, remembering his first days in college. Freshmen drink hard early on: A 1995 Harvard study of college freshmen found that 70 percent binge drink in their first semester. But after students find their social circle (and worship once or twice at the Temple of the Porcelain God), many decide to drink infrequently or not at all.

But others choose to drink throughout college. "When people ask me why college students drink," says Hanson, the sociologist, "I say, 'Why not?'" People in the "real world" have too little time and too many responsibilities to drink heavily night after night. They have to get up early five days a week, work all day, then go home to their families. Co-workers and family members count on them to live up to their obligations. College students are usually responsible only for themselves. All they have to do is go to a few classes and study when it's convenient. Michael Haines, coordinator of Health Enhancement Services at Northern Illinois University, notes that campus life is set up for binge behavior of all kinds. Students stay up one night cramming for a test, sleep in until noon the next day, then drink all night.

Research finds that college students who drink heavily have lower grades than those who drink moderately or not at all. But these students generally aren't chemistry majors whose grades and classes will be critical for graduate school and future careers. They tend to be business or social science majors who will probably end up in jobs that have little to do with their academic studies. "The truth is that most students can go out drinking several nights a week and get by," says Wartenburg, the Swarthmore dean.

College students get into trouble not because they drink to get drunk but because they get drunk to be irresponsible. "I was drunk" is a get-out-of-jail-free card for college students who act like idiots, get into fights, climb into construction equipment, or behave in other unacceptable or embarrassing ways. It works because friends know that drinking makes people lose control and they may want to use alcohol as an excuse for their own behavior, especially sexual behavior. According to the Harvard study, 41 percent of frequent binge drinkers engage in unplanned sexual activity, as opposed to only 4 percent for non-binge drinkers.

But unplanned does not mean unwanted. Students drink because they want to feel uninhibited. Men are less hesitant to approach women because they know that if their advances are rejected, they can laugh it off later, saying they were drunk. Women, who still face a double standard when it comes to sleeping around, can blame one-night stands on alcohol.

So men and women have a strong incentive to attribute sexual   15 behavior to drinking, which can be dangerous. Men may be inappropriately aggressive, and willing women may later claim they did not consent. The popularity of the alcohol excuse also helps explain the higher rates of unplanned and unprotected sex while drinking, because halting "uncontrollable" sex to be responsible would destroy the illusion of chemical compulsion.

Although alcohol has consistent effects on motor skills among people of different cultures, its effects on behavior may have more to do with expectations than with pharmacology. Researchers at Washington University in Seattle have found that students who think they are drinking alcoholic beverages become more animated and aggressive, even if they've had only tonic water. Anthropologists have discovered that alcohol's behavioral effects are shaped by culture. In Europe, people grow up drinking beer or wine as a normal part of family life, so drinking is no big deal and generally doesn't cause problems. Americans, by contrast, have always been ambivalent about drinking. As Hanson notes, we "think dry and act wet": We associate drinking with negative behavior but do it anyway. In addition to a person's "set" (beliefs and expectations), the "setting" where drinking takes place has an important impact on drinking behavior. A young man having wine at a family dinner will not behave the same as he would at a bachelor party.

College drinking behavior usually resembles a bachelor party more than a family dinner, but it also varies with the situation. When students go to a $3.00 all-you-can-drink kegger, they descend into a dimly lit, damp, smoky, and crowded basement. The beer is terrible, there's no place to sit, and everyone is pushing and shoving to get their money's worth before the keg runs out. The only thing to do is drink fast and hard. Students at keggers are mostly underage because they have nowhere else to drink, thanks to the twenty-one law.

Things are usually more festive at college bars and fraternity functions. The beer is flowing, so students can relax and have a good, rowdy time. Drinking takes on a party atmosphere, which means strong sexual overtones. Bars and frat parties keep the music at a throbbing volume, making it difficult to talk.

But at the East 19th Street Café, one of five microbreweries near the UO campus, the music is turned down low so people can talk without shouting and savor the premium ales, porters, and stouts. The brew pubs are probably the closest college equivalent to an adult drinking environment. Some graduate students and twenty-somethings come to 19th Street, but most patrons are undergraduates who also spend a lot of time in the campus bars. No matter how much people had to drink, I never witnessed drunken or boorish behavior by anyone at a brewery.

With an understanding of how set and setting affect drinking behavior, social norms can be used to control problems. People used to   20 wink and laugh at drunk driving. Now it's considered reckless and stupid, and drunk-driving fatalities have fallen dramatically. Many college administrators would like to design programs to encourage responsible drinking, but they are blocked by federal law. Thanks to the Drug-Free Schools and Community Act Amendments of 1989, universities must have an official no-use alcohol policy for students under twenty-one or risk losing federal funds, including student financial aid. "It's hard to teach people how to do something responsibly if it's illegal to do it at all," says Swarthmore's Wartenburg.

Nevertheless, some colleges are succeeding. In the late 1980s, officials at Northern Illinois University realized that the traditional approach of controlling consumption and keeping alcohol away from underage students wasn't working. A 1988 survey found that 43 percent of NIU students were binge drinkers, but students believed 70 percent were. NIU administrators thought that misperception of the campus norm was encouraging drinking. "What people feel is the norm has a rather potent influence on behavior," Haines, the NIU administrator, observes.

So with a slim budget of $6,000, the university began taking out ads in the campus paper during the 1989–90 school year reporting actual binge-drinking rates on campus. It also hired students to dress up like the Blues Brothers and hand out dollar bills to anyone who could report this information correctly. By 1995, perceived binge drinking had fallen to 43 percent. More important, actual binge drinking fell to 28 percent, and alcohol-related problems fell proportionally.

Officials at the University of Oregon are hoping to transplant Northern Illinois's success to their campus. Oregon is also one of many colleges that has set up substance-free dorms for students who want to avoid the mayhem in the regular dorms. "It's a great way for people who don't want to drink to avoid people who do," says Hanson. But there is probably a limit to what colleges and universities can do. The days when colleges served *in loco parentis*[2] are long gone.

The best place for students to learn responsible drinking behavior is at home. "Children follow in their parents' footsteps," says Hanson. "What they learn in the home has more impact than what they pick up from friends or at school." Instead of allowing other students to teach their children "normal" drinking behavior, parents can teach their children to drink in moderation, with food, and in the company of adults.

---

[2]*in loco parentis:* "In the place of a parent" (Latin).

Unfortunately, Hanson says, many parents are reluctant to teach   25
their children responsible drinking when underage drinking is illegal
outside the home and public health campaigns warn against sending
"mixed messages." But accountability is not a mixed message. [The
principle that people are responsible for their behavior even when
drinking should be drilled into young people's heads] by parents as
they are growing up and reinforced in college.

Not that college students would abandon keggers, campus bars,
and frat parties altogether. College is not the real world, and responsible drinking has a different meaning there. "You gotta do it [drink-
ing] in moderation," says Craig, a twenty-three-year-old University of
Oregon senior. "I think that you should go out once a week and get
wasted — that's moderation."

Discussing Vocabulary / Using a Dictionary

1. How is the word "repercussion" (para. 5) related to the "percus-
   sion" instruments in an orchestra?

2. How does a person act when he or she is feeling "uninhibited"
   (para. 14)?

3. Is "boorish" (para. 19) behavior regarded as desirable? What are
   some other words to describe a "boor"?

Discussing Meaning

1. What is "binge" drinking? How does it differ from other kinds of
   drinking?

2. Why, according to Carson, is college an ideal setting for binge
   drinking? What kinds of "secondhand" effects does binge drinking have on other students?

3. What, according to Carson, do "neoprohibitionists" (see para. 6)
   believe about drinking among young people?

4. How, according to Carson, are college administrators blocked
   from designing programs to promote responsible drinking?

Discussing Writing

1. How does Carson describe keg parties, fraternities, and brew
   pubs? Which setting does he present most favorably? How does

his description support his argument that college campuses have a drinking *behavior* problem, not a drinking problem?

2. How would you describe Carson's tone in this article? Is he neutral, skeptical, impassioned, or some combination of these? Do you think Carson agrees with the last student quoted? Why do you think he chooses to conclude his article with this quotation?

Challenging the Selection

1. "People in the 'real world' have too little time and too many responsibilities to drink heavily night after night," Carson states in paragraph 11. Do you agree? Does heavy drinking occur only on college campuses?

2. Carson argues that students should learn to drink responsibly at home. Where do you think people should learn about drinking? Why?

In-Class Writing Activities

1. Describe the drinking scene on your campus. By your estimate, what percentage of the student body are "binge" drinkers? What are the most popular settings for drinking? Is drinking (or drinking *behavior*, as Carson says) a problem at your school?

2. At what age do you think people should begin drinking? At what age should they be legally allowed to purchase alcohol? How much is an excessive amount to drink in an evening?

3. Would you prefer to attend a school where students didn't drink at all, or only in moderation? Why or why not?

RENE SANCHEZ

Surfing's Up and Grades Are Down

[THE WASHINGTON POST NATIONAL WEEKLY EDITION / June 3–9, 1996]

Before You Read

Computers can be a powerful tool for college students, allowing them to word-process term papers, browse the Internet, and send e-mail to classmates. But can exploring cyberspace actually become addictive? How much computer time is too much?

Words to Learn

array (para. 9): a group or range (n.)
venerable (para. 18): respectable because of dignity, age, or tradition (adj.)
correlate (para. 24): to match up with or be parallel to (v.)

A new campus support group called "Caught in the Web" is being formed at the University of Maryland to counsel students spending too much time on computers.

At the Massachusetts Institute of Technology, students unable to break their addiction to playing computer games on campus terminals have new help. At their request, the university will deny them access whenever they try to sign on.

Faculty studying the freshman dropout rate at Alfred University in New York have just found that nearly half the students who quit last semester had been logging marathon, late-night time on the Internet.

Nationwide, as colleges charge into the digital age with high-tech libraries, wired dormitories, and computerized course work, faculty

---

Reporter RENE SANCHEZ *(b. 1965) currently covers schools and education for the* Washington Post. *A graduate of Loyola University of the South, Sanchez joined the* Post *as an intern in 1987 and eventually became a reporter for the newspaper's Metro section. Sanchez is now part of the* Post's *national news staff.*

and campus counselors are discovering a troubling side effect: A growing number of students are letting computers overwhelm their lives.

It is hardly a crisis on any campus — yet. Some college officials   5
say it is merely a fad, and not nearly as harmful as other bad habits students often fall prey to on campuses — such as binge drinking of alcohol. But concern over the issue is spreading.

Some universities now are imposing limits on the time students spend each day, or each week, on campus computers. Other colleges are debating whether to monitor the time students spend on computer games and chat rooms, then program a warning to appear on their screens when it gets excessive.

Some college counselors are creating workshops on the subject and planning to include them in freshman orientation programs. Others already are urging students not to plunge into on-line relationships with strangers.

A growing number of students are letting computers overwhelm their lives.

"More and more students are losing themselves in this," says Judith Klavans, the director of Columbia University's Center for Research on Information Access. "It's very accessible on campuses, and students have time on their hands. We're seeing some of them really drift off into this world at the expense of practically everything else."

Campus officials say that communicating on the Internet or roaming the huge universe of information on the World Wide Web holds an especially powerful lure for many college students because it takes them into a vast new realm of learning and research, usually at no cost. But for students having trouble establishing social ties at large universities, or who are on their own, unsupervised, and facing adult pressures for the first time, it also poses an array of new risks.

At the University of California's Berkeley campus, counselors say   10
they are dealing with a small but increasing number of student cases linked to excessive computer use. Some students, they say, are putting too much emphasis on electronic relationships, are neglecting course work, and, in a few instances, are even being swindled out of money by e-mail strangers they have come to trust.

"There can be a real sense of isolation on a large campus, and for young students or new students, this seems like a safe, easy way to form relationships," says Jeff Prince, the associate director of counseling at UC-Berkeley. "But some go overboard. It becomes their only way to connect to the world. One of the things we're really working on now is helping students balance how many social needs they try to have fulfilled by computers."

Linda Tipton, a counselor at the University of Maryland, which limits students to forty hours a week on campus terminals, says she began noticing some of the same problems arise last year in individual and group therapy sessions.

Some of them, she says, spoke of spending more than six hours a day on-line and considered a computerized forum the only setting in which they could express themselves or relate well to others. A few students told her of dropping or flunking courses partly because they were so preoccupied with the Internet. Others confessed to trying to get multiple computer accounts with the university to circumvent its forty-hour-a-week rule.

"Obviously, this is a wonderful tool, and for many students it's perfectly fine," says Tipton, who is trying to form a campus support group and develop a workshop on Internet addiction. "But for others it's becoming a tremendous escape from the pressures of college life. Students can become whomever they want, for as long as they want, and many other things in their lives, like classes, start to suffer."

Nathaniel Cordova, a graduate student at Maryland, says his problems are not that severe — but he is nevertheless heeding Tipton's advice and trying to cut back on the time he spends on computers. And he says he routinely talks to other students on campus also trying to break habits like his.

"I don't think I'm an addict," Cordova says. "But I admit, sometimes I'll be in my office at eight o'clock at night, and then the next thing I know it's three A.M., and I realize I forgot to eat. It's so easy to get drawn in, and not just in research, but talking to people. You tell yourself, 'Okay, just one more link-up.' But you keep going."

Other college officials, however, say the concern seems exaggerated.

Some say they see few signs of trouble, and others say student interest in computer games or the Web is often intense at first, then fades. One of the venerable rites of college, they contend, is for students to find distractions from their academic burdens. They say this one is much safer than many others causing campus problems.

"There will always be something like this on college campuses," says Richard Wiggins, who manages information systems and teaches computer courses at Michigan State University. "In my day, in the

1970s, it was pinball. We played that all the time to get rid of stress. Usually things like this are not that harmful."

"For some people, it's just a great new way to waste time," says   20
Jeff Boulier, a senior at George Washington University who spends several hours a day on the Internet. "And college students have always been quite dedicated to wasting time."

At MIT, Patrick McCormick, an undergraduate who helps administer computer game systems for the university, says he sees both sides of the trend. A few students in his residence hall dropped classes, or saw their grades sink, after they lapsed into intensive computer use. "But others stay up all night with this stuff and still get 4.0s," he says. "It's very easy to get sucked in, but it isn't always bad."

Still, McCormick notes one problem he spots consistently: Classmates who trust virtually everyone they meet, or everything they read, on-line. "Some people think if it's on a computer screen, it must be true, and they get burned," he says. "You hear them talking about flying their dream lover up, and of course they never show."

This spring, Alfred University in upstate New York decided to examine what the students who dropped out last semester had in common. What prompted the inquiry was that twice as many students as usual — seventy-five, mostly freshmen — did not return for classes there this spring.

Every student at Alfred receives a campus computer account, which is free. So Connie Beckman, the director of Alfred's computer center, decided to check the account records of all the students who had dropped out. She found that half of them had been logging as much as six hours a day on computer games or the Web, usually late at night. "It was the only thing that correlated among so many of them," Beckman says.

University officials say they doubt that is the only, or even the   25
primary, reason many of those students quit. But the discovery has led to several new policies.

Next fall, for the first time, freshmen at Alfred will be told about the dangers of heavy computer use as soon as they arrive on campus. Residence halls, all of which have computer rooms, also will each have a full-time, professional counselor to keep a close eye on late-night computer addicts. Other campuses are studying similar moves.

"We've dealt with alcohol and drugs; we've dealt with TV and video games. Now this looks like the latest pitfall for college students," Beckman says. "They're doing this all night instead of doing their homework, or eating, or sleeping. When they're up until five A.M. playing around on the Web, they're not going to make their eight A.M. classes."

Discussing Vocabulary / Using a Dictionary

1. In paragraph 9, Sanchez writes that the Internet "poses an array of new risks" for college students. Can you come up with three synonyms for the word "array"?

2. Finding distractions is one of the "venerable rites" of college, Sanchez writes in paragraph 18. What connotations does "venerable" have?

Discussing Meaning

1. What steps have some universities taken to respond to computer overuse among students?

2. Why, according to campus counselors, do students tend to get so involved in computers?

3. What do those quoted in the article feel are the most worrisome aspects of excessive computer use? What reasons do some people give for saying excessive use is not harmful?

Discussing Writing

1. The author begins his article with three paragraphs that give examples of computer addiction. Do you find this opening effective? In which paragraph do you find the article's thesis, or main point?

2. Make a list of all the sources quoted in this article. What points of view are represented? How well does Sanchez balance students and faculty, computer advocates and critics?

Challenging the Selection

1. When Sanchez writes in paragraph 5 that computer overuse is "hardly a crisis on any campus — yet," he implies that it might turn into a crisis. Do you agree? Have you seen any signs of this on your campus?

2. What are some typical images of computer experts? Do you think these images influence attitudes toward excessive computer use? Would people be as concerned if students were spending six hours a day doing research in the library, practicing the violin, or playing on the soccer team?

In-Class Writing Activities

1. Draft a letter that a college dean might send to a student informing her that her computer privileges had been suspended because of excessive use. How would you explain the college's decision to intervene? Then write a response from the student in which you justify the amount of time you had been spending on the computer and ask that your privileges be reinstated.

2. Have you (or someone close to you) ever got so involved in an activity that other areas of your life suffered as a result? Describe the experience.

KIRK HOFFMAN

Why We Can't Just Stamp Out Smoking

[THE DAILY NORTHWESTERN, NORTHWESTERN UNIVERSITY / January 15, 1996]

Before You Read

Who's the coolest smoker you can think of? Who's the coolest person you can think of who is publicly opposed to smoking? Which person is cooler?

KIRK HOFFMAN *(b. 1976) was a sophomore when he wrote this essay for the* Daily Northwestern. *A peer adviser in his major fields — theater and economics — Hoffman is also active in many campus organizations. He plans to graduate from Northwestern in 1998.*

Words to Learn

propaganda (para. 6): strongly biased material put out by a person
or group to convince others to
follow a cause (n.)
tarnish (para. 7): to dull the luster
of (v.)

rebellious (para. 7): resistant to authority (adj.)
emphysema (para. 10): lung disease
that causes difficulty in breathing
(n.)

Sniff . . . sniff . . . sniff. What's that smell? It's the pleasant
tobacco-filled air in the corner of Norris 1999. The smoking section.
Nowhere else on campus can you see Northwestern students so re-
laxed and carefree, enjoying a warm cup of coffee and indulging in a
once-popular habit currently being bashed across America.

Since the Surgeon General's first warning about cigarettes,
politicians, the press, and mainstream America have decided that
cigarettes' and smokers' days are numbered. Last year, our fearless
leader President Clinton jumped on the antismoking bandwagon,
supporting new, tougher laws on cigarette sales. Every two-bit news
magazine has to have its weekly segment showing yet another reason why cigarettes
and tobacco companies are secret tools in Satan's plan. Lately, I continue to hear
more of the usual health class textbook comments from the army of antismokers.

> *Antismokers forget
> one simple fact:
> Smoking is cool.*

"It's so dirty!"

"It's not sexy!"

"Don't you know smoking's out? No one who's anyone   5
smokes!"

Well, that's all fine and dandy. Of course, antismokers will all
fail miserably because they forgot one simple fact that cancels out all
the propaganda and laws they try to pass: Smoking is cool.

Cigarettes are so ingrained in American society that attempts to
tarnish their image fail miserably. We all remember how our high
school health classes attempted to tell us that cigarettes weren't cool;
only losers smoked. However, when we looked around, all we saw
were the incredibly cool American figures who smoked. The ultra-
smooth Humphrey Bogart, the hardened tough guy Clint Eastwood,
the super-sexy Ingrid Bergman, the comic genius Denis Leary. The list
goes on and on. Whether anyone admits it or not, every time you see
someone take a drag off a cigarette, you automatically attach a cer-

tain rebellious, exciting personality to that person. Imagine a cop movie where the star cop is a nonsmoker.

In reality, the more antismokers try to tarnish the image of smoking, the cooler it becomes. Many of the new cigarette laws are supposed to make it harder for minors to buy cigarettes by censoring magazine and in-store advertisements. Great plan! So now it's ultra-rebellious for teens to smoke. I'm sure it will be a very effective method in stopping underage smoking.

Also, we can't forget the whole new flood of antismoking ads. My favorite is this ad that begins with a sexy, model-like girl smoking while the camera takes a close-up of her luscious red lips puffing away on a cigarette. Then, a guy comes up to her and says, "Smoking's disgusting. I would never kiss a girl who smoked." My first thought was that I would immediately start smoking just to meet this girl. It was the best free advertising a tobacco company could ever get.

Yes, cigarettes are bad for you. Yes, they cause emphysema and   10
lung cancer. Yes, they cause birth defects if used during pregnancy. Yes, they contain carbon monoxide. But we just can't stamp out smoking because, hey, cigarettes are cool.

Discussing Vocabulary / Using a Dictionary

1. What kind of information is termed "propaganda" (para. 6)? What is Hoffman implying about antismoking messages by using this word to describe them?

2. What are some synonyms for "tarnish" (para. 7)? What are some words that mean the opposite?

Discussing Meaning

1. What are some of the "health class textbook comments" that Hoffman says he hears about smoking (paras. 3–5)? What things, in his opinion, contradict those messages?

2. How, according to Hoffman, do people respond to the sight of someone smoking a cigarette?

3. What does Hoffman suggest is the actual effect of efforts to prevent smoking?

Discussing Writing

1. We say that a writer is being "ironic" when he lets readers know, by context or other verbal clues, that he actually means the opposite of what he says. Can you find an example of irony in Hoffman's piece? How do you know he is being ironic? What effect does this irony have?

2. For much of his essay, Hoffman focuses on the positive aspects of smoking and the futility of efforts to curb its appeal. Why does he admit at the end that "cigarettes are bad for you," and that they cause lung cancer and birth defects? Does this admission strengthen or weaken his position?

Challenging the Selection

1. Both "ultra-smooth" Humphrey Bogart and "super-sexy" Ingrid Bergman died of cancer. Does knowing this fact influence how you respond to Hoffman's depiction of "the incredibly cool American figures who smoked" (para. 7)?

2. Does the antismoking television ad Hoffman describes in paragraph 9 seem aimed at men or at women? Smokers or nonsmokers? Does Hoffman's criticism of the ad seem valid to you? Why or why not?

In-Class Writing Activities

1. Write a short essay in which you either support or criticize Hoffman's opinion. State your points clearly at the outset, and be sure to back up your comments with specific references to Hoffman's piece.

2. Hoffman's essay is an example of "polemical" writing — writing that takes on a controversial topic or that aggressively disputes another point of view. Try writing your own polemic on a topic being debated on your campus. Be creative with your argument; while it's best to avoid angry personal attacks, don't be afraid to attack views with which you disagree.

Discussing the Unit

Suggested Topic for Discussion

"I can resist everything except temptation," said the English playwright Oscar Wilde. How often do we have to give in to temptation before it becomes an addiction? Who should decide when an indulgence becomes excessive?

Preparing for Class Discussion

1. What are some of the common motivations among people who play the lottery, drink heavily, cruise the Internet, and smoke cigarettes? Why do they do it? Why can some resist while others can't?

2. Doctors who study substance abuse have come up with complex ways to analyze how our bodies react to certain chemicals. But as anyone who's ever tried to quit smoking knows, sometimes the mental cravings are as bad as the physical ones. Why are some habits so hard to break? Why do we develop needs that sometimes harm us?

From Discussion to Writing

1. Write an essay titled "There's No Future in _____." Choose a type of behavior that you think is excessive or harmful and state your reasons for opposing it.

2. Addiction is a controversial topic, in part, because it involves the question of what society should do to protect a person against him- or herself. In a free society, should the state play a role in preventing a person from engaging in self-destructive behavior? At what point do a person's bad habits become an issue for others?

3. Pick an addiction you believe is especially harmful. How would you advise people who are hooked this way to kick their habit? Outline a program you think would help them overcome their addiction.

Topics for Cross-Cultural Discussion

1. People from other countries often find American attitudes about health contradictory. We eat high-fat, sugary junk food and then exercise obsessively; we heavily advertise alcohol and tobacco while declaring a "war" on all other drugs. How are attitudes different in your native country? Are people there more or less concerned about addictive substances and activities?

2. What types of harmful habits do people in your homeland have that don't exist here? How does society deal with people who have those habits?

9

Do Words Matter?

As anyone who was ever called a "dork" or a "dog" or a "wimp" in junior high school knows, words can have a powerful effect on how we feel about ourselves. But can other people really "make" us feel a certain way? Not unless we let them, suggest Charles G. Russell and Judith C. White in this chapter's first essay. By using words like "make" and "made," they argue, we act as though others control our feelings, when in fact we do. The next two pieces point out that labels are not insignificant: They have real — and possibly damaging — consequences. In "A Humble Proposal," Hanns Ebensten takes a funny and perceptive look at what's wrong with the word "gay": Why should homosexual men be described with a label that implies they are only merry and frivolous, not serious and courageous? In the last piece, student Charles Choi finds racial ignorance lurking in the menu of a college dining hall.

CHARLES G. RUSSELL
AND JUDITH C. WHITE

Who Controls Your Life?

[ET CETERA / Spring 1993]

Before You Read

Can words really *cause* a person to feel a certain way? Why do we give other people the power to influence how we feel about ourselves?

Words to Learn

attribute (para. 1): to assign to a particular cause or source (v.)

causality (para. 2): the ability to cause (n.)

inadvertently (para. 5): unintentionally; accidentally (adv.)

linguistic (para. 6): related to language (adj.)

ascribe (para. 7): to assign or attribute (v.)

"He made me angry!" "She makes me feel stupid." Feeling angry and stupid and attributing the cause of the feelings to someone else relieves us of the responsibility for our feelings. If others can control when and if we feel angry, happy, stupid, or anything else, they, in effect, control our lives. The words "make" and "made" can play a significant role in our feeling powerless to control our feelings. As long as we accept, without question, the power of others to determine our feelings, we perhaps abandon any chance of controlling our own lives.

CHARLES G. RUSSELL (b. 1937) is professor of communication at the University of Toledo in Ohio and a consultant in management and communications. JUDITH C. WHITE (b. 1946) is president of Scribe Communications, a writing and editing service based in Ann Arbor, Michigan.

When we attribute causality for our feelings with the words "make" and "made," we assert that something we feel or experience happens because someone else makes it happen. If this assertion were, in fact, accurate, we could not change whatever we experience or feel unless the other person permitted the change. Yet feelings change dramatically from angry to amused without others giving us permission to change our feelings. Think about the last time you had a "heated argument" with someone and felt very angry until someone else walked into the room. Did the other person "give you permission" to stop feeling angry, or did you stop feeling angry on your own?

No doubt you recognize that you had the power to feel any way you wanted and that the other person could not really force you to feel anything you did not allow yourself to feel. Even with the recognition that we really can control our own feelings, the words "make" and "made" continue to dominate our conversations and perceptions. If you were to count in one day the number of times you and others attribute responsibility for feelings to someone else, you will probably discover the pervasive nature of "make" and "made" in our communication.

Thinking that others "cause" our feelings relieves us of assuming responsibility for choices we make.

If you want to discover the role of the words "make" and "made" in your perceptions and communication, try confronting the next person who asserts "you made me ____" with a rejection of the assertion. In other words, respond to the assertion that you caused the other person's feeling with a straightforward rejection, something like "I have no control over your feelings, you allow yourself to feel that way." You might not win many friends this way, but you just might contribute to the other person confronting the reality that he/she in fact did allow the feeling to exist.

Additionally you might want to pay special attention to the feelings you experience and determine whether you hold yourself or others responsible for them. When you feel inadequate, happy, or guilty, do you find yourself using the words "make" and "made" to attribute responsibility for the feelings to someone else? If you do, whomever you hold responsible for the feelings also inadvertently gains control over how long and often you experience the feelings.

5

The words "make" and "made" can easily contribute to our forgetting that we, and not others, control our feelings. As long as we assign responsibility for choices we make to others, we will very likely continue doing so, even if these choices do not serve us well. Thinking that others "cause" our feelings relieves us of assuming responsibility for choices we make. This "linguistic cop-out," in effect, ensures that we will continue to allow others to control our lives.

If you want to ensure control over your own feelings, you can begin by not using the words "make" and "made" in ascribing responsibility for your feelings. Recognizing "I allowed myself to feel silly" can reduce the chances I will hold others responsible for my feeling. Once I control my feelings, others cannot determine if and when I experience them, and I therefore gain at least some control over my life. Perhaps we now face an important question: "Do we really want to accept responsibility for our feelings?" If we do, our use of the words "make" and "made" will probably diminish. If we do not want to claim responsibility for our feelings, we can continue to declare "You *made* me feel stupid!"

Discussing Vocabulary / Using a Dictionary

1. What is another way of saying we "attribute causality" (para. 2) to something? Are "attribute" and "ascribe" (para. 7) synonymous?

2. Can you come up with a few synonyms for "inadvertently" (para. 5)? Use one of them in a sentence.

Discussing Meaning

1. According to the authors, how does using the words "make" and "made" influence the way we feel about our ability to control our emotions?

2. How do the authors recommend, in paragraph 4, that you respond to a person who says you "made" him feel a certain way? What are the advantages of confronting the person? What are the hazards?

3. What, in the end, is the question that the authors believe we must ask ourselves about our feelings?

Discussing Writing

1. Who is speaking in the essay's first two sentences? Why do you think the authors begin the essay with quoted statements rather than their own words?

2. If you could state the authors' central point in one sentence, what would it be? How many variations of this central point can you find in the essay?

Challenging the Selection

1. Russell and White suggest that the reader should "respond to the assertion that you caused the other person's feeling with a straightforward rejection" (para. 4). Do you think this is good advice? How do you think the other person might react? Can you think of any other ways to convey the same idea without a confrontation?

2. How well does Russell and White's argument apply to insults or other remarks that people *intend* to cause pain? If someone you respect says to you, "You're the dumbest person I've ever met," are you justified in saying that they "made" you feel stupid?

In-Class Writing Activities

1. Have you ever felt bad about yourself because of something someone said and then later wished that you hadn't "let it get to you"? What was it this person said? Why did you react the way you did? Would you have reacted differently if you had another chance? How?

2. "No man is an island, entire of itself," the seventeenth-century poet John Donne famously wrote. "Every man is a piece of the Continent, a part of the main." Why are we so dependent on others, and why do we let them influence how we feel about ourselves? Is it because we don't want to accept "responsibility," as Russell and White suggest, or are we justified in our feelings? Can we ever truly free ourselves from caring about what others think? Would we be better off if we could? Write an essay stating your view.

HANNS EBENSTEN

A Humble Proposal

[CHRISTOPHER STREET / July 1993]

Before You Read

What's in a name? Would homosexual men win more respect from mainstream society if they weren't labeled with a word as misleading as "gay"?

Words to Learn

cloying (para. 2): excessively rich or sweet (adj.)

vapid (para. 2): lacking zest; flat (adj.)

blithe (para. 2): carefree (adj.)

flaunting (para 2): given to showing off (adj.)

licentiously (para 4): lacking sexual restraint (adv.)

oblique (para 7): indirect (adj.)

whimsical (para. 8): playful (adj.)

spurious (para. 8): false; inauthentic (adj.)

denigrate (para. 8): to put down or belittle (v.)

wanton (para. 17): immoral (adj.)

stalwart (para. 17): strong; robust (adj.)

I am becoming increasingly anti-gay.

I did not understand why this appellation was applied to homosexual men when I first heard it used about fifty years ago, and since then I like it less and less. It is a nauseating word which brings to mind *The Gay Hussar,* one of the most cloying, vapid pieces of music ever composed, and conjures up sickening visions of painfully gay peasants with bells and ribbons around their ankles dancing in

---

HANNS EBENSTEN *(b. 1923) owns his own travel company, from which he operates tours, cruises, and expeditions in such remote locations as the Vilcabamba region of Peru, Easter Island, and Borneo. He has also contributed articles and book reviews on travel to a variety of publications, including* Archaeology, The Advocate, Genre, *and* New York Native.

the square of some village in Mittel-Europa.[1] I am not gay, I have never been gay in my life, not even at some disastrous New Year's Eve parties in my youth with a mask on my face and dressed as a harlequin or as Nijinsky in *L'Après midi d'un Faune.*[2] To be condemned to go through life being gay seems to me to be a very sad and dismal prospect — how loathsome to be constantly merry, joyous, bright, and lively, happy even at a funeral, blithe in adversity. Does this describe me, or most of us? Are we merely brilliantly flashy, flaunting, gaudy, showy buffoons without a sensible thought in our heads?

No, I am not gay; and I believe that opposition to the concept of accepting homosexuals in the U.S. military is due, to a large extent, to this unfortunate name, which damns us with a total lack of seriousness and purpose.

Who wants a light-hearted, licentiously "gay dog," a hilarious man given only to social life and pleasures, to be beside him in the assault on the enemy beach and in the parachute attack?

No, gay will not do: We must find another and more appealing   5
name for ourselves.

> *To be condemned to go through life being gay seems to me to be a very sad and dismal prospect.*

When I was a boy, homosexuality was not a fit subject for discussion. I overheard my parents, their lips primly pursed, acknowledge that Uncle Max was "a confirmed bachelor" and my mother smirked when she confided to the ladies at her coffee parties that her male hairdresser was "quite a lady." It was explained of an unmarried general who was invariably accompanied in public by a handsome young *aide-de-camp* that he "had never met the right woman"; and some actors were rumored to be *so.* Later, at school and in the army, I listened with fascination when the boys talked about weird, mythical creatures of whose existence they had heard but whom none had ever encountered — "queers," men who were "bent," "bum-rushers" and, most distasteful of all, "brown hatters," named thus for the same reason that men who demeaned themselves to their teachers or officers to seek favors were said to have "a brown nose."

---

[1]*Mittel-Europa:* Central Europe.
[2]*Nijinsky:* Vaslav Nijinsky (1889–1950), the great Russian dancer, choreographed and performed the avant-garde ballet *L'Après midi d'un Faune (The Afternoon of a Faun).*

Such talk was restricted to all-male environments. When this unpleasant subject was mentioned in mixed company, and in my home, which was seldom, and oblique references had to be made to someone who suffered from this affliction, the wretch was said to be *tapette*, conveniently breaking into French — the word means a chatter-box — as was customary when anything disagreeable was being discussed while servants were in the room.

In Cockney rhyming slang, in England, queer is equated with "ginger beer," so that some people I knew in London would say of an obviously effeminate man that "he's a bit ginger!" Queer was more often, and more aptly, applied to someone who was ill, specifically ill in the head, demented, rather dotty, or irregular in his or her bowel movements. "Mum got taken all queer," they said. Queer, meaning odd, strange, whimsical, suspicious, spurious, cross, crotchety, and erratic, but which is for an inexplicable reason now being used by homosexuals to denigrate themselves, is offensive in any sense of the word. To queer someone's pitch is not doing him a kindness. Bent, meaning crooked, curved, hooked, or deflected in one's purpose, was the favorite term used by "straight" soldiers and sailors who traditionally accommodated any gentleman who paid for their beer and gave them a gratuity for sexual favors — but these men were hardly quite "straight" and their patrons were only occasionally bent with age and knew quite well what they were doing.

When I came to America, I learned that a gay or queer gentleman who had just left the room is called a faggot, which is a bundle of sticks, twigs, or tree branches. In England, where it must not be confused with a "fag," it used to be applied to a shrivelled old woman. A fag, in England's great public (meaning private) schools, is a young boy who has to serve a senior student and is mistreated and abused in order to teach him that life is invariably unfair; but a fag is not necessarily a faggot.

Before we all became very bold and open-minded and outspoken and permissive, if one met a man whom one liked and with whom after several subsequent meetings, such as taking nature hikes or visiting the zoological gardens or the opera, one felt a certain rapport, one then hesitatingly, daringly asked him: "Do you like the color *green?*" or "Are you" — a pregnant pause for effect — "*musical?*" But not everyone who liked the color green was musical, so this circumspect questioning could and not infrequently did lead to embarrassment and confusion. To be "warm" was also occasionally heard,

10

though I never understood why, and Germans still speak, with approbation or derision, according to their sentiments, of a "warmer Bruder," which sounds like something very nice and cozy to have beside one in bed on a cold night.

So there we have our choices: Do we really want to be gay, queer, bent, faggots, brown hatters, or even warm brothers? There are other collective appellations, but we are not all pederasts, catamites, sodomites, perverts, or onanists. The only other name which is neither condescending nor derogatory is long, awkward on the tongue, a dirty ten-letter word which contains those dread letters s-e-x, but at least it is correct.

Homosexual women are fortunate. They name themselves and are named after the island of Lesbos in Greece, the birth-place of Sappho, antiquity's greatest lyrical poet who lived there with her female lovers in the 6th Century B.C. It is a sensible and dignified name, devoid of any unpleasant traits and associations.

I suggest that homosexual men also look back to the classical Greek and Roman period for a suitable and honorable name. The ancient Greeks believed (and proved in battles) that troops composed of pairs of lovers were superior in valor to other soldiers. The city states of Sparta and Thebes employed such troops of lovers, and it is tempting for male homosexuals to name themselves Spartans or Thebans; but these names are, on reflection, not suitable — by no means all homosexual men are fighters; few of us today lead what is generally now understood to be a Spartan[3] existence; and the most famous of the ancients' troops of lovers, the Theban Sacred Band which consisted of 150 pairs of lovers, of which Plutarch wrote: "A band that is held together by erotic love is indissoluble and unbreakable," was finally defeated, though by overwhelmingly large numbers of Macedonians.

So, instead of taking our new name from the battlefield, let us consider the most famous, accepted, and documented male homosexual relationship of antiquity, that between the Emperor Hadrian and Antinous, a youth who was born in the Kingdom of Bithynia, in what is now northern Turkey. They met in 124 A.D. and remained inseparable, traveling constantly, until Antinous's death. He was broad-shouldered and exceptionally beautiful, with curly hair, as is attested by more than five hundred statues of him which survive, many of

---

[3]*Spartan:* Characterized by self-discipline or restraint.

them portraits taken from life, not idealized, three of the finest being in the museums of Delphi, Olympia, and the Vatican. Eighteen centuries after his death, gazing at the statue of Antinous in the British Museum, the Poet Laureate Lord Tennyson exclaimed: "Ah — this is the inscrutable Bithynian. If we knew what he knew, we should understand the ancient world."

Antinous died on October 30, 130 A.D., by drowning in the river 15
Nile. The inquest continues — was it an accident, murder, or suicide? The distraught Emperor founded a city there in memory of his lover and ordered statues to be raised all over the Roman Empire to his "beloved Bithynian" so that he could be worshipped as a god. There is no better, no more romantic, no more uplifting example of a fine love between two men; and I propose that homosexual men everywhere call themselves Bithynians.

It is an unfamiliar word, and few of us have an affinity with a long-forgotten minor Kingdom on the north coast of Turkey; but after a year or more of general, wide-spread use, this name will seem no more strange than does lesbian — and who, after all, apart from lesbians themselves, knows that this is the name for the natives of a Greek island in the Aegean Sea?

Heads of the U.S. Armed Forces, who are averse to having those wanton, frivolous, erratic gays in the military, will, I believe, have fewer reservations about accepting stalwart, courageous, athletic Bithynians.

Shall we start to call ourselves Bithynians?

Who will begin?

Discussing Vocabulary / Using a Dictionary

1. What do you think a "cloying" (para. 2) piece of music would sound like? What are some other ways to describe something that is "vapid" (para. 2)?

2. What are some examples of "licentious" (para. 4) behavior? What is the root of the word? Write down two synonyms and two antonyms for "licentious."

3. How are the words "wanton," "frivolous," and "erratic" related? Can you come up with three words that would describe someone completely the opposite?

Discussing Meaning

1. How was homosexuality discussed in Ebensten's family when he was a boy? What were some of the terms used for homosexuals?

2. What does Ebensten say were some of the codes gay men once used to approach one another? What was often the result of having to use such coded language?

3. What problems does Ebensten foresee with the name "Spartans" for gay men? Why does he suggest that "Bithynians" is a better choice?

Discussing Writing

1. What does Ebensten mean by his first sentence, "I am becoming increasingly anti-gay"? In what other ways could this sentence be read? Why do you think Ebensten chooses to begin with such a statement?

2. Why does Ebensten inform the reader that he has served in the army? What effect does this fact have on his argument?

3. In paragraph 4, Ebensten asks, "Who wants a light-hearted, licentiously 'gay dog,' a hilarious man given only to social life and pleasures, to be beside him in the assault on the enemy beach and in the parachute attack?" Is Ebensten referring to a real person or an abstract idea? What do you think his purpose is in stating the question?

Challenging the Selection

1. Ebensten writes in paragraph 3 that "opposition to the concept of accepting homosexuals in the U.S. military is due, to a large extent, to this unfortunate name [gay], which damns us with a total lack of seriousness and purpose." Do you agree? How much does terminology affect prejudices? Do you think an army commander opposed to gay men in the military would be convinced by the argument that homosexuals were considered great warriors in ancient Greece? Why or why not?

2. "Homosexual women are fortunate," Ebensten writes in paragraph 12, because "lesbian" is a "sensible and dignified name, devoid of any unpleasant traits and associations." Is this statement accurate? Do you think that homosexuality among women is more accepted in our society than homosexuality among men?

In-Class Writing Activities

1. What do you think gay men should call themselves? Is "gay" an appropriate term? What about "homosexual" or "queer"? Write a short essay in which you argue for a term to be used and list its merits.

2. Consider the struggles other groups have waged to define their identity in America: At various points in time, African Americans have been called "colored," "Negro," and "black"; women can today be "Ms." rather than "Miss" or "Mrs."; people with disabilities are no longer acceptably referred to as "handicapped" or "crippled." Can you think of any other significant name changes? How do you think such changes have come about? Has the different terminology changed how society treats these groups?

CHARLES CHOI

A Beef with Beef Oriental

[THE CATALYST, UNIVERSITY OF SOUTH FLORIDA / October 2, 1995]

Before You Read

Why do some people insist on lumping all Asian cultures together under the term "Oriental"? What is the effect of using such a broad term?

CHARLES CHOI (b. 1977) was a freshman when he wrote this essay for the Catalyst at the New College of the University of South Florida. According to Choi, "The piece not only made people laugh, but made people think, too. In fact, the management no longer cooks up recipes with the label 'Oriental' on them due to student action." Choi expects to graduate in 1999.

Words to Learn

homogeneity (para. 5): the quality of being homogeneous, or of the same kind (n.)
heterogeneity (para. 5): the quality of being heterogeneous, or different (n.)
dogma (para. 6): a set of principles that are held to be the truth (n.)

It was dinnertime, Tuesday, September the 12th, and I had a food card. The two main entrees happen to be the topic of this piece: Southwestern Snapper and Beef Oriental.

Y'know, I have a beef with the term Beef Oriental.

I was born in Hong Kong and raised in America for most of my life by my Chinese parents. I see myself as Chinese and American, something that takes a lifetime to get used to: In America I am seen as Chinese, and in China I am seen as an American. So is the reason I have a beef with the term Beef Oriental because of my heritage?

I have to question the complete and utter ignorance when it comes to the rather sweeping term (Have you ever heard of Chicken European? Try some Fish Negroid.) The plain fact is, Asia just ain't one big province, folks. If you don't even consider the 1.3 billion people living in over forty provinces of China, there happen to be a number of other countries in Asia also. Ask yourself this: Do you see the difference between Thai and Koreans?

> *Have you ever heard of Chicken European? Try some Fish Negroid.*

What struck me was the contrast between the two entrees: Beef   5
Oriental and Southwestern Snapper. The former recognized only a homogeneity among populations in a geographical area (i.e., there are no regional differences in Asia), while the latter recognized a heterogeneity among populations in a geographical area (i.e., there are regional differences in America).

Am I being overly analytical because I might be sensitive over the subject? Am I being politically correct? I'll answer the former by saying that I hate being judged by things I cannot control, among them my genetically predetermined gender, my genetically predetermined appearance, and my age. Am I being politically correct? No. I think what has now been turned into political correctness is sad; I think it started as an exercise in respect, and turned into a belief in dogma.

The fact is, one's culture, heritage, and environment really do shape a person. Would it be good to have a little help in trying to understand other people? I would say yes. Would it be good to judge people only by what little we know about their environment? I would say no.

Should we think about important issues every day of our lives, even when they concern what seem like trifling details? Yes. Actually, I think those are probably the most important of all.

Discussing Vocabulary / Using a Dictionary

1. What does Choi mean by a "homogeneity" among populations (para. 5)? What does a "homogeneous" group of people look like? How is "heterogeneity" (para. 5) different?

2. What connotations does the word "dogma" (para. 6) have? What type of thinking do you associate with the term?

Discussing Meaning

1. In what ways does Choi say being both Chinese and American is difficult?

2. How does Choi respond to the idea that he is being "overly analytical" (para. 6)?

3. What does Choi mean when he writes that "trifling details" are "probably the most important of all" (para. 8)?

Discussing Writing

1. Why does Choi use the word "ain't" (para. 4)? Do you think he knows that the word is ungrammatical? What tone does the word convey? What effect does it have on you as a reader?

2. In writing this essay for a college newspaper, Choi must have assumed that many of his readers had recently eaten in the same dining hall. How do you think you would read the essay differently if you, too, had been faced with a choice between Southwestern Snapper and Beef Oriental? Does the author's argument speak only to the members of his college community, or does it have relevance to a larger audience?

3. Find several instances where Choi asks himself a question and then answers it. Why do you think he does this?

Challenging the Selection

1. Do you think that Choi's essay is trying to be "politically correct"? How do you define "political correctness"? Why do you think Choi feels a need to distance himself from this term?

2. In paragraph 7 Choi asks, "Would it be good to judge people only by what little we know about their environment? I would say no." Do you agree? How should we judge people?

In-Class Writing Activities

1. Imagine that you are the president of an Asian-American student organization at Choi's college and that you want to meet with the head of dining services to protest the term "Beef Oriental." What would you say to convince him or her to change the name? Write several paragraphs explaining how you might use reasoning to argue your point. Be sure to anticipate any objections you think the head of dining services might raise.

2. In his essay, Choi takes what he calls a "trifling detail" — the name of a particular dish in the dining hall — and expands upon it to discuss a much larger issue: the tendency of many Americans to not distinguish among people from very different parts of Asia. Write a similar essay in which you choose something interesting but of minor importance that you have noticed recently and then address its broader significance.

Discussing the Unit

Suggested Topic for Discussion

The three pieces in this chapter deal with the tension between how others see us and how we see ourselves. Charles G. Russell and Judith C. White show how we can take responsibility for our own feelings rather than letting others "make" us feel bad; Hanns Ebensten argues that opposition to homosexual men would lessen if they were not re-

ferred to as "gay;" Charles Choi addresses the cultural ignorance behind the blanket term "Oriental." How, according to the authors, do
words affect the way we think about things?

Preparing for Class Discussion

1. How do you think Russell and White might respond to Ebensten's argument that being called "gay" is damaging to homosexual men? How would Ebensten respond to the idea that people
   should "take responsibility" for their own emotions? On what
   points would the authors agree, and on what would they differ?

2. What are the origins of the key terms discussed in Ebensten's and
   Choi's essays? Why do you think the terms "gay" and "Oriental"
   have endured in popular usage if they are not accurate or appropriate to describe their subjects?

From Discussion to Writing

1. Write an essay in which you describe a time in your own life
   when you learned something about the power of words.

2. Write your own "humble proposal" for change. What term or
   phrase would you like to see retired for good? What do you suggest people should use in its place? Why is this change needed?
   Who would it benefit and how?

Topics for Cross-Cultural Discussion

1. What words are used in America to describe your culture? Are
   they accurate? If you could correct one mistaken idea that many
   Americans have about your culture, what would it be?

2. Whose opinion about yourself do you value the most and why?
   How have American attitudes about your ethnic group or native
   country influenced the way you see yourself?

10

Can We Say What We Want?

Ask an average American to tell you what the Constitution's Third or Seventh Amendment says, and most likely you'll just get a blank stare. Ask that same person what the *First* Amendment guarantees, and you'll probably get an answer immediately: the right to free speech. Why is this particular right so prized in our society? And what should we do about some kinds of speech — for instance racist remarks — that cause great pain and offend many people?

This chapter features three thoughtful and provocative attempts to deal with this thorny issue. Political commentator Barbara Ehrenreich examines how free speech is being threatened at work, where saying the wrong thing (and even wearing the wrong T-shirt) can get a person fired. Syndicated columnist Clarence Page discusses how students are increasingly trying to squelch views they don't like; Page thinks that people of color will benefit more from open debate than from censorship. Finally, Colgate student Jill Glazer looks beyond the rhetoric surrounding "political correctness" to what she sees as the central issue: Why are we so afraid of talking to one another?

BARBARA EHRENREICH

Zipped Lips

[TIME / February 5, 1996]

Before You Read

Where free speech is concerned, should the same standards apply to both the government and private employers?

Words to Learn

flaunt (para. 1): to show off (v.)
obscenity (para. 1): an offensive expression (n.)
libel (para. 1): speech that damages another's reputation (n.)
incendiary (para. 2): tending to inflame or provoke (adj.)
infraction (para. 2): a violation (n.)
alacrity (para. 2): eagerness (n.)

glade (para. 4): a pleasant, open space in a forest (n.)
infringement (para. 4): a violation or encroachment (n.)
rescind (para. 4): to take back (v.)
servile (para. 10): like a servant (adj.)
subjugation (para. 10): the state of being controlled or enslaved (n.)

Earlier this month a fellow named Sam Young was fired from his grocery-store job for wearing a Green Bay Packers T-shirt. All right, this was Dallas, and it was a little insensitive to flaunt the enemy team's logo on the weekend of the N.F.C. championship game, but Young was making the common assumption that if you stay away

---

Writer BARBARA EHRENREICH (b. 1941) is well known for her social and political commentary. She has contributed articles, reviews, and essays to a wide range of publications, including the New York Times Magazine, *Esquire, Harper's, Vogue, and* Time, *where she has been a regular essayist since 1990. Ehrenreich is also the author of several books, including* Fear of Falling: The Inner Life of the Middle Class *(1989),* The Worst Years of Our Lives: Irreverent Notes from a Decade of Greed *(1990), and, most recently,* The Snarling Citizen *(1995).*

from obscenity, libel, or, perhaps in this case, the subject of groceries, it is a free country, isn't it? Only problem was he had not read the First Amendment carefully enough: It says *government* cannot abridge freedom of expression. Private employers can, on a whim, and they do so every day.

On January 10, for instance, a Peoria, Illinois, man was suspended from his job at Caterpillar Inc. for wearing a T-shirt bearing the words DEFENDING THE AMERICAN DREAM, which happens to have been one of the slogans of the United Auto Workers in their seventeen-month strike against Caterpillar. Since the strike ended in early December, the firm has forbidden incendiary slogans like "Families in Solidarity" and suspended dozens of union employees for infractions as tiny as failing to shake a foreman's hand with sufficient alacrity. A fifty-two-year-old worker who failed to peel union stickers off his toolbox fast enough was threatened with loss of retirement benefits.

It is not just blue-collar employees who are expected to check their freedom of speech at the company door. In mid-December, Boston physician David Himmelstein was fired for going public about the gag clause in his employer's contract with doctors, forbidding them to "make any communication which undermines or could undermine the confidence . . . of the public in U.S. Healthcare . . ." or even revealing that this clause is in their contract.

> The lesson for America's working people is: If you want to talk, be prepared to walk.

So where are the guardians of free speech when we need them? For the most part, they are off in the sunny glades of academe, defending professors against the slightest infringement of their presumed right to say anything, at any volume, to anyone. Last fall, for example, history professor Jay Bergman was reprimanded by his employer, Central Connecticut State University, for screaming at a student he found tearing down a flyer he had posted. Now the Anti-Defamation League and the National Association of Scholars are rallying to have the reprimand rescinded. Reprimand, mind you, not firing or suspension.

Or, in 1991, you would have found the New York Civil Liberties Union defending crackpot Afrocentrist professor Leonard Jeffries of New York's City University. Thanks to such support and the fact that CUNY is a public-sector employer, Jeffries still commands a lectern, from which he is free to go on raving about the op-

5

pression of blacks by "rich Jews" and how melanin[1] deficiency has warped the white brain.

Most workers, especially in the private sector, have no such protections. Unless their contract says otherwise, they can be fired "for any reason or no reason" — except when the firing can be shown to be discriminatory on the basis of race, sex, or religion. In addition, a few forms of "speech," such as displaying a union logo, are protected by the National Labor Relations Act, and the courts may decide this makes Caterpillar's crackdown illegal. But the general assumption is, any expansion of workers' rights would infringe on the apparently far more precious right of the employer to fire "at will." So the lesson for America's working people is: If you want to talk, be prepared to walk.

Obviously there are reasonable restrictions on an employee's freedom of speech. A switchboard operator should not break into Tourette's-like[2] torrents of profanity; likewise, professors probably *should* be discouraged from screaming at students or presenting their loopier notions as historical fact. But it's hard to see how a Green Bay Packers T-shirt could interfere with the stocking of Pop-Tarts or how a union sticker would slow the tightening of a tractor's axle. When employers are free to make arbitrary and humiliating restrictions, we're saying democracy ends, and dictatorship begins, at the factory gate.

So we seem to have a cynical paradox at the heart of our political culture: "Freedom" is our official national rallying cry, but *un*freedom is, for many people, the price of economic survival. At best this is deeply confusing. In school we're taught that liberty is more precious than life itself — then we're expected to go out and sell that liberty, in eight-hour chunks, in exchange for a livelihood. But if you'd sell your freedom of speech for a few dollars an hour, what else would you sell? Think where we'd be now, as a nation, if Patrick Henry had said, "Give me liberty or give me, uh, how about a few hundred pounds sterling?"

Surely no one really believes productivity would nose-dive if employees were free to wear team logos of their choice or, for that matter, to raise the occasional question about management priorities. In fact, the economy could only benefit from an increase in

---

[1]*melanin:* Dark pigment in skin or hair.
[2]*Tourette's-like:* Reference to Tourette's Syndrome, a neurological disorder that can cause those affected to swear or shout uncontrollably.

democracy — and enthusiasm and creativity — on the shop floor. Or does the "free" in "free market" apply just to people on top?

When employers have rights and employees don't, democracy it-self is at risk. It isn't easy to spend the day in a state of servile subju-gation and then emerge, at five P.M., as Mr. or Ms. Citizen-Activist. Unfreedom undermines the critical spirit, and suck-ups make lousy citizens.   10

Discussing Vocabulary / Using a Dictionary

1. What effect are "incendiary" (para. 2) slogans intended to have on their hearers? What is the word's literal meaning? Do you think Ehrenreich really believes that the phrase "Families in Soli-darity" is incendiary?

2. Why does Ehrenreich call academia a "sunny glade" (para. 4)? How do the connotations of the word "glade" strengthen the point Ehrenreich is trying to make?

3. How would you characterize a "servile" state (para. 10)? How is "servile" related to "servant" and "serf"?

Discussing Meaning

1. What does Ehrenreich think is wrong with the priorities of free-speech advocates? What are they working on, and what does Ehrenreich think they *should* be doing?

2. What are some examples of speech that Ehrenreich believes should be restricted? What types of restrictions does she oppose?

3. What does Ehrenreich say, in paragraph 8, is a "paradox" in American politics? What examples does she give of this paradox?

Discussing Writing

1. Find several places in her essay where Ehrenreich uses the word "democracy." How does she use the term? What characteristics does she attribute to "democracy"? What does she suggest is its opposite?

2. In paragraph 8, Ehrenreich refers to the famous statement Patrick Henry made during the Revolutionary era "Give me liberty or

give me death." What is she implying about present-day America by changing Henry's statement as she does?

3. Consider Ehrenreich's final sentence: "Unfreedom undermines the critical spirit, and suck-ups make lousy citizens." Why do you think Ehrenreich ends her essay with such an informal tone? Rewrite the sentence in a more formal style: Is your version more or less effective than the original? Why?

Challenging the Selection

1. Is freedom of speech absolute or relative? Ehrenreich protests employers' curbs on speech by union members, with whom she seems to agree, but appears to support the suppression of speech by a professor she calls a "crackpot" (para. 5). Do you find this contradictory? Should some forms of speech be protected and others not? Who should decide, and what standard should be used?

2. "In school we're taught that liberty is more precious than life itself," Ehrenreich writes in paragraph 8, "then we're expected to go out and sell that liberty, in eight-hour chunks, in exchange for a livelihood." How is the concept of political "liberty" different from the "liberty" one feels on a Saturday afternoon at the beach? Which sense of the word is Ehrenreich using?

In-Class Writing Activities

1. Suppose you were a lawyer and Sam Young, the grocery store worker fired for wearing a Green Bay Packers T-shirt, asked you to represent him in a lawsuit against the store. How would you convince a jury that it was unfair for the store to fire Young? Draw on both Ehrenreich's views and your own in making your case. (Or, if you prefer, imagine you are representing the store instead, and defend the firing.)

2. A "paradox" can be either something that on first sight seems false but is actually true, or something that combines two truths that seem contradictory. Ehrenreich thinks American culture is paradoxical because we prize freedom but then sell it away by working 9-to-5 jobs. What things do you find paradoxical about America? Write an essay describing one of them.

CLARENCE PAGE

More Talk Needed — Not Silence

[CHICAGO TRIBUNE SYNDICATION / February 1996]

Before You Read

How should African American students react when they feel slighted, misrepresented, or even invisible on their campuses?

Words to Learn

calamity (para. 5): disaster (n.)
ostensibly (para. 6): apparently; seemingly (adv.)
assimilate (para. 9): to adopt, or become accustomed to, the characteristics of another culture (v.)
draconian (para. 9): extremely harsh (adj.)

heresy (para. 12): a word or action that violates established beliefs or doctrines (n.)
expedient (para. 16): something that serves an immediate purpose (n.)

In the drive by many campuses to make a more hospitable environment for minorities, some overdo it. Instead of finding ways to make students feel more comfortable with one another, they impose speech codes, "sensitivity sessions," and special orientation sessions that try, in effect, to suppress any possibility of offense to women or minorities on campus.

In response have come howls of outrage over "political correctness." Conservatives have waged a culture war against speech codes,

CLARENCE PAGE *(b. 1947), a syndicated columnist for the* Chicago Tribune, *won a Pulitzer Prize for commentary in 1989. A contributor to Public Broadcasting System's "NewsHour with Jim Lehrer" and "The MacLaughlin Group," Page is also a panelist on Black Entertainment Television's "Lead Story." His collection of essays on race,* Showing My Color: Impolite Essays on Race and Identity, *was published in 1996.*

orientation days, "sensitivity sessions," and any other activity that contributes to a sense described aptly by the Wellesley senior who said mournfully, "You have to be a victim to fit in at Wellesley."

Yet, somehow the academy survives. Efforts by well-meaning progressives to "protect" us people of color and other perennial victims from objectionable words or ideas tend to fold rather quickly under the heat of public scrutiny and ridicule.

As new-wave "censors" or academic "McCarthyites,"[1] they tend to have paper teeth compared to the armor of those who have real power in America. While there have been occasional excesses and idiocies, it is true, as British journalist Katharine Whitehorn said in 1991, that "there are a lot more places where you can say 'spic' and 'bitch' with impunity than places where you can smoke a cigarette."

A greater calamity is the array of actions students take upon themselves to squelch ideas or speech they don't like. In one case, for example, students at the University of Maryland woke up one autumn morning in 1993 to find that at least half of the copies of their campus newspaper, the *Diamondback*, had been lifted from their distribution points around campus and dumped into the trash. In their place were leaflets saying, "Due to its racist nature, the *Diamondback* will not be available today. Read a book."

The proper answer to objectionable speech is more speech, not less.

I have long believed that episodes of racial friction on campus are never about the issue that ostensibly touches them off. The most obvious incident provides only a spark for less apparent kindling that has been building up over time.

At Maryland, for example, black students' complaints about the student newspaper sounded painfully trivial at first glance. For example, it showed only white models in a fashion supplement; it misreported Frederick Douglass' name as "Franklin Douglass" in a black history month tribute, and it mistitled W.E.B. Du Bois' *Souls of Black Folk* as *The Sales of Black Folks*. Ironically, the newspaper's efforts to reach out and include black life in its pages had backfired painfully. It had done badly in trying to do good.

---

[1]*McCarthyites:* Supporters of Senator Joseph McCarthy (1908–1957), who led witch-hunts against suspected communists after World War II.

But at an open forum organized by the campus chapter of the National Association of Black Journalists, a litany of abuses, affronts, cruelties, and insensitivities, big and small, came out that touched almost every department on campus. But the biggest overall complaint was a common one heard across the country: They were tired of invisibility.

They wanted to do more than assimilate on white men's terms. They also wanted respect. Since universities are not in the market of dispensing respect, they try shortcuts. Some, like speech codes, can be unnecessarily draconian.

As an African American who made it my task to comfort the af-   10
flicted and afflict the comfortable, as the old quotation goes, it annoys me to hear the authors of speech codes say women and minorities are such sensitive souls that we need special protections from the idiotic statements of the ignorant. The University of Maryland, after careful study and, one presumes, agony, came up with a student-approved speech policy that others should take as a model.

It cautions everyone to "consider the hurt which may result from the use of slurs and epithets," but it does not limit speech. Instead, it says, the educational mission of the university requires "the need for freedom, the right to think the unthinkable, discuss the unmentionable, and challenge the unchallengable."

Let worthy ideas drive out the bad. It is no accident that the creative spirit of black America flourished at the frontiers of struggle, hardship, and risk. Safety stagnates the intellect. The real life of the mind flourishes at the frontiers of conventional thinking, flouting protected borders. The proper answer to objectionable speech is more speech, not less. The intellectual lives of women and people of color need more than babysitters and bodyguards. They also need adversaries. As Susan Sontag[2] said, the most interesting ideas are heresies, whether they come from outside the community or well up from within.

What to do? Garry Trudeau's syndicated "Doonesbury" comic strip stepped into the campus culture war in September 1993, with two weeks of strips that showed a college president struggling with empowerment-hungry students pressing their pluralistic wishes. Alarmed that various ethnic and gender enclaves had "managed to produce a fully segregated campus," the college president thought things couldn't get worse. Then he found out they could. The cam-

[2]*Susan Sontag* (b. 1933): Prominent American author and cultural critic.

pus black students were at the door demanding separate water fountains.

It was the type of fiction that, in many minds, was more true than facts. Many believe the resegregation of America's campuses is just that severe, but I caution, before we throw around the word "resegregate," the campuses must first desegregate.

Students can begin by talking to one another more often across racial lines. Black students, having heard one too many curious questions about how they do their hair and the like, tell me wearily, "I'm tired of trying to educate white students about black folks." White students just as wearily complain, "I'm tired of being called racist every time I try to talk about it." 15

Bitter episodes drive many students, particularly those whose backgrounds left them largely unacquainted with white college life or white people, to seek their own ethnic brethren and sistren as a campus comfort zone. But, for their own good, they should avoid treating their comfort zone as anything more than a temporary expedient, a strategic base of operation from which they can go forth and deal with the larger world. Just as changing demographics require white students to learn more about diversity of other cultures, so must students of color learn how to work in an increasingly multicultural America. No amount of name calling or "unity" checks is going to change that. Black students, in particular, cheat themselves when they pass up golden opportunities to socialize with whites and learn more about America's dominant culture. Before you can change the world, you need to know how it works. There is no better place to begin than in the world as it is represented in the diversity of a multiethnic campus.

In my travels to campuses across the country, I have found that the real victims of the culture wars tend not to be the activists of either the right or the left, righteously armed with their ideology, organization, and particularly in the case of conservative student groups, financial backing from conservative foundations, media, and alumni. The real victims tend to be the vast majority of students who merely want to get a diploma and get out.

It is they who stand on the sidelines of free inquiry rather than engage in candid discussion and debate across racial, ethnic, or gender lines, for fear of offending someone, either on the right or the left. It is they who, in my opinion, are being cheated out of the very mind-broadening experience that campus life should be. They are not indigestible, these students in the middle. It is campus life that has become indigestible to them. They come in all colors and genders. Who will speak up for them?

Discussing Vocabulary / Using a Dictionary

1. What is another way of saying an issue "ostensibly" (para. 6) touched off racial friction?

2. Look up the word "draconian" (para. 9) in your dictionary. What is the word's origin? What would the opposite of a draconian law be?

3. Page writes that "the most interesting ideas are heresies"(para. 12)? What does this statement mean? What meanings does the word "heresy" have in this context?

Discussing Meaning

1. According to Page, what usually happens to efforts to "protect" people of color from objectionable speech? What annoys him about such efforts?

2. What does Page see as the best response to offensive speech? In what ways do people benefit from the open conflict of ideas?

3. Why does Page think that students of color should take opportunities to socialize with whites?

4. Who, in Page's view, are the real victims of "political correctness"? How are they affected by the desire not to offend anyone?

Discussing Writing

1. Pay attention to the way that Page uses the first-person pronouns "I" and "my" in paragraphs 6, 10, and 17. How is his identity and personal experience relevant to the essay? Why does he tell the reader about himself instead of staying in the background?

2. What is the subject of Page's first four paragraphs? How does this introduction relate to the rest of the essay? Would the essay be more or less effective if Page had simply started with the Maryland case at the outset?

Challenging the Selection

1. "Let the worthy ideas drive out the bad," Page declares in paragraph 12. Do you agree with this motto? Will the most worthy ideas — the most persuasive, well-informed, intelligent ones — always win out? Why or why not? What factors other than worthiness influence an idea's acceptance in society?

2. Are the real "victims" of the "culture wars," as Page writes in paragraph 17, those students "who merely want to get a diploma and get out"?

In-Class Writing Activities

1. Write a short essay describing how students of differing race, gender, or ethnic background get along on your campus. What tensions exist among these different groups? What campus activities bring diverse groups of people together? Does your college have any kind of "speech code," and if so, how well does it work? Have there been any attempts to foster greater understanding across race or gender lines?

2. *Black student:* "I'm tired of trying to educate white people about black folks."
    White student: "I'm tired of being called a racist every time I try to talk about it."
    Continue this dialogue. How could these two students come to understand each other?

JILL GLAZER

On Politically Correct Speech

[THE COLGATE MAROON-NEWS, COLGATE UNIVERSITY / February 23, 1996]

Before You Read

Do we need to hide our true beliefs for fear of offending someone? How can we learn what terms other people find hurtful if we don't communicate?

Words to Learn

plethora (para. 1): an excess of something (n.)
compliant (para. 2): obedient or yielding (adj.)

When most people hear the term "political correctness," they cringe. Instantly, they become frightened of offending, scared of being honest, and wary of communication with anyone who is different from themselves. What started as an attempt to make people aware of their language and word choice has triggered a plethora of jokes and attracted a lot of negative attention. However, language is very important. The way we choose to express ourselves reflects our attitudes and beliefs. The way we label or refer to another human being is indicative of how we feel about that person. The language that we use does reflect our own set of values as well as our cultural identity.

While I feel strongly that words are powerful tools and symbolic expressions of what one believes, I know that it is dangerous to restrict another person's right to say anything. I firmly believe in freedom of speech, and also believe that change only comes about through open

JILL GLAZER *(b. 1974) was a senior at Colgate University when she wrote this essay. While at Colgate, where she received her bachelor's degree in 1996, Glazer contributed a biweekly column on gender issues to the* Maroon-News. *She also wrote an article on sentencing guidelines for women and children for the* U.S. Sentencing Reporter.

and honest communication and interaction. People often avoid confronting difficult issues because they are afraid of being labeled offensive. Here at Colgate we try so desperately in our conversations, as well as in our actions, to remain neutral and compliant. However, in doing so, we have become ineffective and fearful of others.

Personally, I would rather know up front what one thinks about issues that are important to me. Many people harbor ideas and beliefs that are radically different from mine. Sharing ideas, no matter how different they are, is educational for both parties. In order to establish one's own political and social identity, one must know what else is out there and why others feel the way they do. Despite popular belief, it is possible to engage in an open dialogue with another person and learn something, and it is possible for a class to discuss race, gender, or class issues without accusations being made or people being silenced. We don't have to be afraid of one another.

You are free to say anything you want to me, but you had better believe that I will express my views to you as well. There is a certain way I like to be addressed, and that is with respect. We all know that there are some labels and words that some of us object to. However, don't you want to know why? I would rather be given the opportunity to tell someone why I do not want to be called a "chick" than have someone not call me that and not recognize the political and social implications of that word. The only way we can learn the distinctions between words like "Hispanic" and "Latina" is if we ask. The only way to truly become educated is to uncover why some of us prefer being addressed as "African American" and not "black." We cannot assume that others know the meaning of the words they use, but we can teach them.

> *The language we use mirrors the attitudes we have.*

Of course, I am making the assumption that people want to learn and do not want to offend. I am often in situations with people who use speech that makes me uncomfortable, and I regularly voice my objections. Sometimes people are open to my suggestions, and sometimes they are not. It is then my right to disassociate from those whom I find offensive. I am not saying that I am always right, because being "right" is very subjective. However, I do not have to surround myself with people who use words I cannot accept.

Whether political correctness has been overdone or misinterpreted is irrelevant. What we should be focusing on is our ability to communicate openly and effectively with one another to bring about positive change. We have to recognize that others have insight into ideas, cultures, traditions, and beliefs that we do not necessarily have. The language we use mirrors the attitudes we have. Speech can, but does not have to, alienate. Some words do have hateful or offensive messages behind them. But the only way to learn is through interaction with others. Obviously, using certain words and not others is not going to eliminate all forms of sex or race discrimination. However, becoming aware of the meanings behind the words we use can make us aware of behavior that also needs to change.

Discussing Vocabulary / Using a Dictionary

1. Write down three synonyms and three antonyms for the word "plethora" (para. 1). Use one of each in a sentence.

2. How is the word "compliant" (para. 2) related to other words with the same root — for instance "complete" and "compliment"?

Discussing Meaning

1. According to Glazer, in what ways is language important? What things do we reveal about ourselves in the way we express our thoughts?

2. Why does Glazer think that people sometimes avoid difficult issues? Does she find this to be the best approach?

3. Why does Glazer say the issue of "political correctness" is "irrelevant" (para. 6)? What things does she think people should focus on? What can we learn by doing so?

Discussing Writing

1. Throughout her essay, Glazer makes generalizations about what "we" do, as in the second paragraph: "we try so desperately . . . to remain neutral and compliant. However, in doing so, we have become ineffective and fearful of others." Is Glazer including herself in this "we"? How would you react differently to her essay if she substituted "some people" for "we"?

2. In the fourth paragraph, Glazer addresses the reader directly, using the second-person pronoun "you." What effect does this direct address have? How does it fit in with the point Glazer is making?

Challenging the Selection

1. How would Glazer respond to the accusation that she is just being "politically correct" or "too sensitive" in objecting to the word "chick" (para. 4)? If a person disagreed with Glazer about the "political and social implications" of the word, and didn't believe it was disrespectful, would he or she be entitled to use it? Why or why not?

2. Glazer states in paragraph 5 that if people use language she finds offensive, she "has the right to disassociate" from them rather than "surround myself with people whose words I cannot accept." What assumptions is she making about her freedom to choose with whom she associates? How would her choices be limited if the offending person were her professor or her boss?

In-Class Writing Activities

1. "We cannot assume that others know the meaning of the words they use, but we can teach them," Glazer writes in paragraph 4. Pair up with a classmate who is different from you in some way and discuss how each of you defines yourself. If you prefer to be known as "African American" rather than "black," for example, or hate being called a "girl," or object to the word "jock," explain why to your classmate. Talk about the connotations and history of words that you wish people wouldn't use in referring to you. Then present the things you learned about each other to the class.

2. You might be surprised to learn that the term "politically correct" got its start as a joke among liberal academics who were making fun of the idea that any one cultural attitude could be called "correct." Why do you think the term now stirs up such emotional responses from both liberals and conservatives? How might calling someone "politically correct" be a useful way to discredit his or her views? Write a short essay analyzing the term and its uses.

Discussing the Unit

Suggested Topic for Discussion

In 1919, Supreme Court Justice Oliver Wendell Holmes, Jr., ruled that "the most stringent protection of free speech would not protect a man from falsely shouting fire in a theater, and causing panic." Ever since then, Holmes's famous statement has served as an example of the limits of free speech. But by the standards of the authors in this chapter, speech these days is *too* limited, and for reasons that have little to do with public safety: Companies can't tolerate employees disagreeing with them, black students don't want a biased newspaper distributed on campus, and "political correctness" won't allow people to express their true beliefs. Do employers have the right to fire workers who challenge management's approach or beliefs? Is using a racist slur the same as shouting "fire" in a theater? Are some forms of expression so dangerous or offensive that they shouldn't be allowed?

Preparing for Class Discussion

1. Both Page and Glazer argue that dialogue between people with very different ideas is valuable. Compare Page's reasons (paragraphs 12 and 16) with Glazer's (paragraphs 2 and 3). Do their views overlap? How are they different?

2. How might Page suggest that the university respond to the racial theories of Afrocentrist professor Leonard Jeffries mentioned in Ehrenreich's essay (para. 5)? Would he and Ehrenreich agree or disagree about the best way to deal with Jeffries?

From Discussion to Writing

1. To what extent is freedom of speech linked to other social factors such as wealth and power? (For example, a number of cities have passed laws against asking people for money on the street, but almost none have banned advertising.) Write an essay in which you discuss freedom of speech in America, both in theory and in practice. Does freedom of speech really apply across class lines?

2. Write about a time when you were censored, or when you held yourself back from speaking your mind. What prevented you from expressing your thoughts? How did you react? In retrospect, do you still think you were right?

Topics for Cross-Cultural Discussion

1. America prides itself on being the land of freedom and liberty, but as the essays in this section show, not all types of speech are always free. Is freedom of speech highly valued in your native country? How do people there view their right to say what they want? What types of speech are punished or not allowed?

2. Do you feel free to express your opinions about America? In your opinion, are immigrants or people of minority cultures less free to express themselves than longtime Americans or white people are?

11

Should English Be the Official Language?

Walk the streets of most American cities (and even some small towns) and chances are you'll find an astonishing variety of food being sold: Chinese, Italian, Indian, Mexican, and many other cuisines have become common in this country. And as you're walking, you're also likely to hear a variety of languages being spoken. But while few people would suggest that everyone should eat the same kind of food, some do wonder if such diversity of languages is beneficial to the country. How can the United States truly be united if its citizens can't even understand one another?

Michael Gonzales starts off the chapter with an account of his experience in his high school's bilingual program. Next, the novelist Chang-rae Lee describes the daily difficulties his mother faced as a Korean immigrant before she learned to speak English. University of Rochester student Rosa Rivera concludes the chapter; in her view, there's no point in trying to unify America by making English the official language, as there's no such thing as a unified American culture anyway.

MICHAEL GONZALES

The Bilingual Ed Trap

[THE WALL STREET JOURNAL / October 18, 1995]

Before You Read

The author of this piece emigrated from Cuba to America at age four-teen; now he's a foreign correspondent for a prestigious New York newspaper. Was his success a result of the bilingual program at school? You might find his answer surprising.

Words to Learn

immersion (para. 2): the act of being submerged or completely involved in something (n.)

melodious (para. 6): having a melody or a pleasant sound (adj.)

waif (para. 6): a helpless or orphaned child (n.)

duly (para. 6): rightfully (adv.)

instill (para. 7): to establish a belief or feeling through persistence (v.)

strife (para. 8): struggle or conflict (n.)

dissipated (para. 9): exhausted or expended (adj.)

hypothesize (para. 10): to guess or speculate (v.)

nativism (para. 10): favoring the interests of native inhabitants of a country over those of immigrants (n.)

MICHAEL GONZALES *is a* Wall Street Journal *staff reporter in New* York.

The push to make English the official language of the United States misses the point. If proponents of such a constitutional amendment aim to prevent Balkanization[1] and preserve the ideal of the melting pot, they would do far better to channel their efforts into radically changing bilingual education programs. Immigrants will learn English if the social engineers will only let them.

I know about bilingual education firsthand. When my family came to this country from Cuba via Spain more than twenty years ago, the New York City public school system, in its infinite wisdom, put me in a bilingual program, despite my family's doubts. The program delayed my immersion into English, created an added wedge between new immigrants and other students, and was sometimes used as a dumping ground for troubled Spanish-speakers more fluent in English.

> *The push to make English the official language of the United States misses the point.*

When I tried to transfer to a regular class, the system threw roadblocks in my way. Administrators finally relented, though it took a lot to convince them. The process was an education in itself, but it wasn't one a fourteen-year-old should be asked to go through.

One year later, the students who had stayed in the bilingual class were still there, and their English-language skills were little improved. They were every bit as bright as I; it was the system that held them back. Sadly, this picture has not improved in the past two decades.

While a bilingual program of short duration that truly aims at quick immersion in the English-speaking culture would be of value, the lobbying groups that support bilingual education appear to have other aims in mind: chiefly, pushing the Spanish language as something in need of protection and creating a multicultural, multilingual nation.

Spanish is my native tongue, and it is the native tongue of every member of my family. I work hard at not losing it and speak it as often as I can, especially in the street. It is a beautiful, melodious tongue, especially suitable for poetry and other forms of literature. It is not a waif that needs the help of some concerned administrator. The language is alive and duly celebrated in Spain and eighteen coun-

[1]*Balkanization:* A division of a territory into smaller, sometimes warring, nations.

tries in Latin America, as well as in any other country where individuals have chosen to add it to the particular inventory of the foreign languages they know.

Paul Hill, research professor at the University of Washington's graduate school of public policy, says one hidden agenda of bilingualism's proponents may be to create demand for teachers who speak a foreign language. He also suggests a more Machiavellian[2] agenda: Instilling in a child a self-consciousness as a member of a separate group virtually ensures that he or she will never fully feel a member of the larger society and will be more vulnerable to claims of ethnic pride, or resentment, by politicians and marketers alike. I fear Professor Hill may be right on target.

As a correspondent, I have witnessed countries such as South Korea and Japan use unity of purpose to compete globally. I have also witnessed strife in countries that are multilingual and multicultural, such as Afghanistan and Cyprus. We should think twice before we toss out the corny goal of having a melting pot.

Yes, Americans, an English-speaking people, had better start learning foreign languages, such as Spanish, in order to better compete in the world. Yes, our diversity is a real strength: Americans of Eastern European, Asian, and Latin American background are leading the charge in opening markets in those regions. But we cannot afford to become dissipated at the center — we have to understand one another, linguistically and culturally, back at the head office.

But if the liberals on one side confuse matters, the conservatives on the other side also send the wrong message with English-only drives. The first law that established English as the official language of a state, in Nebraska in the 1920s, restricted the learning of any other foreign language until secondary education. Any law that risks encouraging isolationism should be opposed. Globalism is real — anyone who doubts it should visit our business schools and see students grappling with how to overcome America's natural seclusion. In addition, if it's fair to speculate about the motives of bilingual-ed supporters, it is also legitimate to hypothesize that supporters of English-only may be animated by nativism, racism, and ignorance.

Far from working toward union, making English an official language risks creating further divisions. It goes against the grain of how

10

---

[2]*Machiavellian:* Referring to the beliefs of Italian statesman Niccolò Machiavelli (1469–1527), who held that politicians will use any means — even deceit — to achieve their ends.

things have traditionally been done in this country, where there is no official religion nor family that represents the state. Reforming bilingual ed and restricting government literature to English does not require an official language. We've done without one for 219 years. We don't need one now.

Discussing Vocabulary / Using a Dictionary

1. What would a program of "quick immersion in English-speaking culture" (para. 5) be like? What are some of the other meanings of "immersion" and how are they related to Gonzales's use of the term?

2. What are some characteristics of a "waif"? (para. 6) What is Gonzales suggesting about Spanish by saying the language is not a waif?

3. What do you think a "social engineer" (para. 1) does?

Discussing Meaning

1. What does Gonzales say were the disadvantages of the bilingual program he entered when he came to the United States? What happened to the students who remained in that program?

2. Why, according to Gonzales, do lobbying groups support bilingual education?

3. How have Gonzales's experiences as a correspondent influenced his opinion on bilingualism?

4. What, in Gonzales's view, are some problems with the English-only drives supported by conservatives?

Discussing Writing

1. How well does the essay's title reflect its major themes? In what ways does Gonzales show that bilingual education is a "trap"?

2. "I know about bilingual education firsthand," Gonzales writes in paragraph 2. How does he use his personal experience as a Spanish-speaking immigrant to support his point of view? Would you find his argument more or less convincing if he claimed that speaking Spanish was no longer important to him?

Challenging the Selection

1. Why do you think the administration in Gonzales's school didn't want him to transfer to a regular class? How might they have defended keeping him in the bilingual program?

2. Should all immigrants to this country speak English as their main language and speak their native tongue only in private situations or "in the street"? Why or why not?

3. In his final paragraph, Gonzales writes, "We have done without [an official language] for 219 years. We don't need one now." Do you agree with this statement? Why or why not?

In-Class Writing Activities

1. Gonzales writes in paragraph 8 that he has "witnessed strife in countries that are multilingual and multicultural." Is conflict inevitable in a multicultural society? How can it be avoided? Is it better for countries to have "unity of purpose," as Gonzales found in South Korea and Japan? Write a short essay in which you state your opinion and your reasons for it.

2. Advocates of bilingual education programs argue that they help students who are smart but can't do regular work because of poor English skills. Opponents, such as Gonzales, argue that such programs do more harm than good and that immigrant students respond better to the challenge of regular classes. What do you think? Explain your position in a short essay.

CHANG-RAE LEE

Mute in an English-Only World

[THE NEW YORK TIMES / April 18, 1996]

Before You Read

Have you ever been in a situation where you couldn't understand what someone was saying because he or she was speaking another language? How did it feel?

Words to Learn

proliferation (para. 1): rapid, abundant growth (n.)

exclusionary (para. 2): excluding others from rights or advantages (adj.)

loathe (para. 5): to hate strongly; to despise (v.)

nasality (para. 6): a nasal sound, as if spoken through the nose (n.)

mimic (para. 6): to imitate or copy (v.)

sundry (para. 8): various (adj.)

harrowing (para. 9): distressing or traumatic (adj.)

When I read of the troubles in Palisades Park, N.J., over the proliferation of Korean-language signs along its main commercial strip, I unexpectedly sympathized with the frustrations, resentments, and fears of the longtime residents. They clearly felt alienated and even unwelcome in a vital part of their community. The town, like seven

CHANG-RAE LEE (b. 1965) was born in Seoul, South Korea, and immigrated to the United States with his family when he was three. He received a bachelor's degree from Yale University and a master's degree from the University of Oregon, where he is currently an assistant professor of creative writing. Chang-rae Lee's first novel, the award-winning Native Speaker, *was published in 1995. In the essay reprinted here, the author responds to a feature story in the* New York Times *about a New Jersey town that was preventing Korean merchants from posting signs exclusively in Korean in the downtown shopping district.*

others in New Jersey, has passed laws requiring that half of any commercial sign in a foreign language be in English.

Now I certainly would never tolerate any exclusionary ideas about who could rightfully settle and belong in the town. But having been raised in a Korean immigrant family, I saw every day the exacting price and power of language, especially with my mother, who was an outsider in an English-only world.

In the first years we lived in America, my mother could speak only the most basic English, and she often encountered great difficulty whenever she went out.

We lived in New Rochelle, N.Y., in the early seventies, and most of the local businesses were run by the descendants of immigrants who, generations ago, had come to the suburbs from New York City. Proudly dotting Main Street and North Avenue were Italian pastry and cheese shops, Jewish tailors and cleaners, and Polish and German butchers and bakers. If my mother's marketing couldn't wait until the weekend, when my father had free time, she would often hold off until I came home from school to buy groceries.

> *Having been raised in a Korean immigrant family, I saw every day the exacting price and power of language.*

Though I was only six or seven years old, she insisted that I go out shopping with her and my younger sister. I mostly loathed the task, partly because it meant I couldn't spend the afternoon playing catch with my friends but also because I knew our errands would inevitably lead to an awkward scene, and that I would have to speak up to help my mother.

I was just learning the language myself, but I was a quick study, as children are with new tongues. I had spent kindergarten in almost complete silence, hearing only the high nasality of my teacher and comprehending little but the cranky wails and cries of my classmates. But soon, seemingly mere months later, I had already become a terrible ham and mimic, and I would crack up my father with impressions of teachers, his friends, and even himself. My mother scolded me for aping his speech, and the one time I attempted to make light of hers I rated a roundhouse smack on my bottom.

For her, the English language was not very funny. It usually meant trouble and a good dose of shame, and sometimes real hurt. Although she had a good reading knowledge of the language from university classes in South Korea, she had never practiced actual conversation. So in America she used English flashcards and phrase books and watched television with us kids. And she faithfully carried a pocket workbook illustrated with stick-figure people and compound sentences to be filled in.

But none of it seemed to do her much good. Staying mostly at home to care for us, she didn't have many chances to try out sundry words and phrases. When she did, say, at the window of the post office, her readied speech would stall, freeze, sometimes altogether collapse.

One day was unusually harrowing. We ventured downtown in the new Ford Country Squire my father had bought her, an enormous station wagon that seemed as long — and deft — as an ocean liner. We were shopping for a special meal for guests visiting that weekend, and my mother had heard that a particular butcher carried fresh oxtails, which she needed for a traditional soup.

We'd never been inside the shop, but my mother would pause before its window, which was always lined with whole hams, crown roasts, and ropes of plump handmade sausages. She greatly esteemed the bounty with her eyes, and my sister and I did also, but despite our desirous cries she'd turn us away and instead buy the packaged links at the Finast supermarket, where she felt comfortable looking them over and could easily spot the price. And, of course, not have to talk.

10

But that day she was resolved. The butcher store was crowded, and as we stepped inside the door jingled a welcome. No one seemed to notice. We waited for some time, and people who entered after us were now being served. Finally, an old woman nudged my mother and waved a little ticket, which we hadn't taken. We patiently waited again, until one of the beefy men behind the glass display hollered our number.

My mother pulled us forward and began searching the cases, but the oxtails were nowhere to be found. The man, his big arms crossed, sharply said, "Come on, lady, whaddya want?" This unnerved her, and she somehow blurted the Korean word for oxtail, soggori.

The butcher looked as if my mother had put something sour in his mouth, and he glanced back at the lighted board and called the next number.

Before I knew it, she had rushed us outside and back in the wagon, which she had double-parked because of the crowd. She was furious, almost vibrating with fear and grief, and I could see she was about to cry.

She wanted to go back inside, but now the driver of the car we were blocking wanted to pull out. She was shooing us away. My

15

mother, who had just earned her driver's license, started furiously working the pedals. But in her haste she must have flooded the engine, for it wouldn't turn over. The driver started honking and then another car began honking as well, and soon it seemed the entire street was shrieking at us.

In the following years, my mother grew steadily more comfortable with English. In Korean, she could be fiery, stern, deeply funny, and ironic; in English, just slightly less so. If she was never quite fluent, she gained enough confidence to make herself clearly known to anyone, and particularly to me.

Five years ago, she died of cancer, and some months after we buried her I found myself in the driveway of my father's house, washing her sedan. I liked taking care of her things; it made me feel close to her. While I was cleaning out the glove compartment, I found her pocket English workbook, the one with the silly illustrations. I hadn't seen it in nearly twenty years. The yellowed pages were brittle and dog-eared. She had fashioned a plain-paper wrapping for it, and I wondered whether she meant to protect the book or hide it.

I don't doubt that she would have appreciated doing the family shopping on the new Broad Avenue of Palisades Park. But I like to think, too, that she would have understood those who now complain about the Korean-only signs.

I wonder what these same people would have done if they had seen my mother studying her English workbook — or lost in a store. Would they have nodded gently at her? Would they have lent a kind word?

Discussing Vocabulary / Using a Dictionary

1. The prefix "ex-" (as in "exclusionary" [para. 2]) has a specific meaning. What is it?

2. Lee writes in paragraph 5 that he "loathed" going shopping with his mother. What are some synonyms for "loathe"? What degree of emotion is suggested by the word?

3. Look up the word "harrowing" (para. 9). What is the root of the word? Can you see the relation of its root to its common modern usage?

Discussing Meaning

1. Who were some of the ethnic groups living in New Rochelle, N.Y., when Lee was growing up there?

2. How did Lee's mother feel about the English language? What did it usually mean to her? What would happen when she tried to speak English in public?

3. What does Lee wonder about the paper wrapping his mother made for her workbook?

Discussing Writing

1. Why does Lee begin his account by saying he sympathizes with the English-speaking residents of Palisades Park? Why does he describe his sympathy as unexpected?

2. Reread Lee's description of the butcher shop incident. How do the small details — for example, that his mother went to the butcher because she needed an ingredient for a traditional soup — shape your reaction to the incident? How does Lee describe the butcher's reaction to his mother's speaking Korean by mistake? Why is this significant?

3. Does knowing that Lee's mother eventually learned to speak English change how you respond to the essay's final paragraphs? Why do you think Lee wants the reader to know that his mother overcame her language barriers and that her personality was the same in English as it was in Korean?

Challenging the Selection

1. Does Lee provide any clues for the questions with which he concludes his essay? How do you think he might answer his own questions? How would you answer them? Why do you think Lee ends his essay this way?

2. What is Lee's attitude toward the bilingual signs? Why does he write that his mother "would have understood" those who complain about Korean-only signs (para. 18)? Do you think she would? Why or why not?

In-Class Writing Activities

1. Suppose that the Palisades Park city council convened a public forum to discuss what to do about Korean signs on the main commercial strip. If you were given a chance to speak, what would you say? How would you address both the Koreans in the

audience and those who wanted the signs changed? What course of action would you suggest?

2. Describe a time when you were embarrassed or ashamed by a situation involving your parents. What happened, and how did you feel? Looking back, why do you think your mother or father behaved the way he or she did?

ROSA RIVERA

Why English-Only Laws Are Useless

[THE CAMPUS TIMES, UNIVERSITY OF ROCHESTER / Spring 1996]

Before You Read
Do you think English should be the "official language" of the United States? Why or why not?

Words to Learn

repercussion (para. 1): an effect — usually indirect — of an action (n.)
invalidation (para. 2): the act of repealing; declaring something void (n.)

mandate (para. 2): to require (v.)
integral (para. 4): essential (adj.)
medium (para. 4): the means or way (n.)

ROSA L. RIVERA (b. 1974) was a senior when she wrote this essay for the University of Rochester's Campus Times. Rivera, former president of the university's Spanish and Latin Students' association, received her bachelor's degree in political science in 1996. She expects to receive her master's degree from the university's Graduate School of Education and Human Development in 1997.

The newest move to bash immigrants in the United States has arrived with the resurgence of the "English-only" movement. The type of legislation called for by this movement is sure to have negative repercussions for American society at large.

In 1996, the Supreme Court agreed to review a lower court's invalidation of Arizona's 1988 constitutional amendment making English the official language of that state. This law mandates that voting ballots be in English only and that English be the official language of all government functions and actions, including government documents. Government officials and employees are to conduct business in English only. Additionally, schools are not allowed to teach in any other language unless the class is specifically geared toward teaching a foreign language.

Legislation that would make English the official language of the United States would affect institutions that are crucial to all Americans: elections, government, and education. Citizens who cannot understand the English language would not be able to understand voter registration forms. They would not be able to vote in local or national elections, even though they have a constitutional right to participate in electoral politics. Government documents that are currently printed in several languages in addition to English would only be printed in English. That would mean that non-English-speaking people applying for housing, health care, welfare, and other social services would no longer have access to these services. In addition, students who do not speak English would not be able to learn — their access to education would be cut off. Should government officials want to help the affected individuals by explaining application procedures or school policies, they would not be able to; according to the law, official business must be conducted in English. Should the proposed legislation be passed, government employees probably would not have the necessary language skills to assist people. There would probably be no hiring preferences given to those with knowledge of a foreign language and, therefore, no motivation to learn one.

Ethnic divisions and racism go a lot deeper than language.

Aside from my concern about the consequences that this proposed legislation might have on a large group, the whole issue strikes me as un-American. This country was founded by immigrants and now it is trying desperately to turn its back on them. Immigrants have it hard enough in this country without being forced to abandon their native language. Language is an integral part of culture; it is the medium through which the culture is passed on from generation to generation. The "English-only" movement (and others like it) is trying to create something in the United States that our rich history prevents: one unified culture.

Presidential candidate Bob Dole and others argue that making   5
English the official language of the United States would unify the country. I disagree. Ethnic divisions and racism go a lot deeper than language.

Discussing Vocabulary / Using a Dictionary

1. Can you determine the meaning of "resurgence" (para. 1) without looking it up? (Hint: First break it into parts: *re* + *surge* + *ence*.)

2. What is another way of saying that a law "mandates" (para. 2) certain things? When a politician wins an election by a large margin, he or she is also said to have a "mandate" from the voters. How are the two meanings related?

3. What does Rivera mean when she writes in paragraph 4 that language "is the *medium* through which culture is passed from generation to generation"? How is this word related to "media" — for instance television and newspapers?

Discussing Meaning

1. What would be some of the consequences of English-only laws for those who do not speak English? How would the law affect government officials?

2. Why does Rivera think that English-only laws are un-American?

3. What, in Rivera's view, is the "English-only" movement trying to create in the United States? What prevents it from succeeding?

Discussing Writing

1. Why does Rivera individually list the services (such as housing, health care, welfare, and education) to which non–English-

speaking people would not have access? How would you respond if she merely said that the "government" should be accessible to all?

2.   Rivera's essay has two main points: that English-only laws harm non–English-speaking citizens and that such laws are useless anyway because American society is so multicultural. What evidence does she provide to support each point? How do the two points work together?

Challenging the Selection

1.   "This country was founded by immigrants and now it is trying desperately to turn its back on them," Rivera writes in paragraph 4. Do you agree? Why or why not? Can you cite any examples of either a welcoming or intolerant attitude toward immigrants in America today?

2.   If English-only laws were passed, people would not be able to participate in elections, Rivera argues, because they would not be able to understand the forms for voters. But consider all the other elements of an election: candidates' speeches, television commercials, newspaper endorsements. Can a citizen vote responsibly without understanding those things too? How could this problem be resolved?

In-Class Writing Activities

1.   Imagine that there is a bill being debated now in your state that would make English the official language. Choose one point from Rivera's essay with which you strongly agree or disagree and use it as the basis of a short letter to your state representative. Urge him or her to vote yes or no on the bill, depending on your position.

2.   Do English-only laws force immigrants to "abandon their native language," as Rivera suggests (para. 4)? What other possible effects (besides reduced access to government services) do you think English-only laws have on immigrant life? Write several paragraphs addressing this issue.

Discussing the Unit

Suggested Topic for Discussion

How important is language to a sense of national identity? Some countries hold together without a common tongue: For example, Switzerland is divided between French and German speakers, and people in China speak many different dialects, including Cantonese and Mandarin. What about the United States? Does a person need to speak English to be truly American?

Preparing for Class Discussion

1. Gonzales argues that bilingualism holds immigrants back; Rivera says that English-only laws harm immigrants; and Lee points out that anyone being excluded by language suffers as a result. Who's right? How can the United States respect both the value of minority cultures and the need for a common way of understanding one another?

2. An old joke goes, "What do you call someone who speaks two languages? Bilingual. What do you call someone who speaks one language? American." Do you think Americans should study foreign languages more in school? Why is learning a language valuable? If you had been given a choice between, say, wood shop and Portuguese when you were in high school, which would you have chosen? Why?

From Discussion to Writing

1. The essays by Gonzales and Lee originally appeared as op-eds, newspaper pieces written in response to a topical issue (the name refers to the material's usual position *op*posite the paper's *edit*orial page). Yet much of the impact of these essays comes from their authors' personal stories rather than their expressed opinions on current events. Following these examples, write a short op-ed piece on a current issue. Try to use your personal experiences or stories to illuminate the issue you are addressing.

2. Write an essay in which you describe some of the different ways you use language. Do you speak one way with your professors and another with your friends? Do you have codes or shorthand that you use with your brothers and sisters that your parents don't understand? Don't forget to include physical gestures, signs, or other unspoken means you use to communicate with others.

Topics for Cross-Cultural Discussion

1. Chang-rae Lee writes that "in Korean" his mother "could be fiery, stern, deeply funny, and ironic; in English, just slightly less so" (see para. 16 of his essay). How are you different in English from the way you are in your native tongue? Are there some things you can express in one language that are impossible to say in the other?

2. How many languages are spoken in your homeland? Are there both "official" languages and local dialects? How does the government there deal with minority cultures and language differences?

12

TV Talk Shows — What's Their Appeal?

Are television talk shows an effective forum for the discussion of important issues, or are they merely a form of entertainment that cynically exploits human pain and misery? This is a question that usually comes up in debates about television talk shows, and it is worth considering as you study the following selections.

In "Freak Parade," Charles Oliver finds television talk shows to be like old-time carnivals with their sideshow freaks, oddities, and sleazy thrills. But not all media critics condemn the talk shows. In "Crowd on the Couch," Elayne Rapping takes a more positive view of the shows: Growing out of 1960s feminism and "consciousness-raising," they permit ideas and feelings that would otherwise remain suppressed to be publicly discussed. Even people who see little value in the shows find them irresistible, as Boston University student Kimberly Smith admits in her brief classification of the features that make a talk show successful. In "How to Produce a Trashy TV Talk Show: The Four Secret Ingredients" (based on the author's steady consumption of popular talk shows during a winter vacation), Smith finds the shows trashy and exploitative — but still she can't stop watching them.

CHARLES OLIVER

Freak Parade

[REASON / April 1995]

Before you Read

Do you enjoy watching television talk shows? If so, what do you like most about them? If not, what features don't you care for?

Words to Learn

vicarious (para. 3): emotions felt by imagining the experiences of others; indirect experience (adj.)

tawdry (para. 3): cheap, showy (adj.)

genre (para. 4): type or class (n.)

exploitative (para. 4): taking advantage of; using for one's own purpose (adj.)

staple (para. 6): a principal commodity (n.)

voyeurism (para. 8): from the French; the act of obtaining sex-ual gratification by secretly watching others (n.)

veritable (para. 10): true, genuine, real (adj.)

sordid (para. 10): morally low; filthy (adj.)

solicit (para. 15): to seek, request, entice (v.)

promiscuity (para. 16): having numerous sexual partners on a casual basis (n.)

jaded (para. 24): dulled by overindulgence (adj.)

Bearded ladies. Siamese twins. Men and women who weigh more than 300 pounds each. Tattooed men. These are just a few of the guests to grace the stages of daytime talk shows in recent months. If those examples remind you of a carnival sideshow, there's a reason.

CHARLES OLIVER (b. 1964) writes on national issues for Investor's Business Daily. *Oliver, who holds a master's degree from George Mason University, currently lives in Los Angeles.*

In the nineteenth century and for the first few decades of this century, carnivals crisscrossed the United States, providing entertainment to people in small towns. Carnivals catered to the dark side of man's need for spectacle by allowing people to escape temporarily from their dull everyday lives into a world that was dark, sleazy, and seemingly dangerous. Of course, the danger wasn't real, and the ultimate lure of the carnival was that you could safely return from its world to your everyday life.

Television and regional amusement parks took their toll on the carnival. Today, the few carnivals in existence are generally sad collections of rickety rides and rigged games. But man's need for dark spectacle hasn't gone away, and a new generation of entrepreneurs has found a way to allow people to experience the vicarious thrill of the dark, the sleazy, and the tawdry — all without leaving the safety of their homes.

The gateways to this dark world are daytime talk shows. Phil Donahue created the mold for this genre, and Oprah Winfrey carried it to perhaps its greatest success. Both their shows are essentially women's magazines on the air, alternating celebrity profiles, services-oriented features, discussion of political issues, and more exploitative episodes. Both mix the tawdry with the serious. Donahue was the man who gave us daytime debates between presidential candidates, and he was also the man who wore a skirt on a show devoted to cross dressing.

However, a new generation of hosts has emerged that trades almost exclusively in the sleaze their audiences demand: Geraldo, Montel, Ricki, Jerry. Their names may not be familiar to you, but they have millions of viewers. "Oprah" alone is watched by seven million households each day. Each has managed to recreate the carnival in a contemporary setting.

One of the main attractions of the old carnivals were the "hoochie coochie" dancers. Men would eagerly wait in line, enticed by the talker's promise that these women would "take it off, roll it up, and throw it right at you." This was the origin of modern striptease. Today, the heirs of Little Egypt[1] are a staple on daytime television. In fact, they are so common that producers really have to try to come up with new angles. Male strippers, female strippers, old strippers, grossly overweight strippers, amateur strippers — these are

---

[1]*Little Egypt:* A once popular carnival dancer.

just a few of the variations that I saw on daytime talk shows in just one four-week period. Of course, these people didn't just talk about their profession; they inevitably demonstrated it. While the television viewer could see the naughty bits only in digitized distortions, the live audiences for these shows were treated to an eyeful.

However, most of the strippers on these shows are attractive young women. Given that the audience for daytime talk is also women, this seems like a strange choice of guests. I can only assume that at least some of the women who watch these shows are intrigued by the profession and wonder what it would be like to be a stripper. By presenting these women strippers — indeed, by actually taking their cameras into clubs for performances — talk shows give those women viewers the chance to live out their fantasies vicariously without risking any of the dangers involved. Based upon the comments offered, female audience members generally seem to sympathize with the strippers who appear on these shows, usually defending them against those brought on to attack the profession.

Of course, at times the subject of stripping is simply an excuse for these shows to engage in emotional voyeurism. A perfect example was an episode of "Jerry Springer" dealing with strippers and family members who disapproved of how they earned their money. Naturally, the strippers couldn't just talk to their parents and siblings; they had to demonstrate their art to them. So while the assembled families and the studio audience watched, the girls stripped naked.

On one side of a split television screen, the home audience saw a lovely young girl strip down to her distorted birthday suit. On the other side, her family, some of them crying, averted their eyes and tried to ignore the hooting and catcalls of the audience.

It was tacky; it was sleazy. It was the perfect daytime moment.   10
Whoever thought of it is a veritable P. T. Barnum[2] of the airwaves. At once, this sordid mess provides the viewer with the voyeuristic thrill of seeing a family conflict that one really shouldn't observe, the vicarious thrill of stripping before an audience, and, ultimately, the confirmation that a dull, "normal" lifestyle is superior to that of the women on the show.

An important part of carnivals was the freak show, an assortment of real and contrived physical oddities: pinheads, fat people, bearded ladies. While the carnival talkers would try to entice people

---

[2]P. T. *Barnum:* Phineas Taylor Barnum (1810–1891), American circus operator and promoter.

into the sideshow tents with come-ons about the scientific oddities inside, the real lure of these attractions wasn't intellectual curiosity. It was terror and pity. The customer could observe these people and think to himself that no matter how bad his life seemed at times, it could be much, much worse.

Daytime talk shows have their own version of the freak show. Indeed, on her now-defunct show, Joan Rivers had actual sideshow freaks. These were politically correct "made" freaks (people who had purposefully altered their bodies), not natural ones. The guest who drew the biggest reaction from the audience was a man who lifted heavy weights attached to earrings that pierced various parts of his body. (I've actually seen this guy perform, and I can say that the audience didn't see his most impressive piece of lifting. But there was no way that it could have been shown on television, at least not without some serious digitizing of the screen.)

More often, talk shows will feature people with physical conditions similar to those who were attractions in sideshows. I've seen various shows do episodes on women with facial hair, and the lives of the very large are always a popular topic. One episode of "Jerry Springer" featured greeting card models who weigh more than 300 pounds. In typical fashion these women were not dressed as they presumably would be in everyday life, but in revealing lingerie. So much the better for gawking, I guess.

Is the public's appetite for talk-show sleaze unlimited? Probably not.

Again, the host will set up one of these shows with some remarks about understanding these people, and to their credit, many of the guests on these programs do try to maintain their dignity. The greeting card models seemed a happy, boisterous lot of people. But more often guests are asked to tell tales of discrimination and broken hearts. It's easy to conclude that they were invited on the show so that the audience could feel sorry for them and feel superior to them.

And speaking of feeling superior, how could anyone help but laugh at and feel better than the endless parade of squabbling friends and relatives who pass through these shows? Judging from the looks of guests on some of these shows, you'd think that the producers comb every trailer park and housing project in the nation looking for them. In fact, most are solicited through telephone numbers given during the show: "Are you a white transsexual stripper whose family disapproves of your Latino boyfriend? Call 1-800-IMA FREK."

The guests then are invited on the show, where they battle it out for the amusement of the audience. A typical example was a show

15

hosted by Ricki Lake on the topic of promiscuity. Ricki began by introducing Shannon, a girl who claimed her best friend Keisha sleeps around too much. Amid much whooping from the audience, Shannon detailed her friend's rather colorful sex life: "It ain't like she getting paid."

Then Keisha came out and accused Shannon of being the one who sleeps around too much. They spent an entire segment arguing. After the break Ricki introduces a mutual friend of the two and asked the question everyone in the audience now wanted to know: "Which one is the real slut?" A dramatic pause. The emphatic answer: "Both of them." The audience erupts.

Conflict is a key element on the new breed of talk shows. Physical fights seem to break out on Ricki Lake's show more frequently than at hockey games. These conflicts are not always mere arguments between friends or family members. Often, there are clear-cut good guys whom the audience is supposed to cheer and bad guys whom the audience boos. These episodes resemble the low-brow morality plays of professional wrestling.

Pro wrestling, in fact, had its origins in the carnival. Sometimes the resemblance to pro wrestling is quite pronounced. Daytime talk shows have a fascination with the Ku Klux Klan. It seems a week doesn't go by without one show bringing on members of the Klan to discuss their views on race relations, welfare, abortion, or child rearing. Usually there'll be representatives from some civil rights organization present to offer an opposing view.

The Klansmen look every inch the pro wrestling "heel." They are   20
invariably overweight and have poor skin and a bad haircut. Watching them sitting there in their Klan robes, shouting racial slurs at their opponents as the audience curses them, I always expect these people to pull out a set of brass knuckles and clobber the "babyface" while the host has his back turned.

More often, though, the villains on talk shows are a little more subtle. The audience seems to value family quite a bit because the most common types of villains on these shows are people who pose a threat to the family: child-deserting wives, cheating husbands, and abusive parents.

One typical show was an episode of "Jenny Jones" where women who date only married men faced off with women whose husbands had left them for other women. The women who dated married men certainly made no attempt to win the audience over. They came in dressed in short skirts or low-cut dresses. They preened; they strutted; they insulted the other guests and the audience members; they bragged about their sexual prowess. "Nature Boy" Buddy Rogers[3] himself could not have worked the crowd better.

Why do such people even show up for these shows? It can't be for the money, since guests receive no more than a plane ticket and a night in a nice hotel. After watching countless shows, I've come to the conclusion that these people really think there is nothing wrong with what they do, and they usually seem quite surprised that the audience isn't on their side.

Is the public's appetite for this sleaze unlimited? Probably not. After all, the carnival came around but once a year. With close to two dozen daytime talk shows competing for viewers, people are bound to grow jaded. Last year, Oprah Winfrey, who already had one of the less sleazy shows, began a policy of toning down the tawdry elements. Even her sensational admission to using crack cocaine during the 1980s came in the middle of an "inspirational" program on recovering addicts. The show, which was already the top-rated daytime program, saw its ratings climb. But for those with a taste for the dark side of life, there'll always be a Ricki Lake or a Gordon Elliott.

[3]*Buddy Rogers:* A wrestler known for his preening and strutting.

Discussing Vocabulary / Using a Dictionary

1. The words "vicarious" (para. 3) and "voyeurism" (para. 8) are essential to the author's explanation of why viewers watch talk shows. Explain how both words describe the relationships of the viewers and the guests.

2. Oliver uses the word "tawdry" several times. Find at least five examples of "tawdry" characters in the essay.

3. "Sordid" (para. 10) is a strong word. Use it in several contexts. What Latin word does it derive from?

Discussing Meaning

1. How do old-time carnivals and current talk shows satisfy the "dark side of man's need for spectacle" (para. 2)? What other "spectacles" also satisfy this need?

2. In paragraph 8 Oliver points out that the strippers on the "Jerry Springer" show not only talk to family members about what they did but also "had to demonstrate their art to them." Why is such programming "emotional voyeurism," according to Oliver? Why are current TV producers the new "P. T. Barnum[s] of the airwaves" (para. 10)?

3. How do the talk shows introduce issues related to "family values"? Why do audiences like to see family arguments?

Discussing Writing

1. Why does the author choose the examples of guests he uses in his opening paragraph?

2. Is the author's reading audience the same people who watch television talk shows? What does he assume about his readers?

3. A common writing strategy is *alliteration* — the repetition of the same first letter in successive or nearby words. Note "*d*igitized *d*istortions" in paragraph 6. Can you find other instances of the author's use of alliteration? Why do you think it is used?

Challenging the Selection

1. If, as Oliver claims, people in the audience find a "vicarious thrill" in observing stripteasers (see paragraph 3), then why do they feel "superior" to them? If the audience applauds and admires what strippers do, then why doesn't the audience feel *inferior* instead? How do you explain the feeling of "superiority"?

2. Consider the author's attitude toward talk shows. In what ways does he himself feel "superior"? Do you think he feels superior to the guests? the audiences? the hosts? Give specific examples from the article.

In-Class Writing Activities

1. What talk-show topics attract you? In a few paragraphs describe an issue you would like to discuss on a talk show and how you would like to appear. Would you feel better or worse once the show was over?

2. Do you think classrooms should try to resemble talk shows? Why or why not? Which talk shows would make the best models for class discussion? Which the worst?

ELAYNE RAPPING

Crowd on the Couch

[ON THE ISSUES / Spring 1994]

Before You Read

What do you think of most talk show topics? Are they bizarre or are they relevant to our time?

Words to Learn

bulimic (para. 2): suffering from "bulimia," an eating disorder (adj.)

formidable (para. 6): causing fear; intimidating; discouragingly difficult (adj.)

avidly (para. 7): eagerly; enthusiastically (adv.)

depoliticize (para. 7): to remove from the influence of politics (v.)

visceral (para. 9): instinctive; arising from the inmost self (adj.)

monolithic (para. 9): characterized by total uniformity, rigidity (adj.)

tremor (para. 10): a shaking; trembling (n.)

welter (para. 12): a confused mass, a jumble (n.)

inculcate (para. 15): to implant in the mind by repetition (v.)

commiserate (para. 16): to feel compassion for (v.)

transfix (para. 17): to hold motionless with amazement (v.)

tangentially (para. 17): incidentally (adv.)

bilk (para. 17): cheat, defraud (v.)

cathartic (para. 18): referring to an emotional release (adj.)

adamantly (para. 19): unyieldingly; inflexibly (adv.)

eradicate (para. 19): to completely eliminate (v.)

Media critic and analyst ELAYNE RAPPING *(b. 1938) is professor of communications at Adelphi University. She writes regular columns on culture, feminism, and the media for the* Progressive *and* On the Issues *magazines, and she has also contributed to such publications as* The Nation, Newsday, *and the* Village Voice. *Rapping's books on the media include* The Looking Glass World of Nonfiction TV *(1987),* Media-tions: Forays into the Culture and Gender Wars *(1994), and* The Culture of Recovery: Making Sense of the Self-Help Movement in Women's Lives *(1995).*

"Today on "Donahue": Lesbian mothers and their straight children!"

"Oprah talks to bulimic incest survivors!"

"On "Geraldo": Husbands who got penile implants to save their marriages!"

"Today — Sally Jessy Raphael talks to prostitutes who formed a union!"

These are a few of my recent daytime talk show favorites. Yes, I   5
admit it, I am apt to spend my late afternoon writing break watching Oprah, or Sally, or even Geraldo — one of the many millions of "enquiring minds" with at least a bit of curiosity about these topics and others even more bizarre.

Nor am I particularly embarrassed about this fact, although I know I'm supposed to be. The truth is, I am interested in every one of the subjects just named. I take them all quite seriously, actually, and have ever since — some twenty-five years ago — I attended my first consciousness-raising group and had my mind — and then my life — blown by the radical ideas and attitudes that burst out of the Pandora's Box labelled "The personal is political."[1] Most every talk-show topic grows out of the analysis and critique of patriarchal family and gender relations "we" sent hurling into public life back then, and the shattering impact this critique has had on everyone's "domestic tranquility" ever since.

> *It's a relief to hear real troubles, real feelings, real rage, controversy, and judgment about the most vexing sex, gender, and race issues of our days.*

And the problems posed are so formidable for those desperate to be heard and helped that they willingly reveal them to the entire nation.

While it's all too easy (and in many ways justified) to hold one's nose and distance oneself from the sensational, exploitative style and tone of these daytime gabfests *cum*[2] public spectacles, I think as feminists we would do better to look a bit more closely at why these shows are so incredibly popular. Why do so many millions watch them so avidly? Why do so many others call the shows' hotlines (thousands of calls a day, just to Geraldo!) with urgent, desperate requests to come on and talk publicly about their problems? The answer, I believe, reveals a lot about the enormous impact of feminist

---

[1]*"The personal is political"*: A motto of the 1960s–1970s counterculture.
[2]*cum*: Together with (Latin).

ideas on public debate and personal experience in the last two decades. And — less hopefully — reveals the enormous power of mass media to absorb, transform, and subtly depoliticize some of that impact.

Way back in the fifties, remember, when television first arrived in our living rooms spouting endless messages about how we should live and what we should buy, there was an easy consensus about sex, romance, and family life on the small screen. One fatherly white male after another — from Walter Cronkite to Ward Cleaver to Ronald Reagan (then hawking avocado-green appliances for General Electric) — told us that premarital sex was forbidden; that marriage, monogamy, and motherhood were women's universal calling; and that father knew best in the bedroom, boardroom, and everywhere else.

But feminism — in some ways a visceral reaction to that monolithic message from a generation of girls to whom it was virtually force-fed from birth — had other ideas. It's no accident, after all, that the first generation of feminists spent so much time and energy attacking media stereotypes. We were the first generation to have our identities and fates so firmly determined by a bombardment of pop culture images. We knew the power of these phony, repressive messages and we were determined to smash them to kingdom come.

Which is what we've been doing. And the rest, as they say, is history. Never again — ask Clarence Thomas, Bob Packwood, Dan Quayle — will traditional male assumptions about sex and gender relations go unchallenged. We haven't, obviously, done away with sexism. But we have wiped a bit of the smug sneer off its face and put a nervous tremor in its authoritative pale male voice.

Not that the questions, challenges, and changes wrought by feminists have been an unmixed blessing — to us or anyone else. Revolutions, after all, are messy, contradictory, and long in coming. And the feminist revolution in gender assumptions and relations has, in many ways, barely begun. That's why there's so much confusion, pain, and desperation in the lives and minds of so many of us. Everyone knows that the old ways don't work; the old answers don't fit. But no one, not even we self-identified feminists, knows exactly what to do about it.

How *does* one handle a parent's or child's coming out, after all? What does a fifty-year-old man do about his wife's sudden impatience with his sexual performance and aggressive demand for "improvement"? What happens when, in the welter of discussion about eating disorders and sexual abuse, a woman suddenly begins to realize that her "weight" problem began decades earlier when her father was molesting her?

Because of feminism, all these issues have been placed on the table, publicly acknowledged as important and discussed as problems to be solved rather than shameful secrets or freakish disabilities. And if people everywhere (especially those with little access to more upscale, expensive forms of support) are turning to the simulated support groups and town meetings we call "talk shows" to get some clue as to how others are thinking about and dealing with these matters, it may be depressing, but it shouldn't be surprising.

In fact — and this is both the good and the bad news — the form and substance of daytime talk shows derive directly from that great political invention of the 1960s: consciousness-raising. In those amazing years, women sat in circles and "spoke bitterness," revealing shameful but liberating truths about our families, our boyfriends, our husbands, our teachers, our bosses. And as we built of our collective, common experiences a theory of personal politics and a strategy for social change, we permanently changed our own lives and those of women everywhere.

When you tune into Oprah or Sally Jessy, you see — in an admit- 15
tedly sensationalized and degraded form — a mediated, depoliticized version of this process. While Ted Koppel holds court in all his masculinist glory, asking his questions, legitimizing the answers he decides are "fit" to be heard, he dictates to us all — on behalf of ABC and IBM — what issues really matter and what people deserve to be heard. But Oprah and Donahue and their clones have developed their own, far more "democratic" form and style. They move freely around their semi-circular sets, allowing a far more open give and take among participants. They also allow people who are never seen or heard (except as objects of "study") on television to appear and even speak for themselves. If we cringe at the stretch denim and polyester, the big hair and bad grammar, we should perhaps consider our own class and appearance biases, as inculcated by the media themselves.

Nor are the "weird" problems presented necessarily so different from the ones we ourselves commiserate over with our most trusted friends. Unconventional, embarrassing, and even demeaning sex, gender and family problems are the staples of much of the conversation we all engage in or overhear in our favorite cafés. Feminism gave us permission to reveal our traumas to a safe group of "sisters." But everyone has the same kinds of worries and weirdness in their lives, even Ron and Nancy Reagan. Their daughter has brought that shameful truth home to America, after all, through the public forum of daytime talk — and I for one am tickled to hear about it. It does so much to discredit the phony "family values" propaganda.

And so, understandably, people from Omaha to Orlando sit at home and watch, and call in and discuss the latest Oprah episode about child abuse, or homosexuality in the priesthood, or married women who have lesbian lovers. And — while they may publicly express scorn and contempt for the shows and their guests — they very often find themselves transfixed by the discussion of a problem which they can at least tangentially relate to. Perhaps the flamboyance and extremity of these cases are bizarre, but something hits home. Women bilked by bigamists, for example, are not so different from the rest of us who have, sometimes, been lied to, exploited, and betrayed by a smooth, manipulative guy.

There is something cathartic about these shows. It's a relief to hear real troubles, real feelings, real rage, controversy, and judgment about the most vexing sex, gender, and race issues of our days. It's a relief — as it was for us in consciousness-raising groups — to see the nods of recognition and hear the words of support from those who have been there, who are there now, who can offer a bit of enlightenment about why they feel so bad about their lives and what might work to change them a bit.

But if talk shows take their substance and form, in large part, from feminism, they certainly find their conclusions, their *raisons d'être*,[3] elsewhere. At each program's end, of course, we are given a set of "solutions" which differ radically from the ones we so adamantly proposed in the 1960s. Back then, we were saying that our gender and family injustices and traumas would never be eradicated until the man-made and -run institutions that created them were radically changed through organized political activism.

You won't hear anything like that from Oprah or Phil. You'll   20
hear "experts" sending those in pain to therapists and support groups, or to self-help shelves. You'll hear sponsors sending viewers to the drugstore for Excedrin, diet Pepsi, or maybe a weekend at Disney World.

---

[3]*raisons d'être:* Reasons for being (French).

And therein lies a tale about social movements and their tricky relationships with the media. That the talk shows exist at all, much less command such enormous and loyal audiences, is a tribute to the power of feminism and a sign of its vulnerability. The issues we have raised aren't going away. The life of Ward and June Cleaver, or Claire and Heathcliff Huxtable for that matter, will never again seem possible.

But if TV can't hide that truth, it can certainly do its best to obscure and confuse its political implications. And as long as NBC and Procter & Gamble continue to produce and fund our mediated public sphere, it most certainly will.

Discussing Vocabulary / Using a Dictionary

1. What is a "visceral" (para. 9) reaction to something? What is the origin of the word and why is it appropriate?

2. What is the literal meaning of "monolithic" (para. 9)? What would it normally refer to? How is it used in the context of this selection?

3. List a few synonyms for "inculcate" (para. 15). Do they capture all the subtleties of the word?

4. What is a "catharsis" (para. 18)? What Greek word is it derived from?

5. What do we mean when we say someone is "adamant" (para. 19)? What is the word's original meaning?

Discussing Meaning

1. According to Rapping, in what ways do current television talk shows grow out of the feminist movement of the 1960s and early 1970s?

2. In what ways do the talk shows differ from feminist meetings? What causes these differences? How are the mass media responsible?

3. What biases might the author's readers have against the people on talk shows?

4. What makes the talk shows "democratic" (see para. 15)? What sorts of programs are not "democratic"? Why aren't they?

Discussing Writing

1. Rapping makes her audience clearly known. What kind of people is she addressing in the essay?

2. Consider the opening paragraphs. What are the show topics meant to suggest? Why has Rapping chosen these particular topics? What attitude toward them does she suggest her readers might have? How does she try to surprise her readers?

3. Rapping analyzes several social movements of the last forty years, such as feminism and "consciousness-raising," and the evolution of television and talk shows. In what ways is this broad analysis effective? Does Rapping cover all the concerns she raises effectively, or does she take on too much in one essay?

Challenging the Selection

1. The author admits that the talk shows are a "sensationalized and degraded form" of feminist consciousness-raising sessions (see para. 15). If this is truly the case, why does she enjoy and promote them?

2. The author ends her essay by criticizing the commercial aspects of talk shows. This, of course, is what allows them to reach such large audiences. Is she herself being biased or elitist in her criticism?

In-Class Writing Activities

1. In a brief essay suggest a few of the ways in which feminism has influenced your discussion of issues or interpretation of culture.

2. The author believes that talk shows are an outgrowth of the feminist movement. Can you think of other examples from current media — movies, music, or other television shows — that have also been influenced by feminism? Discuss one of these examples in a few paragraphs.

KIMBERLY SMITH

How to Produce a Trashy TV Talk Show: The Four Secret Ingredients

[THE DAILY FREE PRESS, BOSTON UNIVERSITY / January 23, 1996]

Before You Read

People often say they are "addicted" to certain types of television shows. What do you think people find so fascinating about talk shows?

Words to Learn

succumb (para. 1): to yield to; to be overcome by (v.)
unison (para. 5): sounding together; behaving in the same way (adv.)

During winter break this year, I found myself (as I do every year) suffering from way too much time on my hands and way too little to do with myself. While I had planned on a month of rest and relaxation, a time to see all my old friends and accomplish all the projects I had been putting off for the past three months, I soon succumbed to boredom after the first week of my exciting vacation. So, for the long remainder of break, I did what most of you probably did on your vacation: I spent my days sleeping late, moping around the house, complaining to my parents about how bored I was, talking on the telephone to my BU friends, and, of course, watching the tube. This last activity is what I found myself most frequently engrossed in.

It never fails to amaze me what a variety of programming is on television these days, especially after spending three months watch-

KIMBERLY SMITH *(b. 1973) wrote this essay as a senior at Boston University, where she received a bachelor's degree in communications in 1996.*

ing the five channels that I receive at school (two networks, two home shopping stations, and the Spanish channel). From twenty-four-hour up-to-date weather coverage and programs about how to correctly groom your pet to moral chats with Mother Angelics, there are shows geared toward every type of person these days. But despite this vast variety of quality television programming I had to choose from, I found myself most frequently tuned to possibly the trashiest genre of television ever invented: the talk show. What's worse is that since I've been back at school I've continued to be a victim of television talk. It's not that I even really approve of these shows. Personally, I think they thrive on exploiting personal problems for profit and are, quite frankly, an insult to human intelligence. I mean, what does it really say about the people of our nation when hundreds of thousands of Americans tune in to see a program about transvestite makeovers or a couple whose pets come between their relationship?

But who am I to talk? For I, like hundreds of other people (and I'm sure many of you), cannot resist tuning into these shows and others like them. It's not something I'm proud of, but I won't deny it either. At least I don't go so far as to set my VCR each day to record Sally Jessy, but if it's on, the topic looks interesting, and I have nothing better to do, then I'm going to watch. So now that I've admitted my fault (my one and only fault), I would like to share the wisdom that I've gained from

I found myself most frequently tuned to possibly the trashiest genre of television ever invented: the talk show.

watching these shows with all those people out there who have managed to resist the talk-show temptation. I give you the formula for the perfect talk show:

The first ingredient needed to make a talk show successful is a host who will be adored by his or her fans. There is no special look required of these people, for in the talk-show business, anything goes as far as appearance — fat hosts, bald hosts, old hosts, short hosts, and hosts with trendy red glasses all do equally well. And as far as personality, anything goes as well. An overly-excited-to-the-point-of-being-annoying female host who drools over her male guests is as popular as her sensitive male rival who sends everyone to therapy for free. But in my opinion, there is only one thing required to make a talk show host a success: He or she must be a washed-up celebrity who can find nothing better for work. Take Tempestt Bledsoe, Maury Povich, Ricki Lake, Vicki Lawrence, Carnie Wilson, and Mark Wahlberg, for example.

The second factor that goes into creating a great talk show is the right audience. These people must be energetic, enthusiastic, and must worship their host practically to the point of kissing his or her feet. They must also be willing to chant out the host's name in unison at a moment's notice. Most important, audience members must not be afraid to ask the guests questions, as well as express their feelings, beliefs, and expert opinions about the topic at hand. It does not matter if they give their opinion of guest number one while the host is in the middle of interviewing guest number five, or even if their opinion doesn't appear to be relevant at all. The fact that they are able to express themselves and cause everyone in the audience to clap and cheer is good enough.

Another element that contributes to the talk-show formula are the guests: The more odd the guests, the better the ratings. People with thousands of tattoos or other self-inflicted defacements of their bodies, people with strange sexual habits, and people who have had out-of-body experiences seem to be some of the favorites. Guests who do not meet any of these criteria must at least possess a horrible rage for another guest and be willing to verbally — or physically — express this rage on the air.

The final secret needed to make a successful talk show is an interesting topic. Again, in this category, pretty much anything and everything goes. And while there is a wealth of creativity as far as show topics go, there are a few tried-but-true ones that work every time. These topics are: surprise engagement proposals; "surprise, I've had a crush on you since second grade"; "my mother-in-law is ruining my marriage"; and "I wish my husband/wife would. . . ." (Anything can be used to fill in this category. Some of my personal favorites are "stop flirting with the opposite sex," "lose 150 pounds," and "get rid of his/her body hair").

Well, there you have it: the secret formula for talk-show success, the knowledge that I gained during my productive winter vacation. For those of you who do not tune into this type of television, I hope that I've given you some valuable insight into the talk-show industry. And for those of you who do watch, I hope that you will now admit to your television-trash addiction. Just remember that wherever you are, whatever time of day, there will always be a talk show to tune in to.

Discussing Vocabulary / Using a Dictionary

1. How does Smith use the verb "succumbed" (para. 1)? What are some other contexts in which you might use this word?

2. Smith uses the word "unison" (para. 5) in its literal sense. Why? How else might the word be used?

Discussing Meaning

1. Why did Smith begin watching talk shows? Why does she continue to watch them?

2. What does Smith mean when she says, in paragraph 2, that she's a "victim of television talk"?

3. Which topics does Smith find especially interesting and why?

Discussing Writing

1. When Smith mentions her "exciting" vacation in the first paragraph and her "productive" winter vacation in the last, how is she using those words?

2. Classification, or sorting information by category, is an effective way to structure an essay. Do you agree with Smith's four categories, or would you add others? Find examples of shows that fit your different categories.

3. Is Smith addressing readers who are familiar or unfamiliar with talk shows?

Challenging the Selection

1. Does Smith really provide her readers with a "secret formula"? Would such factors as a popular host, "an interesting topic," and the "right audience" be "secrets" to producers of talk shows?

2. If Smith finds talk shows to be "trashy" and "an insult to human intelligence" (para. 2), why does she watch them with interest? How does she explain her fascination?

In-Class Writing Activities

1. Analyze another popular type of television show — such as a sitcom or cartoon — and make a brief list of its "secret ingredients."

2. Smith can't resist talk shows even though she puts them down as trash. In a few paragraphs describe a form of entertainment you can't resist even though you don't like to admit it. Why can something that is "trashy" and "insulting" be addictive?

3. Smith's tone toward her subject seems sarcastic at times. Has contemporary society — and television specifically — conditioned us to be sarcastic and somewhat cynical? Write an essay in which you take a position on this question. Draw on your own experience and, if you'd like, examples of particular television shows.

Discussing the Unit

Suggested Topic for Discussion

Why do you think talk shows are so popular? At what audience are these shows aimed, and how do the topics reflect audience interests? Do you consider the shows to be fun or serious? Do you think they exploit human problems or help to solve them?

Preparing for Class Discussion

1. For one of the authors, talk shows resemble sleazy, old-time carnivals, yet for another, they instead resemble "support groups and town meetings." Consider how these different comparisons reflect different attitudes toward the shows. Try coming up with a comparison of your own.

2. Although they both express serious reservations about talk shows, Elayne Rapping and Kimberly Smith admit they watch them eagerly. How do you explain this? What attracts viewers to talk shows despite serious misgivings? Do you think most people watch them with reservations?

3. What do you think attracts guests to these shows? What would encourage people to air private matters in public, especially if they're not paid to do so?

From Discussion to Writing

1. Choose a daytime talk show episode that you found especially compelling (you may have to watch a number of these programs before you find a topic that you like). Take detailed notes about the topic, the guests, the call-in and studio-audience questions, the general direction of the discussion, and the host's responses. Taking Rapping's analysis into account, what deeper political or social issues does the episode you've chosen raise?

2. Write an essay discussing whether television is a positive addition to modern life. Pick one side of the argument, and be sure to use specific examples to support your theory. You might quote briefly from the selections in this unit to support your points.

Topics for Cross-Cultural Discussion

1. What do you think television talk shows say about America? Do you think they paint an accurate or a distorted picture of the American people?

2. How do people from your native country get news? How is the news presented? How do people from your country respond to the type of openness seen on talk shows?

13

Do the Media Promote Violence?

Does violence on television and in films and music increase the potential for real-life violence? If so, should the government place more restrictions on the media, or should individuals — particularly parents — just turn off shows and songs they find offensive or harmful? Educators, public officials, and parents have been debating these questions since the early 1950s when television began to reach mass audiences. More than forty years — and some 350 scholarly articles — later, the debate continues, as the three essays in this chapter show.

In "Forrest Gump versus Ice-T" editor and commentator Mortimer B. Zuckerman acknowledges the escalation of violence and graphic sex in the media but cautions against government restrictions, which, he contends, endanger the free exchange of ideas in the media. Next, pop culture writer John Hamerlinck looks at the roots of the "murder ballad," a musical genre that remains popular to this day. The very persistence of this genre, he claims, reflects the acceptance of violence — particularly against women — in our culture. In "Turn Off the TV before It Ruins Us," *Boston Globe* political columnist David Nyhan has some harsh words to say about America's favorite pastime — watching the tube. Student Rima Vesely concludes the chapter by warning of the damaging effects of media violence on children.

MORTIMER B. ZUCKERMAN

Forrest Gump versus Ice-T

[U.S. NEWS & WORLD REPORT / July 24, 1995]

Before You Read

Should the government restrict violent or sexually explicit material in the media? What are the advantages of such restrictions? What are possible disadvantages?

Words to Learn

prurient (para. 1): appealing to an obsessive interest in sex (adj.)

sociopath (para. 1): one who acts without regard to, or against, the rules of society (n.)

caricature (para. 4): to exaggerate for special effect (v.)

deterioration (para. 5): decline or breakdown (n.)

noxious (para. 6): harmful (adj.)

anarchy (para. 6): a lack of central control or authority (n.)

The cultural silent majority in America is up in arms over the rising levels of violence and prurient images that have seeped into popular entertainment. Gangsta rap is the lightning rod. Popular music for the young has always been in some conflict with middle-class attitudes: When you were a teenager did fifty-year-old people ever like the same music you did? But that consoling thought does not last long when you listen to the extreme preoccupation with sex and violence of an Ice-T or the Geto Boys. It seems the sociopaths are taking over music beamed at our most vulnerable group — the children.

MORTIMER B. ZUCKERMAN *(b. 1937) is editor in chief of* U.S. News & World Report, *chairman of* The Atlantic Monthly, *and chairman and co-publisher of the* New York Daily News. *He is a former associate professor of city planning at the Harvard Graduate School of Design and a former lecturer on city and regional planning at Yale University.*

Hollywood, the country's TV and film factory, is another focal point of public concern. It has long been the mirror of our culture and the creator of many of our national myths and heroes. Once filmmakers used to evoke sexual longings through eye contact or a touch of the elbow. Today they resort to startlingly graphic ways of presenting sex and violence. A recent poll indicates that sexual moderation and fidelity are the norm, both for married people and for those who live together. But on so-called dramatic television, seven out of eight sexual encounters involve extramarital sex.

This might not be quite so bothersome if the kids weren't listening and watching. But they are: Children spend more time watching television than they do attending school. According to the American Psychological Association, a typical child sees eight thousand murders and one hundred thousand acts of violence on TV before graduating from elementary school. Working parents plainly worry about their inability to monitor their youngster's viewing habits — and most would welcome President Clinton's proposal to mandate a V-chip (V for violence) that can be inserted into TV sets to program out certain shows and channels.

The jury is still out on how all that TV violence affects kids in the real world.

For all the concern, we need to keep our cool. The jury is still out on how all that TV violence affects kids in the real world. And many of the four hundred or so films that Hollywood produces every year actually convey traditional virtues and mainstream verities — love, loyalty, honor, duty, and compassion. Just consider *Forrest Gump, Little Women, Black Beauty, The Lion King,* and *The Flintstones.* Even the heavily criticized *Natural Born Killers* was intended to caricature the intersection of violence and media attention in our culture. Hollywood, which has had many movies that have exposed prejudice, racism, and other social problems, also maintains a rating system that informs parents which movies are unsuitable for children.

In the democracy of the marketplace, where individuals make   5
decisions about what they will buy, read, or see, some choices will veer toward the vulgar, the profane, and the excessive. Americans have some sense of this. They may be irritated, or outraged, by pop culture, but the polls tell us they understand that the principal causes of violence and other national problems lie elsewhere than in the entertainment industry. They are all too aware that children are

more affected by the general decline of public morality, the lack of religion, the deterioration of public schools, family breakdown, and poor parenting. They could also point to a culture that emphasizes the individual over the group and that elevates self-expression to a religion. Typical is the Nike ad in which Andre Agassi and Wimbledon champ Pete Sampras stop traffic to play tennis in the middle of a busy street, then hit tennis balls at a bus that follows its route through the made-up tennis court. The tag line is "Just Do It!" Translation: Pursue your own fun despite the rules and the inconvenience to others.

The price we pay for our cultural freedom is that a few noxious weeds may thrive amid the thousand flowers that bloom. Better the rough anarchy of the free market than government, directly or indirectly, telling us what we can hear and watch. We can and should fight bad speech with good speech. We can and should encourage corporate executives to think twice before putting trash on the marketplace. We can and should support those institutions that offset some of the ills of the marketplace — public television and public radio. Our culture would be infinitely poorer without them. And we should beware of politicians who would cripple or destroy these institutions while they exploit popular discomfort with mass entertainment. They must not be allowed to divert attention from the real issues facing America.

Discussing Vocabulary / Using a Dictionary

1. Consider some song lyrics you have recently heard or some movie scenes you have recently viewed. Which lyrics or scenes would you classify as "prurient" (para. 1)?

2. What does the prefix "socio-" tell you about the meaning of the word "sociopath" (para. 1)? What other words share this prefix?

3. Zuckerman accepts a few "noxious" (para. 6) weeds that thrive amid thousands of flowers. What other types of things can be "noxious"? Can this word be used to describe ideas as well as objects?

4. How is the word "anarchy" (para. 6) related in meaning to words such as "monarchy" and "hierarchy"?

Discussing Meaning

1. Although Zuckerman acknowledges that the media are more graphically sexual and violent than ever before, he also maintains that the media — Hollywood, in particular — have had positive effects on viewers. What, according to Zuckerman, are some of these positive effects?

2. Zuckerman asserts that the media aren't the real cause of violence in America. What does he say are the real causes?

3. What does Zuckerman prefer over government regulations of the media, and why?

Discussing Writing

1. Do you think the title of Zuckerman's essay accurately reflects its content? Why or why not? Why might such a title have been chosen for his essay?

2. In several places (in paragraphs 2–5, for example) Zuckerman uses statistics and specific examples to support his arguments. How effective is this support? What other types of statistics and examples might have made his argument even more effective?

3. In the first half of his essay (including the catchy title), Zuckerman sets up the problem of media violence. Then, in the second half, he argues for the "democracy of the marketplace" (para. 5). Does he establish a strong enough bridge between these two halves? Did the first part of Zuckerman's essay prepare you for his conclusion, or did you expect the essay to lead in some other direction?

Challenging the Selection

1. Do you think the movie rating system that Zuckerman refers to in paragraph 4 is effective in preventing children's exposure to violent or sexually graphic films? Can Hollywood police itself?

2. In paragraph 5 Zuckerman uses the example of a Nike ad to support his belief that our culture has elevated self-expression to a "religion"; however, he adamantly supports cultural freedom over government restrictions. Do you see a contradiction in these two views, or can they coexist logically?

3. Zuckerman says in his conclusion that politicians who would restrict sex and violence in the media "must not be allowed to divert attention from the real issues facing America." Do you believe that sex and violence in the media aren't "real issues"? Why or why not?

In-Class Writing Activities

1. Write a brief letter to Zuckerman in which you agree or disagree with his position that individuals, not government, should be responsible for restricting violence in the media. Make sure to give specific reasons for your position.

2. Zuckerman describes ways in which American citizens can "fight bad speech with good speech" (para. 6). Which of these steps could you see yourself pursuing? Can you suggest any other steps that individuals could take to combat media violence?

3. Based on the TV programs, movies, and songs you're familiar with, which would you classify as "noxious weeds" (para. 6) because of their potentially negative effects? Which would you classify as "flowers"? Make a brief list under each category and compare your lists with those of your classmates.

JOHN HAMERLINCK

Killing Women: A Pop-Music Tradition

[THE HUMANIST / July – August 1995]

Before You Read

Can you think of a few popular songs that glorify or actually encourage violence? Do you think that popular music is more violent than it used to be? Why or why not?

Words to Learn

innocuous (para. 1): harmless (adj.)
genre (para. 1): type or class (n.)
misogyny (para. 2): hatred of women (n.)
premeditation (para. 2): planning something in advance (n.)
belie (para. 3): to misrepresent (v.)
homicidal (para. 3): relating to murder; murderous (adj.)
perseverance (para. 8): persistence (n.)

appall (para. 8): to dismay or shock (v.)
perpetrator (para. 8): one who is guilty of something, such as a crime (n.)
ubiquitously (para. 8): universally; occurring everywhere at the same time (adv.)

If there has been anything positive about the flood of media coverage of the O. J. Simpson trial, it has been an increased public awareness of the disturbing incidence of violence against women in our society. According to the Family Violence Prevention Fund, an act of violence occurs every nine seconds in the United States. Even though the mainstream press seems to have only recently recognized this horrible reality, the signs of our tolerance toward domestic violence have long had a prominent profile in popular culture. This tragic phenome-

---

JOHN HAMERLINCK is a freelance writer in St. Cloud, Minnesota, who specializes in the sociopolitical aspects of popular culture.

non has often been reflected in novels and on film, but perhaps the most common occurrence of depictions of violence against women comes in popular music. Indeed, the often innocuous world of pop music has cultivated its own genre of woman-killing songs.

Violent misogyny in popular song did not begin with recent controversial offerings from acts like Guns 'N' Roses and 2 Live Crew. There's an old, largely southern, folk genre known as the "murder ballad." And as long as men have sung the blues, they have told stories of killing the women who have "done them wrong." In a common scenario, a man catches "his" woman with another man and kills them both in a jealous rage. In the 1920s, Lonnie Johnson sang a song called "Careless Love," in which he promises to shoot his lover numerous times and then stand over her until she is finished dying. In "Little Boy Blue," Robert Lockwood threatens to whip and stab his lover; while Robert Nighthawk's "Murderin' Blues" suggests a deliberate value judgment in the premeditation: The song says that prison chains are better than having a woman cheat and lie to you.

> *As long as men have sung the blues, they have told stories of killing the women who have "done them wrong."*

In many of the songs in this genre, the music belies the homicidal lyrics. A song like Little Walter's "Boom, Boom, Out Go the Lights" (later turned into an arena-rock anthem by Pat Travers) features a smooth, catchy, danceable blues riff. Little Walter caresses the song's famous hook so softly that one gets the feeling that perhaps his bark is worse than his bite. There is, however, no doubt that retribution for emotional pain is going to come in the form of physical violence.

This theme is not limited to blues artists. The Beatles provide harsh and frightening imagery in "Run for Your Life," a song which features premeditation along the traditional blues lines. It also incorporates stalking and threats sung directly to the target. The stalking transcends the mind-game variety we find in a song like the Police's "Every Breath You Take"; "Run for Your Life" is pure terror. Charles Manson[1] aside, this Beatles offering is considerably more frightening than "Helter Skelter."

---

[1]*Charles Manson* (b. 1934): Leader of a "family" of drifters who was convicted of murder in the 1969 deaths of actress Sharon Tate and six others in California. "Helter Skelter," the name of a Beatles song, became the title of a book and movie about the Manson murders.

Another song in this vein is "Hey Joe," which was a minor hit   5
for a band called the Leaves in the 1960s and was later covered[2] by
numerous artists, including an electrifying version by Jimi Hendrix.
Thanks to Hendrix, the song became a garage-band staple in the sixties and seventies: Many a young vocalist cut his rock-and-roll teeth
singing that musical question: "Hey, Joe / Where you goin' with that
gun in your hand?" (The same bands probably also played Neil
Young's contribution to the genre, "Down by the River.")

The woman-killing genre has also been embraced by the MTV
generation. One of the video age's most recent additions to the catalog of murder songs comes from the "man in black," Johnny Cash,
who is only one of many country artists to record such songs. Cash
recently released a single called "Delia's Gone" from his latest album,
American Recordings. The stark and eerie video, which features Cash
digging a grave for his victim, even made its way into an episode of
MTV's "Beavis and Butt-Head."

Occasionally the genre attempts to even the odds by arming the
victim: For example, in Robert Johnson's "32-20 Blues," the heart-
broken man gets his revenge despite the fact that the victim had a
".38 Special." And sometimes the gender tables are turned: For example, Nancy Sinatra covered "Run for Your Life" shortly after the
Beatles recorded it, changing the prey from "little girl" to "little
boy." In real life, however, the victims are overwhelmingly women,
and their primary form of defense usually consists of a mere piece of
paper called a restraining order.

It should quickly be pointed out, however, that these songs do
not *cause* violence. Their singers are not wicked, evil people. The perseverance of this genre, however, certainly reflects a disturbingly casual level of acceptance in society when it comes to so-called "crimes
of passion." When we hear tales of real domestic abuse, we are ap-
palled. Often, however, we rationalize the perpetrator's actions and
say that we can understand how he could be driven to commit such a
crime. Shoulders shrug and someone ubiquitously adds, "Well, we
live in a violent society." Just as metal detectors and X-rays have become an unquestioned, accepted part of the airport landscape, our
culture comfortably places violence and terror in pop music's love-
song universe.

"I-loved-her-so-much-I-had-to-kill-her" songs are not about love;
they are about power and control. But if the beat is good and the

---

[2]*covered:* To "cover" a song is to record a new version of it.

chorus has a catchy hook, we don't need to concern ourselves with things like meaning, right? We can simply dance on and ignore the violence around us.

Discussing Vocabulary / Using a Dictionary

1. Why do you suppose that Hamerlinck uses the word "innocuous" (para. 1) to describe pop music? What are a couple of synonyms for this word?

2. "Misogyny" (para. 2) contains the root "gyn," which is based on the Greek word for "women." What other words share this root?

3. From what Latin word does "appall" (para. 8) derive? How does the current use of "appall" relate to this origin?

4. List a few comments, other than the one Hamerlinck refers to in paragraph 8, that are "ubiquitous."

Discussing Meaning

1. What is a "murder ballad" (para. 2)? Which songs — past and contemporary — fit this description?

2. What, according to the author, does the persistence of the "woman-killing genre" of music (para. 6) say about cultural attitudes toward violence against women?

3. In paragraph 8, Hamerlinck refers to "crimes of passion." Why are these more excusable than other types of crimes?

4. According to Hamerlinck, what are "I-loved-her-so-much-I-had-to-kill-her" songs really about?

Discussing Writing

1. We often think of a "tradition" as something positive. What effect or mood does the title create by calling the murder of women a "tradition" in pop music?

2. Hamerlinck uses many examples to support his argument that violence against women is nothing new in pop music. Identify a few phrases or sentences he uses to introduce these examples. How do these transitions bring coherence to his argument?

3. In his final paragraph, Hamerlinck uses *irony* (saying one thing and meaning something quite different) to drive home his point. Write an ironic statement of your own about media violence.

Challenging the Selection

1. Hamerlinck says that misogynist songs "do not *cause* violence" (para. 8). Do you agree? Do you think that such songs have any role in causing — or perpetuating — violence against women? Why or why not?

2. In paragraph 8 Hamerlinck writes, "Just as metal detectors and X-rays have become an unquestioned, accepted part of the airport landscape, our culture comfortably places violence and terror in pop music's love-song universe." Do you agree that all of society is "comfortable" with such violence? Can you think of examples that contradict Hamerlinck's statement?

In-Class Writing Activities

1. What other "traditions" have developed in popular music? Describe two or three of them and explain why you think they are either positive or negative.

2. Think of a song you know fairly well that describes or glorifies violent acts. (You can use one of Hamerlinck's examples if you wish.) Do you think of this song differently now that you have read Hamerlinck's essay? Why or why not?

3. Draw a time line that spans the years of your musical awareness (say, the 1980s and the 1990s) and fill in songs that fit the "murder ballad" description. Then write briefly about any trends you see. (For example, do you notice a persistence in the "woman-killing genre" that Hamerlinck describes, or do you see a trend toward more generalized violence? Do you think pop music has become more or less violent than it used to be?)

DAVID NYHAN

Turn Off the TV before It Ruins Us

[THE BOSTON GLOBE / September 16, 1996]

Before You Read

Write down the names of the television shows you watch regularly. List a few of the ways these shows have affected your thinking or behavior.

Words to Learn

meretricious (para. 10): flashy, showy, vulgar (adj.)

baleful (para. 13): menacing or evil in influence (adj.)

soporific (para. 17): causing sleep or drowsiness (adj.)

corrosive (para. 18): destructively wasting or eating away (adj.)

I'm not a doctor, but I play one when I'm talking about TV.

And the American Medical Association and I agree: Television is bad for kids.

Young people not only would kill to watch TV; they do kill from staring goggle-eyed at the box, a truly infernal machine that delivers two hundred thousand acts of violence to the typical youngster's brain pan before he's old enough to drive.

Every kid in America, on average, witnesses sixteen thousand murders on TV before reaching the ripe old age of eighteen. And you wonder why they throw candy wrappers on the sidewalk or refuse to give an old lady a seat on a crowded bus? Geddoudda here, witch, or I'll blow you away!

DAVID NYHAN, *a columnist and an associate editor for the* Boston Globe, *writes three columns a week on politics and current affairs. Since joining the* Globe *in 1970, Nyhan has worked as a Massachusetts State House bureau chief, a labor writer, and a congressional, White House, and national correspondent.*

Four hours a day is what the average kid watches. That twenty-   5
eight hours per week, over the year, is more time than he spends in
school (less than one-fourth of the day for less than 180 days).

The AMA has studied the phenomena of self-hypnotic television
consumption and concluded: Aaaaarrrrrrgh!!!

Did you know that wherever television-watching is introduced,
homicide rates double within a decade and a half? The babies born to
households where TV was just coming in grow up (if they're lucky) to
be fifteen-year-olds in communities with twice as many homicides.

Little kids who OD on TV kick and punch and bite much more
frequently than the little monsters who do not have their sensitivities
dulled by the repetitive and mindless violence of the cathode ray
projector.

How bad does it get for a teenager who watches a lot of TV? He
or she is fatter, sicker, more likely to drink and smoke and drug, and
more likely to engage in premature sexual conduct that can be harmful to him or the kid he's messing with.

TV is an open sewer running into the minds of the impression-   10
able, and progressively desensitized, young. It is a conveyor belt of
cynicism, of self-gratification, of violence-
inducing behavior, of role modeling gone
Our future is rotting,   wrong, of tasteless drivel. The more meretri-
one channel at a   cious the content, the more successful the sale
time.   of same. TV is repackaged dross on video for
the ages, syndication rights reserved.

It is ruining the country. Our society's rot owes more to television
than any other single cause. As the dominant medium, it overwhelms
the periodic, valiant, and ultimately futile appeals to a higher morality
and a more inspirational way of dealing with the rest of humanity.

Television makes everyone cynical, more convinced that no one
is honest, no one pure, no one even admirable. All the politicians are
crooks, the athletes crooks, the journalists cynics, the businessmen
greedheads, the clergy corrupt, the movie stars perverse.

Six out of ten family meals take place under the baleful glare of a
working TV set. More than half of America's kids have TV sets in
their bedrooms, where they can pig out on whatever vile fare is low-
est common denominator of the day.

We already have 1.6 million Americans behind bars. That's almost 2 percent of our total employment rate. Most of them are
young, most are uneducated, and most are coming out, eventually, to
a community near you. They watched too much TV when they were

kids, raised in single-parent, often violence-racked households where they got cuffed around when they weren't staring at some stupid television program.

Does it get any better if we shut off the tube and ask them to listen to music? Not much. Three out of four of the top-selling CDs of 1995 use cuss words and exalt guns, rape, or murder, according to a *Providence Journal-Bulletin* report. 15

Between grades seven to twelve, teenagers drain in 10,500 hours of rock music — that's more hours than they spent in class in all the years between second grade and graduating from high school.

The impact on our kids of electronic media — ranging from the soporific to the truly horrific — is the single biggest problem our society faces. It's a much bigger deal than the deficit or taxes or "job-loss anxiety" labels tossed about in the election campaigns.

The degrading of our human capital by the corrosive moral erosion of television and the related video-audio industries is a challenge of immense significance. The politicians nibble around the edges for slivers of political advantage.

But the dumbing-down of a generation, the deadening of moral sensitivity in millions of youngsters, is a much greater threat than anything rumbling in the Middle East. Our real problem is the Middle West, and the rest of Middle America. Our kids are bathed in filth, in trivia, in meaningless violence, in false happy endings, in cynical nattering from false media gods.

It's a disease. It requires prevention. And vaccination. And, occasionally, something drastic, like amputation. In my family we still talk about one Super Bowl eve when my sister got so mad at the stupefied gazes on the faces of her four kids that she lugged the TV set into her car, drove to the reservoir, and tossed it in, leaving it sitting cockeyed and unplugged on the ice she forgot to take into account. 20

The AMA is on the right side on this one. Our future is rotting, one channel at a time.

Discussing Vocabulary / Using a Dictionary

1. In what way is television a "baleful" (para. 13) influence? What image of television does the author create with his use of the word?

2. What is the derivation of the word "soporific" (para. 17)? Try using the word in another context.

3. What is the difference between "corrosion" (see "corrosive," para. 18) and "erosion"? Do the words derive from the same root?

Discussing Meaning

1. How much time do children spend watching television, according to the author? How much time do they spend in school?
2. Why does the author believe that watching television causes violent activity? What other types of media does he believe also cause violence?
3. Besides violence, what other negative effects does the author attribute to television viewing?

Discussing Writing

1. Nyhan's essay is loaded with negative adjectives describing television. Make a list of these adjectives. How many pertain to morality? How do the adjectives affect your response to the author's position?
2. Consider the author's central analogy — he plays a "doctor" when discussing television (para. 1). How does he reinforce this analogy? Point to words or images in the essay that are directly related to the opening analogy.

Challenging the Selection

1. What facts does the author use to support his argument that watching television causes young people to act in a more violent way? How does he prove his assertion that people in prison "watched too much TV when they were kids" (para. 14)? Are you persuaded by this reasoning?
2. Why does Nyhan apply his argument about television and violence only to children and young people? Do you think adults are also adversely affected by what they watch? What shows might have the most negative impact on older Americans?
3. Near the opening of his essay the author complains about kids throwing candy wrappers on the sidewalk (para. 4), yet at the conclusion of his essay he applauds his sister for tossing her television set into a reservoir. Do you see a logical inconsistency here?

In-Class Writing Activities

1. Does the author ignore any positive aspects of television? Write a brief essay about something on television that had a positive impact on your life.

2. Imagine that you are an executive at one of the leading television networks. Write a letter to the newspaper in which you defend your programming decisions against Nyhan's criticisms.

RIMA VESELY

Over Exposure

[THE DAILY IOWAN, UNIVERSITY OF IOWA / February 27, 1996]

Before You Read

Did your parents restrict your viewing of violent television shows and movies when you were growing up? Did these restrictions, or lack thereof, make any difference in your behavior? What, if anything, would you do as a parent to monitor or curb your children's access to violent material on television, film, the radio, or the Internet?

Words to Learn

blatant (para. 3): obvious or conspicuous (adj.)
deteriorating (para. 4): declining; lessened (adj.)
manipulated (para. 5): designed to create a certain effect (adj.)

RIMA VESELY (b. 1975) was a junior at the University of Iowa when she wrote this editorial for the Daily Iowan. *Vesely, who reported for a newspaper in Cape Town, South Africa, in the summer of 1996, is currently metro editor for the* Daily Iowan.

Adult values have seeped into children's minds through the easily accessible adult world. The result is a society in which values are rarely monitored and violence is increasingly becoming the norm. From television to the Internet to magazines, many children can no longer be called children.

A twelve-year-old and a thirteen-year-old dropped a five-year-old out the window of a Chicago housing project. Three thirteen-year-old boys were charged with plotting to set off a homemade bomb, the instructions for which were derived from the Internet. A fifteen-year-old boy was arrested for allegedly starting a fire that killed five members of his family. Violent "children" are not a new phenomenon. But children are becoming older emotionally as the technological world around them offers exposure to "adult" ideas. To say the problem is a "lack of family values" is to simplify what is happening, since every family has some sort of values. It's more apt to point to the lack of control and explanation children receive.

> The constant repetition of violent themes has affected the way children think.

The exposure to violent actions has changed the traditional role of the child. It's true that many traditions need to be changed, but when the result is destructiveness, the evolving pattern of violence needs to be examined. Increasingly, children are put into a societal category whose boundaries are becoming more and more fuzzy. Although children are told that they cannot make their own decisions, the blatant exposure to adult values has given them free rein to decide what they can learn.

People raged at Tipper Gore when she protested the messages in violent rap music. But she had a good point. Kids cannot be expected to think in nonviolent ways if they are continuously exposed to violent themes. The increase in violence is such that the government feels a need to offer regulations. Congress recently voted to require the makers of television sets to include a feature to block out material rated as offensively violent or sexual. The law also bans pornography over computer networks and institutes penalties for those convicted of distributing "indecent" sexual material to minors. While government control is not the answer, what should be applauded is the recognition that continuous exposure to graphically violent and sexual material has led to a deteriorating view of the value of human life in the minds of some minors.

Violence is not new, it's a part of human nature. However, the   5
constant repetition of violent themes has affected the way children
think. Violence is fed to kids daily through manipulated images that
glare at them through television screens, sing to them through violent
rap music, and beckon to them on computer screens. What children
are exposed to needs to be controlled, and it needs to be restricted
through parental leadership.

Discussing Vocabulary / Using a Dictionary

1. What are some examples of "blatant exposure to adult values"
    (para. 3) that children get through the media? Can you think of
    other words, besides "blatant," that the author might have used
    in this context?

2. What other types of things are "manipulated" (para. 5) in mod-
    ern society? Can you think of a couple of synonyms for this
    word?

Discussing Meaning

1. Vesely disputes the notion that "children are becoming older
    emotionally" (para. 2) because of a lack of "family values."
    Where does she place the blame?

2. What mixed messages do children get about their role in deciding
    what shows and songs they can watch and listen to?

3. Why does Vesely see recent government actions to curb violent
    and sexually explicit material in the media as a positive sign?

4. According to Vesely, what ultimately should be done about
    media violence?

Discussing Writing

1. Why, in paragraph 2, does Vesely put "children" in quotation
    marks?

2. Vesely often resorts to general statements and concepts, such
    as "'adult' ideas" (para. 2). Pinpoint other generalities that
    could have been more clear and vivid if supported with specific
    examples.

3. In paragraph 5 Vesely uses something that writers refer to as "parallel structure" — that is, she uses three phrases with a similar grammatical structure (each, for example, begins with a strong verb): "Violence is fed to kids daily through manipulated images that *glare* at them through television screens, *sing* to them through violent rap music, and *beckon* to them on computer screens." (Italics added.) What is the effect of this parallel structure?

Challenging the Selection

1. Do you think the author is correct in grouping all children into one societal category with "fuzzy" boundaries (para. 3)? Can children be grouped so simplistically?

2. Can children's exposure to violent and sexually explicit material in the media really be controlled effectively through "parental leadership," as Vesely suggests in paragraph 5? What limitations might this form of control impose?

In-Class Writing Activities

1. List other factors, aside from "the technological world around them" (para. 2), that might be causing today's children to grow up faster than children in previous generations. Can these factors be reduced or regulated? By whom?

2. In a brief essay reflect on your own childhood. Were the boundaries placed on your behavior strict or "fuzzy"? What kind of boundaries would you (or do you) set for your own children? (In your essay, you can describe limits on exposure to media violence, or limits on any type of activity.)

3. The *Journal of Adolescent Health Care* concluded in 1990 that the negative impact of TV on children can be reversed through two measures: parental disapproval of violent acts on TV and school-based programs that teach children how to view TV critically. Briefly outline a parental plan of action; then outline a school-based plan.

Discussing the Unit

Suggested Topic for Discussion

Can the media really influence human behavior, or do the media merely reflect — rather than affect — society? Should anyone be responsible for protecting the public, especially children, from possibly negative aspects of the media (for example, violent or graphically sexual material)? If so, who? What are the benefits and drawbacks of having people or institutions "protect" us from aspects of the media? Is it possible to develop criteria that could be used to determine which TV shows, movies, music, and so on should be restricted?

Preparing for Class Discussion

1. Can you think of a time when television, music, or some other medium affected your behavior or thoughts either positively or negatively? What were the specific effects? Were they lasting or fleeting? Do you think the positive effects of the media outweigh the negative, or vice versa?

2. Try to come up with a list of factors that make a TV show, movie, or song potentially harmful. Do you find it easy or difficult to come up with such a list? Given the list that you've created, do you think that people could and should be protected from such factors? Why or why not?

From Discussion to Writing

1. Zuckerman and Vesely both address the effects of government regulation of the media. Are their views similar or dissimilar? Do you agree with one view more than the other? Why? Reflect on these questions in a brief essay. You might also want to compare Zuckerman's and Vesely's views to Nyhan's.

2. Assume that you have been named director of a local television or radio station. What types of programs or music would you air? Would you develop any standards for your staff that spell out which types of programs or music to actively seek out and

which types to avoid? Outline a mission statement for your station, including any broadcast standards you can think of.

3. Write an essay reflecting on what a particular medium (for example, television, radio, or the Internet) will be like in the next century — twenty-five, fifty, and one hundred years from now. Do you think this medium will be more or less violent or sexually graphic than it is now? What other changes do you predict for this medium?

Topics for Cross-Cultural Discussion

1. In your country, does the government censor music, movies, and other media? If so, what criteria does it use? Do people see violence in the media as a serious problem?

2. Do any popular songs in your country have "woman-killing" lyrics? If so, do people speak out against such lyrics? If not, what do you think explains the absence of such lyrics?

3. Are children in your country growing up faster now than they did when you were a child? If so, are the media a factor in this change? What other influences might be causing children to grow up fast?

14

A Student Debate:
Is Affirmative Action
Necessary?

Affirmative action — choosing members of groups that traditionally have faced discrimination for educational and employment opportunities — has been a controversial policy since 1978, when the Supreme Court ruled in a landmark case that universities are entitled to consider race as a factor in admissions. Proponents of affirmative action say that the policy, though it may be imperfect, is the only way to ensure that minorities are fairly represented in business, government, and education. Opponents, however, say that using race as a factor in deciding who receives educational and job opportunities can lead to "reverse discrimination" and other problems. Nowhere is the controversy stronger than on campus, where students — perhaps affected by affirmative action policies while applying to college — prepare for a job market where such policies may determine the opportunities that they will receive.

This chapter sets up a kind of debate among four students who hold a range of opinions about affirmative action. Although these students aren't responding directly to one another — and, in fact, have never met — their diverse views represent the kind you might overhear in your school's classrooms, auditoriums, and dining halls. Erin Mansur-Smith, reflecting on a time when she was kicked off a boys' football team for countering sexist remarks, asserts that affirmative action is a way to "make the boys play fair." Next, Dan McAllister argues that affirmative action actually hurts those it is intended to help by, among other things, admitting "unqualified" minorities into top schools. Then Ted Koerth proposes a new kind of affirmative action that would make income instead of race the primary consideration in deciding who should receive preferential treatment in employment and education. Finally, Dominique Apollon argues that affirmative action policies are necessary to remedy past and present discrimination.

ERIN MANSUR-SMITH

It's Not Whether You Win or Lose — It's Whether or Not You're Allowed to Play the Game

[THE KANSAS STATE COLLEGIAN, KANSAS STATE UNIVERSITY / April 18, 1995]

Before You Read

Do you remember when you first encountered discrimination in some form or another? Do you think that something could have been done at the time to put an end to the discrimination? Have you ever been present when someone else was discriminated against? Did you defend this person, or did you remain silent?

ERIN MANSUR-SMITH (b. 1971) is a 1995 graduate of Kansas State University, where she studied prelaw, English, and theater. Currently, Mansur-Smith is pursuing a master's degree in theater at Kansas State. In 1995 she read this piece, written when she was a senior, on National Public Radio's Morning Edition.

Words to Learn

bar (para. 4): to prohibit or banish (v.)

bully (para. 4): to intimidate with superior strength or authority (v.)

inception (para. 5): beginning (n.)

revamp (para. 5): to revise or renovate (v.)

It was summertime and I was ten, the star quarterback of the neighborhood football team. I could spit farther, throw harder, and tackle just as well as anyone. I was also the only female member.

We'd been playing all morning and the other team had requested a break. While it would have been neater to see someone pass out from heat exhaustion, we were ahead by a million points anyway, and feeling generous, we agreed to reconvene in the cool of the evening. They went home, but my team plopped down to rest on the playing field, wiggling on the ground, worn bare of its grass by our running that afternoon, and swatting at mosquitoes as they swarmed in for the feast. We talked about what we were going to be when we grew up: cowboys, race car drivers, firemen, and doctors.

Affirmative action is a way to make the boys play fair.

I'd given a lot of thought to my future occupation but hadn't shared my secret dreams with the others. I wanted to be a railroad engineer like my father. The idea of going a hundred miles an hour in a vehicle that weighed ten tons appealed to me. When I told the guys what I wanted, they laughed. I couldn't do it, they said, because I was a girl. I was required by law to be a ballet dancer or a mommy. It was my first taste of sexism, and I didn't care for it. I pointed out that if I were a good enough quarterback, I could be a train driver if I wanted to. Girl or not. The logic didn't help me. Later, when the game continued, I found myself replaced as star thrower. Suddenly, I couldn't do all the things I'd always done before well enough to play. The lines had been clearly drawn, and I was on the other side. My team won that day and many days afterwards, but the chance to play quarterback never came again.

When I listen to the arguments against affirmative action, I think about being barred from the football field that afternoon. I remember the pride and anger I felt in the pit of my stomach that kept me from getting an adult to insist that I be allowed to play. I hear affirmative action called a race-counting game, a way for the government to bully businesses into hiring people who may not be qualified. I hear it places a burden upon minorities and women, forcing them to work against doubts regarding the strength of their abilities. Still others say it doesn't go far enough, placing the bite on large businesses while still allowing smaller fish to continue sexist and racist hiring practices. As for myself, I see it as a way to make the boys play fair.

Affirmative action has done a lot for countless women and mi-   5
norities over the years, but it didn't hand them jobs. It didn't throw open the doors of boardrooms and executive offices. And while it hasn't solved the problems it set out to with its inception thirty years ago, the idea of being without it scares me. Affirmative action has blown a whistle to make all the contestants on the field look up to see the star players they won't let play for whatever reason. It makes them acknowledge us and our right to participate. It needs to be re-vamped to fulfill that function again.

I didn't go get an adult to insist I be allowed to play in the game that day. I almost wish I had. I would have worked twice as hard to prove myself half as good as any of the boys on the team, and I would have succeeded.

Discussing Vocabulary / Using a Dictionary

1. How is the idea of being "barred" (para. 4) from something re-lated to the presence of physical bars? That is, what is the rela-tionship between the figurative and literal meanings of "bar"?

2. From what language is "inception" (para. 5) derived? What are some synonyms for this word?

3. What does the prefix "re-" mean in "revamped" (para. 5)?

Discussing Meaning

1. Why, according to the other football players, can't Mansur-Smith be a railroad engineer? What "law" requires her to be "a ballet dancer or a mommy" (para. 3)?

2. What does the author mean when she says, "The lines had been clearly drawn, and I was on the other side" (para. 3)? Why did she never get to play the quarterback position again?

3. What are some of the common perceptions about affirmative action that Mansur-Smith describes? How does she feel about affirmative action?

4. Why does the idea of being without affirmative action "scare" the author (para. 5)? Is her fear obscure or clear?

Discussing Writing

1. Mansur-Smith bases her argument for affirmative action on a personal experience that has an emotional appeal for the audience. Does her personal anecdote make you more sympathetic to her? Would it be easy to refute her argument with a counter-anecdote that makes a similar type of emotional appeal?

2. Mansur-Smith moves from her personal story to a more general discussion of affirmative action, then back to her story. Is this an effective way to organize writing? Would her essay have been more or less effective if she had just ended with the general discussion of affirmative action and not returned to her initial anecdote? Why?

3. In paragraph 3 Mansur-Smith uses an incomplete sentence (a sentence fragment) for effect. What is this fragment? What effect does it have?

Challenging the Selection

1. Mansur-Smith makes several sweeping statements about affirmative action that she does not support with examples. For example, she says that "affirmative action has done a lot for countless women and minorities over the years" (para. 5), but she never explains specifically how it has done so. Does this vagueness weaken the credibility of the author's argument, or does the initial anecdote about the football game suffice to show the benefits of affirmative action? Can you find other instances where the author makes statements that she doesn't support with specific examples?

2. The author claims that affirmative action "needs to be revamped" (para. 5), yet she doesn't offer any proposals for improving the policy. Is this is a serious omission, or does the article seem complete without such proposals?

In-Class Writing Activities

1. Mansur-Smith compares affirmative action to a referee who has "blown a whistle" (para. 5) to call attention to unfair practices. This type of comparison is known as a *metaphor*. In a few sentences or a paragraph, create your own metaphor comparing affirmative action to something or someone. You may want to compare your metaphor with those of your classmates.

2. In a brief essay, describe a childhood experience that has affected you to this day. Why did this experience have such lasting effects? How did it change you?

DAN McALLISTER

A Misguided Policy

[THE SPECTATOR, HAMILTON COLLEGE / March 1, 1996]

Before You Read

What factors should determine whether someone is qualified or unqualified for college admission? How important should S.A.T. scores be? What importance should be assigned to other factors, such as high school grades, special talents, and racial or ethnic background?

Words to Learn

median (para. 3): referring to the middle value in a range of numbers or values (that is, a value preceded and followed by an equal number of values) (adj.)

exploitation (para. 4): using other people for one's own gain (n.)

scrutinize (para. 6): to examine carefully (v.)

notorious (para. 6): known widely and unfavorably (adj.)

DAN MCALLISTER *(b. 1976) is the arts and entertainment editor of* Hamilton College's Spectator.

As with most social planning, affirmative action began with good intentions, though the road to hell has not been paved so efficiently since the Great Fall.[1] The preferential treatment of certain minorities over the past few decades has had a disastrous impact on our society. The tragic consequences of this program, however, have not impacted the majority but the very minorities whom it was designed to help.

The first area in which minorities are hurt by preferential treatment is education. Many colleges and universities have strived to ensure that the number of minority students at their institutions is an accurate representation of the minority population as a whole. Thus, these institutions attempt to enroll African Americans as roughly 11 percent of the student body. While there are a few dozen schools in this country with S.A.T. scores of entering freshman in excess of 1200, as of 1983 there were fewer than 600 African Americans in the entire United States scoring in this range. This meant that the Ivy League alone could not achieve representational proportions of African American students without lowering standards with respect to S.A.T scores.

> *The preferential treatment of certain minorities over the past few decades has had a disastrous impact on our society.*

The response of top-tier institutions, therefore, was to lower their standards. At the University of California at Berkeley, for example, the median S.A.T. scores of the incoming black students is 952, versus 1181 for the university as a whole. An administrator called the incoming classes "wonderfully diverse" because they represent minorities in proportion to the general population of California. How "wonderfully diverse" are Berkeley's graduating classes? The sad reality is that 70 percent of African American students who enroll there do not graduate. What truly makes this situation a tragedy, however, is that the median S.A.T. score of 952 is above the national average for college-bound seniors. This means that the African American students who failed at Berkeley would have prospered at other institutions. They were not unqualified, just unqualified for Berkeley.

This situation, unfortunately, is not unique to Berkeley. Most other top-tier universities have similar tales of high drop-out rates of minorities given preferential treatment in admissions. The psychological and economic consequences of failing out of college are disas-

---

[1]*the Great Fall:* Biblical reference to humans' "fall from grace" with God that originated with Adam and Eve's sinning in the Garden of Eden.

trous, certainly too great a price to pay so that some administrator can brag about his institution being "wonderfully diverse." This is exploitation at its worst.

A second area in which minorities, particularly blacks, have been hurt by affirmative action policies is the workplace. From the turn of the century to the early 1960s, the income of blacks slowly but steadily rose each year relative to that of whites. During the civil rights era, blacks' incomes increased by leaps and bounds, both in absolute terms and relative to whites', and did not begin to level off until the early 1970s, after the federal government had established affirmative action policies for businesses. At first glance, it seems that affirmative action is merely a harmless failure. Upon closer inspection of the facts, however, one is truly exposed to the harm it has done. Throughout the 1970s, the median income of college-educated blacks increased so that by the 1980 census, college-educated black couples were actually earning more than their white counterparts. Uneducated blacks did not fare so well, and their median income relative to whites actually fell by over 10 percent. So while the top fifth of African Americans increased their relative incomes, the bottom three-fifths — those whom affirmative action was intended to help — saw their relative incomes decline. Other ethnic minorities have also fared just as poorly since the institution of affirmative action. Relative incomes of Puerto Rican families fell by nearly 30 percent, and Mexican American family incomes also decreased relative to those of whites.

Why this tragic decline among the least fortunate members of the country? The most likely explanation is that with the government scrutinizing the hiring and firing practices of corporations, employers are unlikely to take risks with an unqualified minority candidate. In a notorious lawsuit against Sears, the Equal Employment Opportunity Commission charged the corporation with under-representation of women among its commission salespeople, despite the fact that not one woman had charged the company with discrimination. The great irony was that Sears had been a pioneer in the affirmative action movement and had maintained a close record of its own performance in the recruiting of women and minorities. The records the company kept turned out to be the very evidence used against it in the federal case. With the federal government constantly scrutinizing Sears for under-representation of women and minorities, it is easy to imagine what might happen if a member of a minority group were actually fired from a job. Thus, the reluctance of companies to take risks in the hiring of minorities. Thus, the decline in relative income of minority groups since the institution of affirmative action.

Discussing Vocabulary / Using a Dictionary

1. What is another meaning of the word "median" (para. 3)? How does this meaning relate to McAllister's use of the word?
2. "Exploit," the root of "exploitation" (para. 4), can have a positive meaning when used as a noun. What is this meaning?
3. List some people or actions that are "notorious" (para. 6). What makes them so?

Discussing Meaning

1. In what ways, according to McAllister, do affirmative action policies hurt minorities?
2. How do top-tier universities achieve representational proportions of minority students? Why does McAllister disagree with this practice?
3. What does McAllister say has happened to the incomes of college-educated blacks in recent years? What has happened to the incomes of blacks without a college education?
4. How, according to McAllister, will the Equal Employment Opportunity Commission's lawsuit against Sears affect the hiring practices of other businesses?

Discussing Writing

1. McAllister clearly states his thesis — or main idea — in his first paragraph. What is his thesis? How well does he support it?
2. Unlike other authors in this unit, McAllister uses several numerical statistics. Do these statistics lend him more authority on the topic of affirmative action? Why or why not?
3. This essay is clearly divided into three sections: an introduction containing the thesis, a discussion of affirmative action's effects on education, and a discussion of the policy's effect on the workplace. McAllister does not, however, provide a strong conclusion. What advantage does he miss out on by this omission?

4. McAllister writes with a great deal of certainty about his subject. How does his tone affect you? Do you think he sounds self-assured or arrogant?

Challenging the Selection

1. McAllister seems to assume that prospective college students must do well on the S.A.T.s to succeed in "top-tier institutions" (para. 3) and that applicants with lower S.A.T. scores are "unqualified" to attend these institutions. Does he provide adequate evidence for these positions? What kind of information or statistics might have made his argument more effective?

2. McAllister doesn't mention the sources of his statistics. Do you think this omission makes his argument less credible? Why or why not?

3. Although McAllister examines the negative impact of affirmative action on those people it is intended to help, he doesn't look at the policy's effects on majority groups. Do you think this omission is a serious or insignificant one?

In-Class Writing Activities

1. McAllister assumes that S.A.T. scores are important in determining success in college. In a brief essay, defend or oppose this assumption. Make sure to support your position with specific reasons and examples.

2. Imagine that you are an admissions officer at a college (it can be your college or an imaginary institution). Come up with a list of criteria — ranging from most important to least important — for admitting students. Then, in a paragraph, explain why you set the priorities you did. You may want to compare your priorities with those of your classmates.

TED KOERTH

Economic Affirmative Action

[THE CAVALIER DAILY, UNIVERSITY OF VIRGINIA / April 9, 1996]

Before You Read

What factors other than membership in a minority group might be used to determine who should benefit from affirmative action? Why do you think these other factors are important?

Words to Learn

saga (para. 1): a long, detailed story (n.)

askew (para. 2): crooked; awry (adv.)

reparation (para. 2): referring to the act of making amends (adj.; usually n.)

qualm (para. 3): a feeling of doubt or uneasiness (n.)

demographics (para. 4): the study of characteristics of particular human populations (n.)

rampant (para. 7): unrestrained or extravagant (adj.)

animosity (para. 8): strong hatred; hostility (n.)

inherent (para. 8): existing naturally or essentially in something (adj.)

Two words probably do not exist which can stir up more of a conversational frenzy than affirmative action. The debate surrounding such policies presents itself daily in the media, a seemingly never-ending saga destined to go back and forth forever.

Proponents of such policies argue that they not only give an advantage to underrepresented minority groups, but they help to settle

---

TED KOERTH (b. 1977) was a freshman when he wrote this editorial for the Cavalier Daily at the University of Virginia, where he plans to double major in government and Spanish. Writing about this column, Koerth says, "I believe that the government should widen the scope of affirmative action policies so as to benefit people of disadvantage, not just those who have traditionally benefitted from them."

some cosmic score that went askew during the first two hundred years of American history. People who oppose affirmative action measures argue that they encourage acceptance of underqualified applicants and that sufficient reparation time has elapsed. A growing majority of those opponents think that minorities do not deserve the push they get, hence the rise in complaints of reverse discrimination.

Despite the deeply felt emotions both sides of the debate harbor, a fair way to reform affirmative action's current state does exist. Many of the qualms some have with affirmative action have to do with the fact that it is based solely on race, for race is natural and unintentional. None of us chooses our race. So to treat someone differently because of his or her race demonstrates a glaring ignorance on the part of the prejudiced. We must consider, however, the opposite side of the coin which often does not receive as much thought. If we cannot judge people poorly because of their race, we cannot judge them superior for the same reason, nor should we use race to decide that a certain class of individuals needs a helping hand from any other.

The affirmative action debate roars on in the United States, with animosity on both sides building constantly.

Here the affirmative action argument comes into play. The problem starts when race becomes the basis for giving out advantages such as college admissions. Choosing minority groups for special treatment in admissions implies that those groups lack the ability to achieve those things on their own, a bigoted assumption totally without founding. Granted, simple demographics demonstrate that certain ethnic groups are more highly represented in certain classes, but we cannot consider that an exclusive phenomenon, given that no group of people has all the same characteristics. Therefore, a generalization implying that any certain number of racial groups needs help lacks reason. For that reason, we need to fix affirmative action.

If two students have had the exact same opportunities during their lives but one is an American Indian and the other Caucasian, the American Indian will receive acceptance priority if her academic achievements are similar, simply because she belongs to an underrepresented group. That implies that an American Indian who achieves is out of the ordinary — a foolish assumption.

Take another example: Two students, one white and one Asian American, score the same on standardized tests and are equally

5

qualified for a job. The white student, however, comes from a lower class, single-parent family, and the Asian student comes from the family of an affluent judge. If those two have equal academic achievements, affirmative action as it now exists would likely give a boost to the Asian student, though he has lived an easier life. The extra efforts the Caucasian student made go unnoticed, and he receives no boost.

For those reasons, America needs an affirmative action system that gives a boost not to members of groups that unfortunately suffered from past discrimination, because the days of rampant discrimination in the United States have passed for the most part. Continuing to pay back groups who previously had to deal with prejudice unfairly punishes other racial majorities for the sins of their ancestors. Instead, we need a system that gives a boost to those who have had to overcome considerable financial, physical, or other obstacles to achieve what they have achieved. Such a policy would not shut any ethnic group out of the process, it would only include anyone who has succeeded without financial assistance. If it occurs that a majority of those who benefit from that system still come from minority groups, that is fine. At least they have benefited from a system that recognizes their situation, not just their skin color.

The affirmative action debate roars on in the United States, with animosity on both sides building constantly. Our current system supposes a certain inherent inferiority of minority groups who in the past have experienced discrimination — an inferiority that simply does not exist. If the government were to institute an equal opportunity system that tries to help those who have had to deal with financial and physical obstacles, we could ease tensions and deal more fairly with admissions policies. Until we can respect the abilities of all ethnic groups, our country will divide its people along racial lines, as the tension rises to a fever pitch.

Discussing Vocabulary / Using a Dictionary

1. What is the historical meaning of "saga" (para. 1)? How does it relate to Koerth's use of the word?

2. In what contexts, other than the one in paragraph 2, is the word "reparation" used?

3. What are some things, other than discrimination, that can be "rampant" (para. 7)?

4. What are some Latin roots of the word "animosity" (para. 8)? How do they relate to the current use of the word?

Discussing Meaning

1. Why does Koerth think that race is an inappropriate basis for affirmative action programs? How can such programs hurt minorities?
2. What, according to Koerth, do current affirmative action policies fail to account for? Why are they unfair?
3. Does Koerth think that racial discrimination remains a serious problem in America today?
4. What solution does Koerth offer to remedy the problems he sees with current affirmative action programs?

Discussing Writing

1. In paragraphs 5 and 6 Koerth presents two brief examples to illustrate what he considers to be problems with current affirmative action programs. What do you think of these examples? Are they adequate to make his point or too simplistic?
2. Koerth waits until the end of his essay, after he has given an overview of problems with current affirmative action policies, to present his proposal for amending these policies. Do you think this is an effective strategy, or do you think his essay would have been more effective if he had presented his proposal at the beginning?

Challenging the Selection

1. In his example of the white student and the affluent Asian student in paragraph 6, Koerth says that current affirmative action programs would "give a boost to the Asian student, though he has lived an easier life." What obstacles in the Asian student's life might Koerth be overlooking in such a generalization?
2. In paragraph 7 Koerth says that "the days of rampant discrimination in the United States have passed for the most part." Can you think of any examples that counter this statement?

3. Do you think that Koerth's proposal, if implemented, would work? Would it truly be a fair system for helping those who are most disadvantaged in our society? Why or why not?

In-Class Writing Activities

1. Even if you are an avid supporter of affirmative action, you might see ways in which it could be improved. In a brief essay, sketch out some of your ideas for making affirmative action programs more effective.

2. Think of some issue — political, social, or economic — about which you are undecided. Discuss the issue objectively, as Koerth has sought to do, showing the strengths and weaknesses of opposing arguments about it. Then, in your conclusion, propose a possible compromise.

DOMINIQUE APOLLON

A Quest for Justice

[THE CAVALIER DAILY, UNIVERSITY OF VIRGINIA, March 26, 1996]

Before You Read

The author of the following essay claims that affirmative action is an extremely touchy subject. Just how sensitive are Americans when discussing this issue? How does your class react when the words "affirmative action" are mentioned?

DOMINIQUE APOLLON (*b.* 1974) *wrote this essay when he was a senior at the University of Virginia, where he received a bachelor's degree in American government in 1996. As an undergraduate, Apollon won the 1996 Best Writer Award from the* Cavalier Daily *and in 1995 was a Ralph Bunche Fellow of the American Political Science Association. Currently, he is pursuing a doctorate in political science at Stanford University.*

Words to Learn

wager (para. 1): to bet (v.)

amicable (para. 1): friendly (adj.)

belligerent (para. 1): hostile; eager to fight (adj.)

reflexively (para. 1): done by reflex, without thought (adv.)

futile (para. 1): having no useful effect or result (adj.)

wholesale (para. 1): done extensively and indiscriminately (adj.)

retrenchment (para. 1): reduction or elimination (n.)

herald (para. 1): to proclaim (v.)

unscathed (para. 3): unhurt (adj.)

facetiously (para. 3): playfully; humorously (adv.)

detrimentally (para. 5): harmfully (adv.)

alleviate (para. 6): to reduce or make more tolerable (v.)

Just hearing the two words "affirmative action" in racially mixed company these days causes all sorts of anxiety, discomfort, and symptoms of tension in most of us. In fact, I would wager many readers already quit reading this column for whatever reason. Whether we are friends or virtual strangers, amicable or belligerent, the words "affirmative action" make the hairs at the back of our necks stand up on end. As our faces reflexively wince, our shoulders slightly rise in a futile biological attempt to hide our head like a turtle when the issue is raised. The rise of vocal conservative public figures, the 1995 federal contractors Supreme Court case, and the University of California Regents' action to abolish all affirmative action policies for women and minorities within the next two years collectively have done their best to force Americans to reevaluate the nearly twenty-year-old attempt to seek justice for segments of our American populace underrepresented in the cross-section of measures of success. The case for wholesale retrenchment heralded by many Americans, however, has yet to convert this columnist given current practices and realities, especially in terms of the realm of higher education, easily the most defensible area of affirmative action policy.

While the words mean many different things to different people, to me, affirmative action signifies giving preference to an historically underrepresented applicant, all other factors being essentially equal for, say, employment or a spot in a college class. I do not think of arbitrary quotas, "set-asides," or the logically bankrupt term "reverse discrimination."

As far as college admissions are concerned, anti–affirmative action camps argue that scores of so-called unqualified black students are admitted at the expense of white students who appear to be more qualified. But the whole issue of qualifications is rather fuzzy. What criteria are outsiders using to judge some black students unqualified? S.A.T. scores? While standardized tests are addressed later, consider that the ingredients for college success do not translate from a simple test score. Even those students entering with high test scores do not necessarily succeed in college or add much to the overall intellectual and social atmosphere at a particular institution. Meanwhile, there are long histories of admissions preferences of multiple sorts, many of which continue virtually unscathed by the swords of public opinion. As Paula McClain, professor and chairwoman of the department of government and foreign affairs, facetiously asked during one of her more informal Minority Group Politics course lectures, "Shouldn't in-state students feel less qualified than out-of-state students who scored higher on average than they did? What about students from underrepresented Western states or those who get admissions preference because their parents or grandfathers attended the University of Virginia? Aren't they unqualified?" Furthermore, consider a recent *Los Angeles Times* article alleging that several California Regents and even Republican California Governor Pete Wilson, a very visible anti-affirmative action enthusiast, may have arranged some set-asides of their own for (ahem, unqualified?) University of California applicants whom they knew personally.

> *Our country still contains deep problems of inequality that are partially historically based and must be addressed in order to guarantee that all Americans have at least a roughly equal chance at success.*

When a black student drops out of college, many folks instantly latch onto negative stereotypes of blacks' intelligence, concluding that the student must not have been qualified from the start. In no way are the qualifications of white dropouts similarly questioned on as wide a basis. Even Fourteenth Amendment considerations of equal protection under the laws remain fuzzy from the higher education standpoint given the broad range of what constitutes a "qualified student." But the convincing aspects of the resistance to the conservative anti-affirmative action movement hardly stop here. Consider the recent research of Stanford psychology professor Claude Steele. Steele, the twin brother and ideological opposite of black conservative Shelby Steele, author of the 1990 book *The Content of Our Character,* has conducted research, highlighted in a *New York Times Magazine* article, linking black students' poorer performance on standardized tests to "stereotype vulnerability."

During a four-year period, Steele tested the performance of white   5
and black college students on the same tough verbal-skills questions in
the Graduate Record Exam. Divided into two separate racially mixed
groups, the first group believed its exam was "a genuine test of your
verbal abilities and limitations," while the second group believed the
research was for the "psychological factors involved in solving verbal
problems." The black students in the second group performed as well
as white students, while the black students subjected to the pressure of
"stereotype vulnerability" in the first group performed significantly
worse than all other students. Eight additional experiments showed
that stereotype vulnerability detrimentally affects women who are told
that a given math test highlights "gender differences." And perhaps
even more interesting, the negative impact of stereotype vulnerability
appeared in white men who took a tough math test after their proctor
announced Asians tend to outperform whites. Shouldn't this research
lead us to further question the wisdom of so rigidly judging who is
"qualified" to attend particular universities?

The absolutely wholesale nationwide scrapping of affirmative action policies, for which many self-identified conservatives call, is almost impossible to justify, especially in terms of higher education.
Our country still contains deep problems of inequality that are par-
tially historically based and must be addressed in order to guarantee
that all Americans have at least a roughly equal chance at success.
There are valid arguments on both sides of the issue. Sometime soon,
we must take steps to alleviate the sheer discomfort and tension
caused by the mere mention of the words "affirmative action" before
a sensible and, most important, effective compromise will be reached.

Discussing Vocabulary / Using a Dictionary

1. Apollon uses "wager" (para. 1) as a verb, but it can also be used
   as a noun. What is the meaning of "wager" when used as a
   noun?

2. What is the Latin root of the word "amicable" (para. 1)? Can
   you think of a word that has the same root and a similar meaning?

3. What are some other meanings of the word "wholesale" (para.
   1)? How, if at all, do they relate to Apollon's use of this word?

4. List a few words opposite in meaning from "facetiously" (para. 3).

Discussing Meaning

1. What are some of the events that, according to Apollon, are caus-
    ing Americans to challenge affirmative action policies? Why does
    Apollon think these policies are still necessary?

2. What criticisms does Apollon launch against those who judge
    some black students as "unqualified"? What problems does he
    have with this description?

3. In paragraphs 4 and 5 Apollon discusses research done by Claude
    Steele on students taking standardized tests. What did this re-
    search show? What point is Apollon trying to make by citing this
    research?

Discussing Writing

1. Apollon begins his essay by describing affirmative action as an
    issue bristling with controversy. Did his opening cause you to pay
    closer attention to his argument? Did you experience any of the
    reactions he describes in his first paragraph?

2. Much of the essay centers on the question of what makes a po-
    tential student "qualified" to attend a particular institution. How
    does Apollon break down the traditional notion of the "quali-
    fied" student? How convincing and complete do you find his ar-
    gument?

3. Apollon never directly defines "stereotype vulnerability" (para.
    4). Do you think this is a serious omission, or were you able to
    determine the meaning of this concept by the context he pro-
    vides?

Challenging the Selection

1. Apollon claims that "our country still contains deep problems of
    inequality" (para. 6). Should he provide more support for this
    statement, or is it undeniably true?

2. In his last paragraph Apollon says that there are "valid argu-
    ments on both sides of the [affirmative action] issue," but he
    never spells out any anti-affirmative action arguments. Would
    the essay have been more effective if he had detailed, then re-
    futed, the opposition to affirmative action, or is his approach
    sound?

In-Class Writing Activities

1. "Racism is no longer a serious problem in America today." In a brief essay, defend or refute this statement, drawing on evidence from personal experience, observations, and current events.

2. Apollon criticizes in his essay the assumption that standardized test results really reflect students' abilities and qualifications. In an essay of your own, take a critical look at some other widely held assumption in our society (for example, that television is a bad influence). In what ways does this assumption oversimplify reality? What do you see as a more realistic view?

Discussing the Unit

Suggested Topic for Discussion

How alive is racism in America today? Is affirmative action a necessary remedy for racial injustices, or does it create other problems that are just as serious? Do better alternatives to affirmative action exist, or are current policies the only way to assure fair access to opportunities in education and business? What do you see as the future of affirmative action in the United States?

Preparing for Class Discussion

1. Imagine that affirmative action policies aren't, and have never been, in place. How, if at all, would opportunities in education and business be different for you and for others you know? Would you be better or worse off? Think of those who belong to a different race or economic class from yours. Would they be better or worse off? Jot down some notes on these questions.

2. Do you think that affirmative action sometimes hurts the very groups it was intended to help, as two of the authors in this chapter argue? Or do you think that the positive effects of affirmative action outweigh any negative effects? State and support your position in a few paragraphs.

From Discussion to Writing

1. Dan McAllister and Dominique Apollon take quite opposite positions in the affirmative action debate. For one thing, McAllister assumes that standardized tests can determine people's real abilities, while Apollon strongly criticizes such tests. For another, McAllister thinks that affirmative action policies hurt minorities, while Apollon says exactly the opposite. Script an argument between McAllister and Apollon, or between any two authors in this chapter. On what points are they most strongly opposed? Do you see any areas in which they might find common ground?

2. Now that you have considered a variety of opinions about affirmative action, write an essay in which you state and support your opinion about current affirmative action policies. Should current policies be kept, scrapped, or reformed? Why? What social, political, and economic factors affect your view? In supporting your argument, make sure to draw on evidence from your own experiences and observations, the essays in this chapter, current events, and other sources.

Topics for Cross-Cultural Discussion

1. Does your native country have any policies that are similar to affirmative action policies in the United States? If so, compare and contrast the U.S. policies to those in your country. If not, why do you think such policies haven't been enacted? How would people in your country react to them?

2. What factors determine who is "underprivileged" in your native country? How are those factors different from those considered in the United States?

3. One college student from South America says he is insulted by U.S. applications that ask him to specify his race, thus placing him in a "box." Does it bother you to specify your race or nationality on forms in the United States? Why or why not? Do you think that Americans are too caught up in racial and ethnic categories, or do you think that attention to such categories is necessary to promote justice, as is the intention of such programs as affirmative action?

15

Opposing Views: What Should Be Done about Date Rape?

Most rapes in America are committed by a person the victim knows: a classmate, a co-worker, a neighbor, a family member, a recent date, or a long-term romantic partner. Acquaintance rape is an especially serious concern on college campuses, where, according to a controversial study, one in four women is a victim of rape or attempted rape. (Other studies have placed this figure as low as 4 percent.) Just as statistics vary widely, so do opinions about what should be done about acquaintance rape on campus. Some say that colleges must bear a share of the responsibility for preventing sexual violence, prompting some schools — for instance, Antioch College in Ohio — to institute rules governing students' sexual conduct. Others criticize such policies, saying that, ultimately, only individuals can prevent rape.

The question of responsibility is central to this chapter and the focus of a debate between two feminists, Camille Paglia and Helen Cordes. In "Rape and Modern Sex War," Paglia, arguing that men always have been and always will be sexually aggressive, contends that "every woman must take personal responsibility for her sexuality." Cordes, responding directly to Paglia's essay, argues that the notion that women are wholly responsible for preventing rape is a throwback to the days when the "blue balls" defense was used to justify men's sexual aggression. This notion is insulting to both sexes, according to Cordes, and could endanger advances that have been made in gender relations.

CAMILLE PAGLIA

Rape and Modern Sex War

[UTNE READER / January–February 1993]

Before You Read

What, if any, steps do you take to lessen the risk that you will be involved in sexual misconduct, either as a victim or a perpetrator? For example, do you limit your consumption of alcohol at parties or take part in educational programs aimed at preventing acquaintance rape? To what extent should people other than potential attackers or victims (for example, parents, school administrators, and society in general) be responsible for preventing sexual misconduct?

Words to Learn

pervasiveness (para. 2): the state of being present everywhere; commonness (n.)

inquest (para. 2): an investigation or inquiry (n.)

testosterone (para. 8): male sex hormone (n.)

resolute (para. 8): characterized by determination (adj.)

delirium (para. 10): a state of mental confusion (n.)

subliminal (para. 12): beneath the level of conscious perception (adj.)

CAMILLE PAGLIA *(b. 1947) is professor of humanities at the University of the Arts in Philadelphia. She is the author of* Sexual Personae: Art and Decadence from Nefertiti to Emily Dickinson *(1990),* Sex, Art, and American Culture: Essays *(1992), and* Vamps and Tramps *(1994).*

voracity (para. 14): limitless appetite (n.)

motif (para. 14): a recurrent or dominant theme (n.)

covet (para. 14): to desire something, especially something that belongs to another (v.)

prudent (para. 15): possessing good judgment (adj.)

espouse (para. 16): to support (v.)

propaganda (para. 17): information distributed by a particular interest to promote a cause (n.)

manipulativeness (para. 17): the state of influencing others, often by deceitful means (n.)

transgression (para. 17): violation of a law or some other rule (n.)

Rape is an outrage that cannot be tolerated in civilized society. Yet feminism, which has waged a crusade for rape to be taken more seriously, has put young women in danger by hiding the truth about sex from them.

In dramatizing the pervasiveness of rape, feminists have told young women that before they have sex with a man, they must give consent as explicit as a legal contract's. In this way, young women have been convinced that they have been the victims of rape. On elite campuses in the Northeast and on the West Coast, they have held consciousness-raising sessions, petitioned administrations, demanded inquests. At Brown University, outraged, panicky "victims" have scrawled the names of alleged attackers on the walls of women's rest rooms. What marital rape was to the seventies, "date rape" is to the nineties.

The incidence and seriousness of rape do not require this kind of exaggeration. Real acquaintance rape is nothing new. It has been a horrible problem for women for all of recorded history. Once fathers and brothers protected women from rape. Once the penalty for rape was death. I come from a fierce Italian tradition where, not so long ago in the motherland, a rapist would end up knifed, castrated, and hung out to dry.

But the old clans and small rural communities have broken down. In our cities, on our campuses far from home, young women are vulnerable and defenseless. Feminism has not prepared them for this. Feminism keeps saying the sexes are the same. It keeps telling women they can do anything, go anywhere, say anything, wear anything. No, they can't. Women will always be in sexual danger.

One of my male students recently slept overnight with a friend in a passageway of the Great Pyramid in Egypt. He described the moon and sand, the ancient silence, and eerie echoes. I will never experience   5 that. I am a woman. I am not stupid enough to believe I could ever be safe there. There is a world of solitary adventure I will never have. Women have always known these somber truths. But feminism, with its pie-in-the-sky fantasies about the perfect world, keeps young women from seeing life as it is.

We must remedy social injustice whenever we can. But there are some things we cannot change. There are sexual differences that are based in biology. Academic feminism is lost in a fog of social constructionism.[1] It believes we are totally the product of our environment. This idea was invented by Rousseau.[2] He was wrong. Emboldened by dumb French language theory, academic feminists repeat the same hollow slogans over and over to each other. Their view of sex is naive and prudish. Leaving sex to the feminists is like letting your dog vacation at the taxidermist's.

The sexes are at war. Men must struggle for identity against the overwhelming power of their mothers. Women have menstruation to tell them they are women. Men must do or risk something to be men. Men become masculine only when other men say they are. Having sex with a woman is one way a boy becomes a man.

> *A girl who goes upstairs alone with a brother at a fraternity party is an idiot. Feminists call this "blaming the victim." I call it common sense.*

College men are at their hormonal peak. They have just left their mothers and are questing for their male identity. In groups, they are dangerous. A woman going to a fraternity party is walking into Testosterone Flats, full of prickly cacti and blazing guns. If she goes, she should be armed with resolute alertness. She should arrive with girlfriends and leave with them. A girl who lets herself get dead drunk at a fraternity party is a fool. A girl who goes upstairs alone with a brother at a fraternity party is an idiot. Feminists call this "blaming the victim." I call it common sense.

For a decade, feminists have drilled their disciples to say, "Rape is a crime of violence but not of sex." This sugarcoated Shirley

---

[1]*social constructionism:* A school of thought holding that human behavior is shaped primarily by external (social), rather than internal, factors.
[2]*Rousseau:* French philosopher Jean-Jacques Rousseau (1712–1778), who argued that people are good by nature but that social influences corrupt them.

Temple nonsense has exposed young women to disaster. Misled by feminism, they do not expect rape from the nice boys from good homes who sit next to them in class.

Aggression and eroticism are deeply intertwined. Hunt, pursuit, and capture are biologically programmed into male sexuality. Generation after generation, men must be educated, refined, and ethically persuaded away from their tendency toward anarchy and brutishness. Society is not the enemy, as feminism ignorantly claims. Society is women's protection against rape. Feminism, with its solemn Carry Nation[3] repressiveness, does not see what is for men the eroticism or fun element in rape, especially the wild, infectious delirium of gang rape. Women who do not understand rape cannot defend themselves against it.

The date-rape controversy shows feminism hitting the wall of its own broken promises. The women of my sixties generation were the first respectable girls in history to swear like sailors, get drunk, stay out all night — in short, to act like men. We sought total sexual freedom and equality. But as time passed, we woke up to cold reality. The old double standard protected women. When anything goes, it's women who lose.

Today's young women don't know what they want. They see that feminism has not brought sexual happiness. The theatrics of public rage over date rape are their way of restoring the old sexual roles that were shattered by my generation. Because nothing about the sexes has really changed. The comic film *Where the Boys Are* (1960), the ultimate expression of fifties man-chasing, still speaks directly to our time. It shows smart, lively women skillfully anticipating and fending off the dozens of strategies with which horny men try to get them into bed. The agonizing date-rape subplot and climax are brilliantly done. The victim, Yvette Mimieux, makes mistake after mistake, obvious to the other girls. She allows herself to be lured away from her girlfriends and into isolation with boys whose character and intentions she misreads. *Where the Boys Are* tells the truth. It shows courtship as a dangerous game in which the signals are not verbal but subliminal.

Neither militant feminism, which is obsessed with politically correct language, nor academic feminism, which believes that knowledge and experience are "constituted by" language, can understand pre-

10

---

[3]*Carry Nation* (1846–1911): American reformer and activist known for her dramatic public demonstrations against the drinking of alcohol. (Nation is often portrayed as wielding an ax at bars and saloons.)

verbal or nonverbal communication. Feminism, focusing on sexual politics, cannot see that sex exists in and through the body. Sexual desire and arousal cannot be fully translated into verbal terms. This is why men and women misunderstand each other.

Trying to remake the future, feminism cut itself off from sexual history. It discarded and suppressed the sexual myths of literature, art, and religion. Those myths show us the turbulence, the mysteries, and passions of sex. In mythology we see men's sexual anxiety, their fear of woman's dominance. Much sexual violence is rooted in men's sense of psychological weakness toward women. It takes many men to deal with one woman. Woman's voracity is a persistent motif. Clara Bow,[4] it was rumored, took on the USC football team on weekends. Marilyn Monroe, singing "Diamonds Are a Girl's Best Friend," rules a conga line of men in tuxes. Half-clad Cher, in the video for "If I Could Turn Back Time," deranges a battleship of screaming sailors and straddles a pink-lit cannon. Feminism, coveting social power, is blind to woman's cosmic sexual power.

To understand rape, you must study the past. There never was   15
and never will be sexual harmony. Every woman must take personal responsibility for her sexuality, which is nature's red flame. She must be prudent and cautious about where she goes and with whom. When she makes a mistake, she must accept the consequences and, through self-criticism, resolve never to make that mistake again. Running to Mommy and Daddy or the campus grievance committee is unworthy of strong women. Posting lists of guilty men in the toilet is cowardly, infantile stuff.

The Italian philosophy of life espouses high-energy confrontation. A male student makes a vulgar remark about your breasts? Don't slink off to whimper and simper with the campus shrinking violets. Deal with it. On the spot. Say, "Shut up, you jerk! And crawl back to the barnyard where you belong!" In general, women who project this take-charge attitude toward life get harassed less often. I see too many dopey, immature, self-pitying women walking around like melting sticks of butter. It's the Yvette Mimieux syndrome: Make me happy. And listen to me weep when I'm not.

The date-rape debate is already smothering in propaganda churned out by the expensive northeastern colleges and universities, with their overconcentration of boring, uptight academic feminists

---

[4]*Clara Bow* (1905–1965): American actress in silent films.

and spoiled, affluent students. Beware of the deep manipulativeness of rich students who were neglected by their parents. They love to turn the campus into hysterical psychodramas of sexual transgression, followed by assertions of parental authority and concern. And don't look for sexual enlightenment from academe, which spews out mountains of books but never looks at life directly.

As a fan of football and rock music, I see in the simple, swaggering masculinity of the jock and in the noisy posturing of the heavy-metal guitarist certain fundamental, unchanging truths about sex. Masculinity is aggressive, unstable, combustible. It is also the most creative cultural force in history. Women must reorient themselves toward the elemental powers of sex, which can strengthen or destroy.

The only solution to date rape is female self-awareness and self-control. A woman's number one line of defense is herself. When a real rape occurs, she should report it to the police. Complaining to college committees because the courts "take too long" is ridiculous. College administrations are not a branch of the judiciary. They are not equipped or trained for legal inquiry. Colleges must alert incoming students to the problems and dangers of adulthood. Then colleges must stand back and get out of the sex game.

Discussing Vocabulary / Using a Dictionary

1. What does the prefix "sub-" mean in "subliminal" (para. 12)? What other words share this prefix?

2. What is another, more literal meaning of "espouse" (para. 16)? How does this meaning relate to Paglia's use of the word?

3. Paglia turns the adjective "manipulative" into the noun "manipulativeness" (para. 17) by adding the suffix "-ness." Turn a few other adjectives into nouns by adding this suffix.

Discussing Meaning

1. According to Paglia, in what ways have feminists exaggerated the "incidence and seriousness" (para. 3) of date rape?

2. Why, according to Paglia, will women always be in sexual danger? How, in her judgment, does the feminist position on date rape worsen this danger?

3. What does Paglia say that young women should do to prevent being raped? What is her opinion of women who don't take such precautions?

4. In what ways, according to Paglia, has feminism "cut itself off from sexual history" (para. 14)? What attitudes of men toward women does she say are part of the "mythology" of sex?

5. What does Paglia see as the "only solution to date rape" (para. 19)?

Discussing Writing

1. Where does Paglia first state her thesis, or main idea, in this essay? At what points does she restate this thesis in different ways?

2. As her title indicates, Paglia places the rape controversy in the context of modern sex war. Go through the essay and identify the words, phrases, and images that reinforce the comparison between rape and war. What do you think of this comparison?

3. How would you describe Paglia's tone in this article — serious or tongue-in-cheek, modest or swaggering? What language, examples, or other aspects of her writing make you react in this way? In general, do you find her writing offensive, entertaining, thought-provoking, or some combination? Why?

Challenging the Selection

1. Throughout her article Paglia makes many general statements about feminism. For example, in paragraph 4 she says, "Feminism keeps saying that the sexes are the same." Do you think she provides adequate support for such statements? Why or why not?

2. In paragraph 10 Paglia says, "Hunt, pursuit, and capture are biologically programmed into male sexuality. Generation after generation, men must be educated, refined, and ethically persuaded away from their tendency toward anarchy and brutishness." Do you think that men, by nature, are brutish? Can you think of any examples that contradict Paglia's statement?

3. Why do you think Paglia singles out "expensive northeastern colleges and universities" (para. 17) as a special target? Would she

be more sympathetic to date-rape incidents on less privileged urban campuses? What has the type of school got to do with the issue?

In-Class Writing Activities

1. Construct two lists comparing the different kinds of language that Paglia uses to describe males and females. Which list strikes you as more positive? Why?

2. Paglia says, "A girl who lets herself get dead drunk at a fraternity party is a fool. A girl who goes upstairs alone with a brother at a fraternity party is an idiot. Feminists call this 'blaming the victim.' I call it common sense" (para. 8). Write a few paragraphs in which you consider Paglia's remarks. Do you agree or disagree with her on this matter?

3. In paragraph 12 Paglia describes the 1960 film *Where the Boys Are,* in which women fend off many sexual advances from men. In a few paragraphs, describe a television show or movie in which a character must deal with another's sexual aggression. How did he or she handle the situation? Do you think that the scene was portrayed realistically? Why or why not?

HELEN CORDES

The Blue Balls Bluff

[UTNE READER / January–February 1993]

Before You Read

Are we ever justified in defending bad behavior by saying "I just couldn't control myself," or is this statement always just an excuse? Can you think of any times when your behavior seemed beyond your control? How did you handle the situation?

Words to Learn

gonads (para. 1): sex organs (n.)

imperiously (para. 1): done in a domineering or overbearing manner (adv.)

cohort (para. 1): an associate or colleague (n.)

screed (para. 2): a long, monotonous piece of writing (n.)

petulant (para. 2): short-tempered or contemptuous (adj.)

rampant (para. 2): unrestrained or extravagant (adj.)

patronize (para. 4): to treat someone in a condescending manner (v.)

perpetuate (para. 5): to continue or prolong (v.)

inane (para. 7): lacking sense or substance (adj.)

ludicrous (para. 7): laughable or ridiculous (adj.)

censure (para. 8): official condemnation (n.)

vilify (para. 8): to put down or defame (v.)

cloister (para. 9): to separate people from larger society, often in an effort to protect them (v.)

HELEN CORDES (b. 1954) is a contributing editor for the Utne Reader, *for which she wrote this direct response to Camille Paglia's argument in the previous essay. Before joining the* Utne Reader, *Cordes worked as a freelance writer for alternative periodicals in Denver and as a radio reporter in Washington, D.C.*

I thought the old "blue balls" defense — you remember, that's the one where backseat Romeos claimed they couldn't halt their sexual advances because their aching gonads imperiously demanded relief — went out with air raid shelters and doo wop. But now there are those like Camille Paglia who are bringing back blue balls with a vengeance. According to Paglia and her cohorts, men really *can't* control their urges. Rape for men is just doin' what comes naturally. And gals, don't bother fighting it — just get used to it again.

It's not surprising that these antifeminist screeds seem irresistible to America's magazine editors (mostly male? just a wild guess), but it is ironic. In the past few years, men have become increasingly petulant about "male-bashing," complaining that feminists have accused them — particularly the white and privileged among them — of being responsible for all the world's major woes, including rampant violence against women. Even politically correct guys protest that extremist feminist statements like "all men will rape if they can" just go too far. "Look," they respond indignantly, "I don't rape, no one I know rapes or beats his wife — why do you women keep saying men are such animals? How do you think that makes us feel?" Then along comes Paglia with the same message — that men rape whenever they can — and, curiously enough, many men give her a rousing cheer.

Paglia's prescription for "prudent" and "cautious" behavior won't save women from sexual violence.

Both extremist views — the contention that men have insistent urges and some feminists' belief that all men rape — are dangerous. Men are right to be outraged at stereotypes about their gender. But they're wrong to accept Paglia's forgiving view of their "biological programming." Lots of men might like to believe that "masculinity is aggressive, unstable, combustible" because that line is a great excuse for self-indulgent behavior. But can most men seriously agree with statements such as "Generation after generation, men must be educated, refined, and ethically persuaded away from their tendency toward anarchy and brutishness"? Do all real men dream of the "fun element in rape, especially the wild, infectious delirium of gang rape"? Do normal men really get off on hurting women? Is this the "truth about sex" we need to tell our sons and daughters?

The truth about sex — and the "sex wars" between men and women — is at once more complicated and more ordinary than that.

Sure, I'll buy Paglia's line that men are sexually violent toward women because they fear being dominated by women. I fear (as women have always feared) being dominated by men. So if a man is patronizing me, can I shoot him? ("He led me on, officer. What else could a red-blooded woman do?") And yes, seeking sex *is* usually motivated in part by pure sexual desire, but both men and women also use sex to substitute for other inadequacies in their lives. Honest women are quick to confide that they use sex to shore up their egos or as a bargaining chip for attention and affection. And truly honest men will tell you the same thing.

The reason for the sex wars — for women feeling that men are   5
sex-obsessed predators who will rape at will, and for men feeling that women are distrustful, uptight, and too quick to cry rape — is that too little has changed. Too many men perpetuate the adolescent blue balls theory — and why should they give it up? Pretending that it's uncontrollable sexual urges that make them aggressively demand sex gives men control, power, and a feeling that they are entitled to sexual favors. And who wants to give that up? In the face of abusive behavior from certain men, many women are giving up all too readily, returning to their mothers' attitude that men are after only one thing. And although it's not fair, it's also not surprising that women occasionally react badly to well-meaning men who are genuinely trying to overcome the conditioning that pushed them to be sexually aggressive.

Both sides are retreating into bitterness and antagonism, when in truth the long view reveals real hope for the future. Look at how much closer we've gotten to egalitarianism and harmony between the sexes in the past twenty-five years. As working women become the norm, men are no longer expected to be wage slaves. Women's experiences of and complaints about abusive behavior have been heard, and institutions have responded — women who have been raped, sexually harassed, and battered can now get help in every region of the country.

Progress like this is what makes it especially annoying and depressing to see Paglia's views gaining legitimacy. Her awestruck view of male sexuality, and her inane suggestion that women view it as a blind force of nature instead of morally accountable behavior, are ludicrous throwbacks to the blue balls days.

Women *should* let men know when their behavior is offensive. But individual complaints are toothless without societal and institutional awareness, dialogue, and censure. The feminist movement that Paglia and others vilify has brought about these critical societal attitudes and structures. For just one example, look to the way rape victims are now treated by the police. When rape victims go to the police they can now hope to be met with respect, thanks to feminist efforts to sensitize officers, many of whom didn't take the crime seriously before.

I agree with Paglia that women would do well to avoid drunken frat parties and solo campouts. But her prescription for "prudent" and "cautious" behavior won't save them from sexual violence. Women are raped and harassed everywhere and anytime — often in situations that are not remotely "dangerous" or "provocative." Instead of cloistering women and allowing men free rein, why don't women and men talk and work together for change, so that they can find ways to be peaceably intimate again?

Discussing Vocabulary / Using a Dictionary

1. "Imperiously" (para. 1) is related to the adjective "imperial." How are these words connected in meaning?

2. "Patronize" (para. 4) also has a positive meaning. What is it?

3. What is the Latin root of "censure" (para. 8)? What is the meaning of this root?

4. List a few synonyms for "vilify" (para. 8). Can you think of social movements or institutions, other than the feminist movement, that are sometimes vilified?

Discussing Meaning

1. What is the "blue balls defense"? Why, according to Cordes, is it back "with a vengeance" (para. 1)?

2. Cordes describes "extremist views" about rape in paragraph 3. What are these views, and why are they harmful, in her opinion?

3. According to Cordes, what progress have men and women made in the past twenty-five years? How, in her view, do the "sex wars" (para. 5) threaten this progress?

4. In the end, what solution does Cordes offer for preventing rape and promoting positive relations between the sexes?

Discussing Writing

1. In the last sentence of her first paragraph, Cordes says, "And gals, don't bother fighting [the "blue balls" defense] — just get used to it again." How would you characterize her tone in this statement? Why do you think she included such a statement?

2. At a few points in her essay, Cordes acknowledges areas in which she agrees with Paglia. For example, in paragraph 4 she says, "Sure, I'll buy Paglia's line that men are sexually violent toward women because they fear being dominated by women." Can you find other places where she acknowledges agreement with Paglia? What is the effect of this strategy? Does it make you more sympathetic to Cordes's argument or does it make her seem indecisive?

3. In paragraph 4 Cordes turns one of Paglia's arguments — that men are sexually aggressive toward women because, among other things, they fear being dominated by women — on its head. "So if a man is patronizing me," Cordes asks, "can I shoot him?" Did you find this counter-argument effective or simplistic? Do you think Cordes is being serious when she asks this question?

Challenging the Selection

1. At a few points in her essay, Cordes makes unsupported generalizations. For example, in paragraph 2 she says that many men give Paglia — and her argument that men rape whenever they can — "a rousing cheer." Do these generalizations, particularly about men (to whom Cordes seems to want to be fair), undercut her credibility? Why or why not?

2. At the end of her essay Cordes suggests that "women and men talk and work together for change, so that they can find ways to be peaceably intimate again," but she doesn't suggest specific ways for achieving this dialogue or countering opponents such as Paglia. Do you think that this vagueness makes Cordes's argument weak, or do you think it is enough that her essay calls attention to a potential threat to advances in gender relations?

In-Class Writing Activities

1. To what extent are our sexual urges biological, and to what extent are they influenced by outside factors such as the media? What implications do these causes and influences have for efforts to prevent date rape and other forms of sexual aggression? Write a few paragraphs in which you reflect on these questions. You might want to compare your opinions with those of your classmates.

2. In paragraph 8 Cordes writes, "Women *should* let men know when their behavior is offensive. But individual complaints are toothless without societal and institutional awareness, dialogue, and censure." Write a brief essay in which you agree or disagree with this statement. Make sure to support your argument with specific reasons and examples.

Discussing the Unit

Suggested Topic for Discussion

Who should be responsible for preventing date rape and other forms of sexual aggression? Is it an unfortunate truth that primary responsibility must rest with potential victims, as Paglia contends, or is that argument unfair, unsound, and even dangerous, as Cordes maintains? To what extent should college administrators, parents of victims and aggressors, and other social institutions be held accountable for preventing rape? What do you think should be done to prevent date rape on your campus?

Preparing for Class Discussion

1. Draw a line down a sheet of paper and write this statement on one side: "All responsibility for controlling sexual aggression must rest with the aggressor." On the other side write "All responsibility for controlling sexual aggression must rest with the potential victim." Then, under each statement, try as best you can to list reasons that support the statement. (You don't necessarily have to agree with these statements; the reasons you list might be opinions that you've heard in the media or other sources.) When you're done, reflect on both lists. Did the act of trying to support each statement affect your view of who's re-

sponsible for preventing sexual aggression? How? Do you side strongly with one view, or do you see "gray areas" in the question of responsibility?

2. Are you familiar with any organizations or programs on your campus that are aimed at preventing rape? If so, how effective do you think they are? If you aren't familiar with any such programs, what kinds of prevention efforts do you *think* should be in place? (For example, do you think that workshops or codes of sexual conduct would be effective?) What are the limitations of rape prevention programs?

From Discussion to Writing

1. Based on your reading, class discussion, and your personal reflections on this chapter, write an essay on the question of who should be responsible for preventing date rape and other forms of sexual aggression, particularly on college campuses. Provide specific reasons for your stand and make sure to support your argument with examples from your reading, personal observations, and, possibly, your class's discussion of the question.

2. Paglia contends that men and women will never achieve sexual harmony, whereas Cordes argues that we've already made significant strides in improving gender relations and that a revival of the "blue balls" defense endangers this progress. Write an essay in which you side with Paglia or Cordes or take another position that balances their views. Be sure to support your position with evidence and examples from your own experiences and observations, Paglia's or Cordes's essay, or other sources.

Topics for Cross-Cultural Discussion

1. How, if at all, are young people in your native country educated about rape or sexual aggression? Is one sex held more accountable for preventing rape? Why?

2. How is rape treated in your native country? Is acquaintance rape considered a crime? Can a husband be convicted of raping his wife? What does the law expect a woman to do to convince a court that she has been raped?

The Periodicals:
Information for Subscription

American Enterprise: bimonthly. $5/issue, $28/yr. Magazine of economics, domestic and foreign policy, politics, and public opinion. Subscription address: *American Enterprise*, P.O. Box 2012, Marion, OH 43301; or call 1-800-596-2319.

Black Collegian: semi-annual. $5/issue, $8/yr. Career and self-development magazine for African American students. Subscription address: Black Collegiate Services, Inc., 140 Carondelet St., New Orleans, LA 70130-2526; or call (504) 523-0154.

Boston Globe: daily. General newspaper covering local, national, and international news. Rates vary according to location and frequency of delivery. Subscription address: *Boston Globe*, 135 Morrissey Blvd., P.O. Box 2378, Boston, MA 02107-2378; or call 1-800-622-6631.

Campus Times: weekly. $18.75/academic yr. A student newspaper of the University of Rochester. Subscription address: *Campus Times*, CPU 277086, Campus Post Office, Rochester, NY 14627-7086; or call (716) 275-5943.

Cavalier Daily: daily weekdays. $49.95/academic yr. A student newspaper of the University of Virginia. Subscription address: *Cavalier Daily*, Newcomb Hall Basement, Charlottesville, VA 22904; or call (804) 924-1086.

Chicago Tribune: daily. General newspaper covering local, national, and world news. Rates vary according to location and frequency of delivery. Subscription address: *Chicago Tribune*, 777 West Chicago Ave., Chicago, IL 60610; or call 1-800-874-2863.

Christopher Street: monthly. $3/issue, $27/yr. Magazine of literature, arts, and politics for the gay community. Subscription address: That New Magazine, Inc., 28 W. 25th St., 4th Fl., New York, NY 10010; or call (212) 627-2120.

Colgate Maroon-News: weekly. $30/academic yr. A student newspaper of Colgate University. Subscription address: *Colgate Maroon-*

News, Colgate University, 13 Oak Dr., Hamilton, NY 13346; or call (315) 824-7744.

Commonweal: biweekly. $2/issue, $39/yr. Journal of opinion published by Catholic lay people. Reviews public affairs, religion, literature, and the arts. Subscription address: Commonweal Foundation, 15 Dutch St., 5th Fl., New York, NY 10038-3719; or call (212) 732-0800.

Daily Beacon: daily weekdays. $165/academic yr. A student newspaper of the University of Tennessee, Knoxville. Subscription address: *Daily Beacon*, 1340 Circle Park Dr., 5 Communications Bldg., Knoxville, TN 37996-0314; or call (423) 974-5206.

Daily Free Press: daily weekdays. $100/academic yr. A student newspaper of Boston University. Subscription address: *Daily Free Press*, 842 Commonwealth Ave., Boston, MA 02215; or call (617) 232-6841.

Daily Iowan: daily weekdays. $40/yr. in town, $75/yr. out of town. A student newspaper of the University of Iowa. Rates vary according to location and frequency of delivery. Subscription address: *Daily Iowan*, 111 Communications Center, Iowa City, Iowa 52242; or call (319) 335-5783.

Daily Northwestern: daily weekdays. $48/academic yr. A student newspaper of Northwestern University. Subscription address: *Daily Northwestern*, 1999 Sheridan Rd., Evanston, IL 60208; or call (847) 491-7206.

Et Cetera: quarterly. $30/yr. Journal of general semantics. Subscription address: International Society for General Semantics, Box 728, Concord, CA 94522; or call (510) 798-0311.

Glamour: monthly. $2.50/issue, $15/yr. Articles on fashion, health, and lifestyle. Primarily for young women. Subscription address: *Glamour*, P.O. Box 53716, Boulder, CO 80322; or call 1-800-274-7410.

The Humanist: bimonthly. $4.75/issue, $24.95/yr. General interest magazine covering philosophy, science, and broad social issues. Subscription address: Circulation Manager, *The Humanist*, 7 Harwood Dr., P.O. Box 1188, Amherst, NY 14226-7188; or call, 1-800-743-6646.

Kansas State Collegian: daily weekdays. $75/academic yr. A student newspaper of Kansas State University. Subscription address: *Kansas State Collegian*, Student Publications Inc., Kedzie Hall 103, Manhattan, KS 66506; or call (913) 532-6555.

Michigan Daily: daily weekdays. $170/academic yr. A student news-paper of The University of Michigan. Subscription address: *Michigan Daily*, 420 Maynard St., Ann Arbor, MI 48109-1327; or call (313) 764-0550.

Minnesota Daily: daily weekdays. $85/yr. A student newspaper of the University of Minnesota. Subscription address: *Minnesota Daily*, 2301 University Ave. S.E., Ste. 1, Minneapolis, MN 55414-3070; or call (612) 627-4080.

The New Republic: weekly. $2.95/issue, $69.97/yr. Journal featuring current events, comments, and reviews. Subscription address: Subscription Service Dept., *The New Republic*, P.O. Box 602, Mount Morris, IL 61054; or call 1-800-827-1289.

Newsweek: weekly. $2.95/issue, $41.08/yr. Current news and com-mentary on events in the nation and the world. Subscription ad-dress: The Newsweek Building, Livingston, NJ 07039-1666; or call 1-800-631-1040.

New York Times: daily, with large Sunday edition that contains the *New York Times Magazine* and the *New York Times Book Re-view*, as well as other supplements. Rates vary according to loca-tion and frequency of delivery. Considered the definitive source for current events, daily, national, and international news, and business and arts reporting. Subscription information: call 1-800-631-2500.

Old Gold and Black: weekly. $50/academic yr. A student newspaper of Wake Forest University. Subscription address: *Old Gold and Black*, P.O. Box 7569 Reynolda Station, Winston-Salem, NC 27109; or call (910) 759-5280.

On the Issues: quarterly. $3.95/issue, $14.95/yr. A feminist, humanist magazine of critical thinking, dedicated to fostering collective re-sponsibility for positive social change. Published by Choices Women's Medical Center, Forest Hills, NY. Subscription ad-dress: *On the Issues*, P.O. Box 3000, Dept. OTI, Denville, NJ 07834.

Reason: monthly. $2.95/issue, $26/yr. Magazine for individuals inter-ested in economic, social, and political issues stressing free mar-kets and individual liberties. Subscription address: *Reason*, P.O. Box 526, Mt. Morris, IL 61054; or call (815) 734-1102.

Reconstruction: quarterly. $8/issue, $25/yr. Journal presents com-mentary on African American politics, society, and culture. Sub-scription address: *Reconstruction*, 1563 Massachusetts Ave., Cambridge, MA 02138; or call (617) 495-0907.

Rock Writing: annual. Journal of student essays published by the English department of Slippery Rock University and distributed on campus for free. For more information write: Slippery Rock University, English Department, Slippery Rock, PA 16057; or call (412) 738-0512.

Rolling Stone: biweekly. $2.95/issue, $25.94/yr. Magazine featuring articles on rock music, pop culture, and national affairs. Subscription information: call 1-800-568-7655.

Spectator: weekly. $80/academic yr. A student newspaper of Hamilton College. Subscription address: *Spectator*, Hamilton College, 198 College Hill Rd., Clinton, NY 13323; or call (315) 859-4100.

Stanford Magazine: quarterly. $4.50/issue, $18/yr. Alumni magazine published by the Stanford Alumni Association. Subscription address: Stanford Alumni Association, Bowman Alumni House, Stanford, CA 94305-4005; or call (415) 725-0672.

Technology Review: 8 × yr. $3.75/issue, $30/yr. Magazine reviewing recent developments in technology. Published by the Association of Alumni and Alumnae of the Massachusetts Institute of Technology. Subscription address: *Technology Review*, P.O. Box 489, Mount Morris, IL 61054; or call 1-800-877-5230.

Time: weekly. $2.95/issue, $59.94/yr. Magazine of current national and world news. Published by Time Inc., Time & Life Building, Rockefeller Center, New York, NY 10020-1393. Subscription information: call 1-800-843-TIME.

USA Today: daily weekdays. General newspaper covering national and international news. Rates vary according to location and frequency of delivery. Subscription address: *USA Today*, Director of National Customer Service, P.O. Box 4179, Silver Spring, MD 20914; or call 1-800-USA-0001.

U.S. News & World Report: weekly. $2.95/issue, $39.75/yr. Magazine covering current national and world news. Subscription address: *U.S. News & World Report*, P.O. Box 55929, Boulder, CO 80322-5929; or call 1-800-333-8130.

Utne Reader: bimonthly. $4.99/issue, $18/yr. Presents general interest articles and reviews selected from independently published newsletters, magazines, journals. Subscription address: *Utne Reader*, Box 7460, Red Oak, IA 51591-0460; or call 1-800-736-UTNE (8863).

Wall Street Journal: daily weekdays. $.75/issue, $164/yr. Newspaper reporting on national business and finance. Subscription address: *Wall Street Journal*, 200 Burnett Rd., Chicopee, MA 01020; or call 1-800-JOURNAL.

Washington Post National Weekly Edition: weekly. $1.95/issue, $48/yr. Weekly supplement of the *Washington Post* summarizing the week's news, with additional feature articles. Subscription information: call 1-800-333-3889.

West: weekly. Published as a Sunday magazine supplement to the *San Jose Mercury News*. Rates vary according to location and frequency of delivery. Subscription address: *San Jose Mercury News/West*, Knight-Ridder, Inc, 750 Ridder Park Dr., San Jose, CA 95190; or call (408) 920-5796.

Acknowledgments (continued from p. ii)

Nell Bernstein, "Goin' Gangsta, Choosin' Cholita." Reprinted by permission of the author. Nell Bernstein is editor of *YO! (Youth Outlook)*, the Youth Press of Pacific News Service, San Francisco.

Brian Brady, "America's Real Fear." Reprinted by permission of the author and the *Old Gold and Black.*

Ed Carson, "Purging Bingeing." Reprinted, with permission, from the December 1995 issue of *Reason* magazine. Copyright 1995 by the Reason Foundation, 3415 S. Sepulveda Blvd., Suite 400, Los Angeles, CA 90034.

Linda Chavez, "There's No Future in Lady Luck." Reprinted by permission from Linda Chavez, (c) 1995.

Charles Choi, "A Beef with Beef Oriental." (c) 1996 the *Catalyst*, New College of the University of South Florida. Reprinted by permission of the author and the *Catalyst.*

Helen Cordes, "The Blue Balls Bluff." Reprinted with permission from *Utne Reader,* January/February 1993.

Meghan Daum, "Safe-Sex Lies." Copyright (c) 1996 by The New York Times Co. Reprinted by permission.

Debra Dickerson, "Who Shot Johnny?" Reprinted by permission of *The New Republic.* (c) 1996, The New Republic, Inc.

Viet D. Dinh, "Single White Female." Viet D. Dinh is Associate Professor of Law, Georgetown University Law Center. "Single White Female" was first published in *Reconstruction* (Vol. 2, No. 3, 1994) and is reprinted by permission of the author.

Hanns Ebensten, "A Humble Proposal." *Christopher Street,* July 1993. Reprinted by permission of the author.

Barbara Ehrenreich, "Zipped Lips." *Time,* February 5, 1996. (c) 1996 Time Inc. Reprinted by permission.

Kate Epstein, "The Classroom Gender Balance: Who Speaks More, Men or Women?" From the *Michigan Daily,* March 25, 1996. Reprinted by permission of the author and the *Michigan Daily.*

Herbert J. Gans, "Fitting the Poor into the Economy." Reprinted by permission of the author. Gans is Robert S. Lynd Professor of Sociology at Columbia University. This article is based on materials in his recent book *The War against the Poor: The Underclass and Antipoverty Policy,* Basic Books, 1995–96.

Henry Louis Gates, Jr., "On Honoring Blackness." From *Colored People* by Henry Louis Gates, Jr. Copyright (c) 1994 by Henry Louis Gates, Jr. Reprinted by permission of Alfred A. Knopf, Inc.

Jill Glazer, "On Politically Correct Speech." (c) the *Colgate Maroon-News.* Reprinted by permission of the author and the *Colgate Maroon-News.*

Michael Gonzales, "The Bilingual Ed Trap." Reprinted by permission of the *Wall Street Journal,* (c) 1995 Dow Jones & Company, Inc. All rights reserved worldwide.

Ellen Goodman, "When Mars Eclipses Venus." (c) 1995, The Boston Globe Newspaper Co./Washington Post Writers Group. Reprinted with permission.

John Hamerlinck, "Killing Women: A Pop-Music Tradition." From *The Humanist,* July/August 1995. Reprinted by permission of the author.

Kirk Hoffman, "Why We Can't Just Stamp Out Smoking." (c) the *Daily Northwestern*. Reprinted by permission of the author and the *Daily Northwestern*.

"Interracial Dating: Yes or No?" Reprinted with the permission of the *Black Collegian Magazine*, from the March/April 1993 issue.

Charisse Jones, "Light Skin versus Dark." *Glamour*, October 1995. Reprinted by permission of the author.

Eric Kim, "Have You Ever Met an Asian Man You Thought Was Sexy?" Reprinted by permission of the author.

Ted Koerth, "Economic Affirmative Action." Reprinted by permission of the author and the *Cavalier Daily*.

Chang-rae Lee, "Mute in an English-Only World." Copyright (c) 1996 by The New York Times Co. Reprinted by permission.

Erin Mansur-Smith, "It's Not Whether You Win or Lose — It's Whether or Not You're Allowed to Play the Game." The *Kansas State Collegian* (c) 1996. Reprinted by permission of the author and Student Publications, Inc., Kansas State University.

Dan McAllister, "A Misguided Policy." (c) the *Spectator*. Reprinted by permission of the author and the *Spectator*.

Jo McGowan, "Take Your Shoes Off My Books." Copyright (c) Commonweal Foundation, 1993.

David Nyhan, "Turn Off the TV before It Ruins Us." By David Nyhan, September 16, 1996. Reprinted courtesy of the *Boston Globe*.

Charles Oliver, "Freak Parade." Reprinted, with permission, from the April 1995 issue of *Reason* magazine. Copyright 1995 by the Reason Foundation, 3415 S. Sepulveda Blvd., Suite 400, Los Angeles, CA 90034.

Clarence Page, "More Talk Needed — Not Silence." Reprinted by permission of Tribune Media Services.

Camille Paglia, "Rape and Modern Sex War." From *Sex, Art and American Culture* by Camille Paglia. Copyright (c) 1992 by Camille Paglia. Reprinted by permission of Vintage Books, a Division of Random House, Inc.

Elayne Rapping, "Crowd on the Couch." From *On the Issues* magazine, Spring 1994. Reprinted by permission of *On the Issues*.

Valerie Richard, "Love Sees No Color." Reprinted by permission of the author.

Rosa Rivera, "Why English-Only Laws Are Useless." Reprinted by permission of the author.

Charles G. Russell and Judith C. White, "Who Controls Your Life?" Reprinted from *ETC: A Review of General Semantics*, Spring 1993, with permission of the International Society for General Semantics, Concord, California.

Rene Sanchez, "Surfing's Up and Grades Are Down." (c) 1996, the *Washington Post*. Reprinted with permission.

Kimberly Smith, "How to Produce a Trashy TV Talk Show: The Four Secret Ingredients." Reprinted by permission of the author.

Knight Stivender, "Somewhere a Room of One's Own." Reprinted with permission from the University of Tennessee *Daily Beacon* and the author.

Deborah Tannen, "Gender Gap in Cyberspace." Reprinted by permission of the author.

Garry Trudeau, "My Inner Shrimp." Copyright (c) 1996 by The New York Times Co. Reprinted by permission.

Rima Vesely, "Over Exposure." Reprinted by permission of the author and the *Daily Iowan*.

Sean T. Wherley, "Coming Out: A Process of Dilemmas." Reprinted by permission of the author and the *Minnesota Daily*.

Dan Zevin, "Roommatism." From *Rolling Stone*, October 20, 1994. Copyright (c) by Dan Zevin. By Straight Arrow Publishers Company, L.P., 1994. All rights reserved. Reprinted by permission.

Mortimer B. Zuckerman, "Forrest Gump versus Ice-T." Copyright, July 24, 1995, *U.S. News & World Report*.

Index of Authors and Titles